STORIES FROM HOME

For Dad and John

Stories from Home
English Domestic Interiors, 1750–1850

MARGARET PONSONBY
University of Wolverhampton, UK

ASHGATE

Published by
Ashgate Publishing Limited
Gower House
Croft Road
Aldershot
Hants GU11 3HR
England

Ashgate Publishing Company
Suite 420
101 Cherry Street
Burlington, VT 05401-4405
USA

Ashgate website: http://www.ashgate.com

British Library Cataloguing in Publication Data
Ponsonby, Margaret
  Stories from home : English domestic interiors, 1750-1850.
  – (The history of retailing and consumption)
  1.Interior decoration – England – History – 18th century 2.Interior decoration – England – History – 19th century 3.Consumption (Economics) – England – History – 18th century 4.Consumption (Economics) – England – History – 19th century 5.Middle class – England – History – 18th century 6.Middle class – England – History – 19th century 7.Great Britain – Social conditions – 18th century 8.Great Britain – Social conditions – 19th century
  I.Title
  306.3'0942'09033

Library of Congress Cataloging-in-Publication Data
Ponsonby, Margaret, 1952-
  Stories from home : English domestic interiors, 1750-1850 / Margaret Ponsonby.
    p. cm. – (History of retailing and consumption)
  Includes bibliographical references and index.
  ISBN 0-7546-5235-1 (alk. paper)
  1. Interior decoration–England–History–18th century. 2. Interior decoration–England–History–19th century. 3. England–Social life and customs–18th century. 4. England–Social life and customs–19th century. I. Title. II. Series.

NK2043.A1P66 2006
747.0942'09033 – dc22

2006005437

ISBN: 978-0-7546-5235-9

Printed and bound in Great Britain by MPG Books Ltd. Bodmin, Cornwall.

Contents

Illustrations and Tables

Illustrations

The author has been unable to trace copyright owners for items in the Birmingham Archive collection, except where stated, and therefore offers her apologies and requests that they contact the publishers for inclusion in any future editions.

Tables

Preface

Since beginning my academic life as a Design Historian my main area of interest has been the material culture of the home, in particular the challenge of understanding how homemakers in the past made meaning out of the contents of their homes. My first attempt at a research project on the subject was as an undergraduate, and dealt with working-class homes in the 1950s. A major part of the research was talking to women who had bought and made their own soft furnishings, and retailers who had sold the fabric. I quickly realized that their story was not written in the accounts of domestic interiors of the period since most delighted in the development of the Contemporary Style. My homemakers had been very slow to respond to Modernist ideas about interiors and had quite different expectations for their homes. As my interests shifted back in time to the eighteenth and nineteenth centuries I felt sure that the experience of homemaking for ordinary homemakers and what their homes meant to them would be equally elusive. Although there are a great many books that deal with the contents of the home for the eighteenth and nineteenth centuries they mostly concentrate on how the style of domestic interiors changed over time, the general trends, the big picture, rather than the individual homemakers. But how to rectify this when the individual homemakers were long dead and could not contribute oral testimonies? During the research for my MA and PhD degrees I have gathered documentary evidence of homemaking and struggled to extract individual stories from the material. It was only after a year had elapsed from completing my thesis that I could stand back from the material and see a structure that would allow me to explore the process and meaning of homemaking for individuals. This book provides a few ways of cutting through the layers of evidence but does not cover all the possibilities; there are many other themes that could have been developed, particularly the place occupied by children in the home. But this book is as much about the methods it employs for examining documentary evidence as any conclusions it reaches.

My most recent research is a natural progression to my work on eighteenth- and nineteenth-century homemaking and how we make sense of it in the present. I am now engaged in research that examines how historic interiors are interpreted at historic house museums. I might easily have chosen another form of representation, such as film or television portrayals of historical domestic interiors. However, the fascination for me about historic house museums is the tangible evidence, so often lacking unfortunately in other aspects of my research. In historic houses the material culture of the past survives but does not automatically reveal its meaning. The interpretation process reconfigures the context, and ideas about how this should be done have changed over time. In addition the interiors and objects have aged and have often been changed through restoration and conservation, which all transforms the meaning that the interiors have now from what they meant to their original owners. By combining an examination of how interpretation has developed in historic house museums with the evidence of homemaking in the past this book is inviting comparisons and further reflection on historic domestic interiors and the stories that they contain.

During my various research projects I have been fortunate in my supervisors and examiners who have given generously of their time and provided enthusiastic and stimulating discussions of my ideas. I would now like to thank Helen Martin, Gillian Naylor, John Styles, Charles Saumarez Smith, Lisa White and in particular Nancy Cox and Judith Attfield for all their efforts on my behalf. The University of Wolverhampton has supported my research in a variety of ways and I have benefited from the strong research culture that prevails in the History and Governance Research Institute. I am aware that colleagues in other institutions are less fortunate. In addition, my research has benefited enormously from a number of grants from external bodies. Winterthur Museum and Library, Delaware, has generously awarded me two Research Fellowships. Its wonderful collections and excellent facilities made working there a great pleasure. I also enjoyed discussions with many members of staff at Winterthur who shared their expertise with me, in the library, in the museum collections and over a great many lunches and dinners. I would like to thank in particular Maggie Lidz, Susan Buck and Linda Eaton. Writing this book was greatly aided by my obtaining sabbatical time through the Arts and Humanities Research Board (now Research Council) Research Study Leave Scheme. I was also fortunate in obtaining a scholarship that enabled me to attend the Attingham Society's summer school, which really introduced me to studying the English country house, and that has grown into an interest in historic house museums more generally. Through the Society I have met many interesting people who have helped my research and in the process become valued friends. I would like to thank Deborah Lee Trupin, Helen Hughes, Kristin Herron, Ann Lee Bugbee and in particular Jack Braunlein

My archival research has taken me to a great many libraries and record offices and I am grateful for all the help I have received. In particular I would like to thank West Sussex Record Office, Chichester; Shropshire Record Office, Shrewsbury; Lichfield Joint Record Office; Coventry Archives; Staffordshire Record Office, Stafford; Birmingham Museum Services at Birmingham Museum and Art Gallery, Soho House and Aston Hall. I spent more time at Birmingham Central Library than anywhere else and, unlike Prince Charles I have a great fondness for the building and will be sad to see it go in a few years' time. The staff of the Local Studies and History and the Archives departments were always kind and helpful.

I would like to thank all the friends and colleagues who have contributed to my work, in particular Helen Clifford, Lesley Whitworth, Carolyn White, Richard Nylander, Leslie LeFevre-Stratton, Malcolm Wanklyn, John Benson, Lisa Taylor, Paul Lewis, Paula Bartley, David Hussey and Karin Dannehl, who have all helped me by offering advice and acting as a sounding board to my ideas, for which I am very grateful.

Introduction

Reading Domestic Interiors, Past and Present

Extraordinary Homes Are Normal

Stationers sell special photograph albums in which, in addition to photographs, the history of a family can be recorded. Spaces are provided for the dates of birth, marriage and death of the different generations. Alongside the information are cut-out sections for the photographs to be inserted: a visual family tree and a potted family history in one. But for many people this would not provide a suitable method of recording their particular family's history. Perhaps some of the necessary photographs have not survived and exact information is not available. Even more problematic are the details of family life that do not fit neatly in the boxes provided: divorce or the death of a partner, remarriage, stepchildren, children born outside marriage, adopted and fostered children. These experiences of family life, with the exception of divorce, occurred in many families throughout the period 1750–1850, just as they do today. Real family life is always messier and less perfect than idealistic representations of it.

Just as these family history albums assume a generic formula that does not reflect the true individuality of family life, so too do many histories of the domestic interiors where family life was acted out. Generic interiors that are a simplistic reflection of period and country do not tell us about the individual nature of home life, the needs and desires, taste and aspirations of particular homemakers. This book is seeking to reconstruct individual domestic interiors, and to explore how to achieve this through incomplete and fragmentary source material, for a period before photographic evidence can be used and outside living memory. The purpose is to retrieve the narratives of domestic life contained in the material evidence of home interiors and the homemaking and consumption practices of the people who inhabited them. The main aim is to acknowledge the kinds of homes that are usually dismissed as too ordinary to warrant attention – homes inhabited by the middle stratum of society by individuals who were not known for any particular achievement.[1] Such 'ordinary' people represent the majority of homemakers and, while they were not the originators of new fashions for interiors, the evidence suggests that their homes were too varied and interesting to be described in generic terms, as is usually the case. Homes were highly individual: many were comfortable and attractive, but likewise many were messy, untidy and badly organized, or at least made use of compromises in their layout and the disposition of their furnishings. Each home has a story to tell, and by observing the details of home furnishings and homemaking practice in a variety of examples these come to light. While the treatment is of specific interiors the book employs a new method of examining the design and materiality of interiors: a cultural history approach for interpreting this type of artefact. As June Philipp has observed, in order 'to discover the experience of people in the past, what they made of it, and with what effect, expressive behaviour or social action must be painstakingly attended, its forms uncovered and its meanings construed.'[2] Here it is the minutia of furnishing decisions, the highly individual arrangements that reveal how a home was organized by its inhabitants that will be uncovered to ascertain the use and meanings that people attached to the domestic environment, and how that evolved during the period.

There is a huge interest in domestic interiors of the past and how people inhabited them. Documentaries and historical dramas, on television and film, show interiors that viewers enjoy on various levels; they might study them for 'accuracy', or be fascinated by the archaic arrangements or even get ideas for furnishing their own homes. All of these interiors have been arranged for our consumption and are therefore representations of the past. In many instances these representations rely on images of typical interiors and stereotypical uses, derived from such sources as narrative paintings, advice and prescriptive literature, which are themselves representations.[3] Media and cultural studies warn against taking representations as reality since the message would always be mediated by the viewer/reader. Homes differed from the ideal in the past just as in the present. Ideals and *mores* even when desired were difficult to achieve in the real world. So homes did not faithfully follow the image even if they followed the general trend. Location, age, gender, sex, occupation and marital status influenced homes. Individual homemakers made individual homes. Therefore, while being aware that the general trends and influences on the domestic environment are important we must, in addition, seek evidence of actual homes to understand how they functioned for their inhabitants and the meanings that were attached to home furnishings.

The Home as a Physical and Social Construct

Before looking at the evidence of actual homes the general trends can be summarized of how the home evolved as a response to the changing nature of domestic life. These trends will provide the backdrop to the individual homes and therefore the departures and divergences can be better appreciated. How homes looked and functioned was not static but evolved over time, with some significant changes taking place during the period. The home was as much an idea as well as a physical place and the two aspects evolved together. At its most fundamental level the home provided a place to live, work and bring up a family. But beyond such basic requirements the home also needed to project the right image, which was closely connected with a person's position in society, their family background, their occupation and their aspirations. This was far more complex than suggested by the 'keeping up with the Joneses' kind of competitive consumption. In the later-eighteenth century the homes of the middling sort were often a place for working and were an extension of the family business. Customers and clients regularly migrated from the shop, workroom or office into the family accommodation to be entertained or to view stock.[4] While it might have been desirable for a home to keep up with fashion over-elaborate interiors were avoided. A home should demonstrate refinement and good taste and show your status but not appear foolishly extravagant. The home was an extension of the working life of the family, not just because it was often physically joined, but as a statement about the credit worthiness, the reliability and work ethos practised by the inhabitants.

We can begin to see that furnishing the home was not simply about creating an attractive and comfortable place to live. There were cultural implications attached to how the home was furnished, how it was organized, and the level of cleanliness practised. This last attribute was particularly important for the moral welfare of the family. During the period religion played an important role in most peoples' day-to-day life. As well as regular church attendance the home also provided the backdrop to the religious life of the family, whatever their denomination. This function of the home is well demonstrated in Joseph van Aken's c. 1725 depiction of a family saying grace before a meal. He deliberately chose the appropriate furnishings for a pious family: the room is clean, the meal humble and the tablecloth spotlessly white with the crisp lines of the press still clearly visible.[5] The role of the housewife was important for enhancing the image of the home. The house needed to be well cared for with polished and scrubbed surfaces, while some of the furnishings, especially textile items, gave further evidence of her handiwork. Such attitudes prevailed throughout the eighteenth century and were inculcated by young girls through instruction from their mothers and from published sources such as conduct books.[6]

During the nineteenth century religious opinions, whether Methodist or Anglican, through the Evangelical revival, intensified the moral attitudes connected with the notion of what constituted a home.[7] The use of the home for family prayers to some extent increased for a time, but beyond that the home was meant to provide a safe haven from the sinful outside world, particularly for women and children. Related to these ideas was the desire for the home to be divorced from the world of work. Homes became the private world of domesticity and contrasted with the public world of work and business.

By the early-nineteenth century industrialized production of goods had affected the quantity and quality of the contents of the home. As a result furnishings were more varied, many goods were cheaper, textiles were more readily available and shops were better stocked. Homes therefore filled up with objects. But the religious or moralistic role of the home also dictated that certain goods were esteemed. Furnishings that suggested comfort, particularly upholstered items that gave the impression of a secure and cosy interior, were valued. The middle-class housewife was not expected to go out to work or even to work in the family business; instead she should enhance the domestic environment with her handiwork. Embroidery and other needlework were essential elements for beautifying the home but a host of other skills were also expected, such as painting china, pokerwork, and pictures made of shells or scrolls of paper.[8]

While essentially a private world the home performed a public role through providing a suitable backdrop for entertaining visitors. In the eighteenth century food had been prepared in rather basic ways by middling households. By the nineteenth century sophisticated cooking ranges allowed food to be cooked in a variety of ways. The Staffordshire potters provided a greater variety of ceramics for serving and eating food. The greater use of forks affected table manners.[9] A wider choice of foodstuffs, including new imported items, made meals more interesting. All these developments led to more elaborate ways of serving food and the rituals connected with meals.[10] The role of the housewife had also subtly changed. Whereas in the eighteenth century she was expected to work in the kitchen and perform many household duties herself, by the nineteenth century more servants were present to perform most of the cleaning and cooking, at least in the wealthier sections of the middle class. The housewife's chief duty was supposed to be managing the home and her servants. She was expected to be an elegant hostess for her guests and appear ornamental even if the reality still involved a great deal of hard work.

These were the ideals that the advice books promulgated.[11] These were the general ideas that were followed by most middling-sort and later middle-class homemakers. But the reality of homemaking was more complex. It was impossible to recreate the perfect image of the home that advice books suggested so every homemaker, even if only in minor things, 'broke the rules', by design or force of circumstance. It is the evidence of these discrepancies that provides us with an insight into homemaking practice.

For various reasons these discrepancies have not been adequately dealt with in other texts on domestic interiors. The emphasis in many books about historic interiors has been on wealthy homes and the leaders and innovators of fashion. This has resulted in London housing and consumption receiving more attention than other parts of England.[12] The country homes of the elite have received attention especially following Marc Girouard's ground-breaking analysis of how the country house functioned and how it related to historical development.[13] The emphasis here, however, is on ordinary and non-metropolitan homes that represent the majority of homemakers. While they were followers rather than leaders in fashion, the trends were interpreted by individual homemakers to create meaning in their own domestic environments. The focus is on the home as the creation of homemakers, with the influence of fashion, prescriptive literature or retailers in the background.

Humble British homes have been addressed in various studies, although the particular concerns of the present work have not been fully covered. For example, James Ayres has dealt with the traditions that prevailed in vernacular homes; he uses an archaeological viewpoint and stresses a non-changing, or at least slowly evolving, tradition.[14] The huge number of examples in his research produces an overview of continuity in the face of changing circumstances rather than individual stories. Lorna Weatherill conducted research into the material culture of homes between 1660 and 1760. Her work consisted of collating inventory evidence to plot ownership by region and occupation.[15] Her emphasis was on using quantitative analysis to gauge levels of ownership, to some extent to explore the changing use of the home but focusing less on the associative meaning of home furnishings. One of the few texts dealing with historical research to address this issue has been Amanda Vickery's *The Gentleman's Daughter: Women's Lives in Georgian England*, in which she shows great insight in her reading of documentary sources.[16] By analysing the use of language in letters and diaries, for example, she has established how objects in the home took on extraordinary significance for their owners and could be invested with meaning and memories. Vickery explores the relationship between homemakers, especially female, with their possessions; but she only deals with a few families, all north-country gentry.

The effects of industrialization, urbanization and of social change have resulted in research and some discussion on the nature of the home. Some studies have taken the evolution of a middle class as a starting point for the discussion.[17] Others have particularly focused on the changing roles for women in society. Domestic ideology and separate spheres have provided the main focus for analysis of nineteenth-century homes. Much of this work uses prescriptive literature to study homes rather than actual examples.[18] By looking at the period 1750–1850 the development of the domestic ideology and its influence on interiors can be seen. But this is not the whole story. There were still highly individual interpretations of the ideal.

In recent years a number of strands of influence have contributed to the stance taken here. Design history has become increasingly interested in ordinary objects and ordinary homes rather than those of celebrated designers.[19] Material culture studies in the United States have explored the narratives of home life as told through the furnishings used by homemakers.[20] Similarly, cultural anthropology encourages the wider cultural implications to be reconstructed and helps to put the objects through which people expressed themselves into a cultural context. This third influence comes particularly from the studies of Attfield, Miller and Cieraad, who have used ethnographic techniques derived from anthropology and cultural studies for understanding homemaking practice in the mid- to late-twentieth century.[21] It is not possible to produce an ethnographic study of earlier periods; the people are no longer available to observe and speak to in order that their attitudes can be interpreted. Instead the qualitative analysis of documentary sources approximates as closely as possible this approach. Rather than extract information from documents they have been closely studied as complete artefacts. The presence or not of objects, their place in the home, their storage, their means of acquisition, the reasons for their disposal, their relationship to other household goods and their relationship to the homemaker all produce nuances of ownership, use and meaning.

Qualitative Analysis of Documentary Sources

The period 1750 to 1850 is too distant for oral history or ethnographic studies. It is slightly too early for photographic evidence. Detailed comments and descriptions in diaries are unusual. Pictures of interiors are rare and tend to be of exceptional homes such as those of artists and designers. In England probate inventories ceased to be a requirement by the mid-eighteenth century and only survive in small numbers for a few areas after that date.[22]

However, the use of a qualitative approach to the sources that exist allows an exploration of the material culture of interiors and how they might have functioned. The main source used here are lists of house contents. Some are probate inventories, others are inventories made for a variety of reasons. Other lists of contents were made for house sales. The quantities of these lists that survive enable analysis of home contents to be made. Their varied nature can be accommodated in a qualitative approach and they offer a rich source to the historian of domestic interiors. They give an indication of what homes contained, how they were used as arenas of social and cultural behaviour and meaning.

Using qualitative analysis of inventories differs significantly from the more widely adopted quantitative method. Quantitative analysis requires large numbers of records to be used to produce data that says something about the contents and use of interiors in a general way. There are various problems and limitations to this procedure. For the data to be reliable the method used for selecting the sample would need to take into account any biases in selection or survival.[23] Pat Hudson has written in defence of quantitative methods but still she warns that it is difficult to achieve a representative sample. In her view, 'an independent random sample' is the most representative.[24] A large sample might appear to offer representative findings, but it is unlikely that biases can ever fully be eliminated and the discrepancies are simply lost in the aggregated whole.

By contrast, a qualitative approach can make use of small samples, even an individual inventory. The idea of lived experience is borrowed from cultural studies to gain an idea of how individuals organized their homes as mediations of the prevailing ideals of the period, and as expressions of the particular circumstances of their lives. Whereas in quantitative analysis everything is reduced to averages and means and no individual household emerges, in the qualitative approach analysis applies to the individual. Rather than plotting ownership over time, and by place and occupation, the emphasis is on how these separate items were arranged and incorporated into a concept of 'the home'.

Inventories were made for a variety of reasons. Probate inventories were made for legal purposes on the death of a person with assets; but inventories could be made for other reasons, not always known, such as when a family were moving or going away temporarily, to establish ownership of goods at the renewal of a lease, or following bankruptcy. Descriptions of items in inventories were brief, often omitting information about, for example, the materials from which objects were made. They almost never commented on the style of the object. Age, quality and condition were not always given. These aspects are important for judging the fashionability and the appropriateness of an object in a particular context. John Styles has commented on the tendency for quantitative methods to reduce contents of homes to categories without taking into account 'the enormous range of variation and differentiation' of goods that consumers selected.[25] Although inventories lack obvious descriptive information, much can be learned from close analysis. The wording and manner of listing often suggest attributes for the goods.

In addition, inventories were usually listed by named rooms, and this provides information about usage and meaning.

If the circumstances surrounding an inventory being made or the background of the maker of the inventory are known this can aid analysis. For example, the inventories used here for mid-nineteenth-century inhabitants of Chichester all come from the same document.[26] This notebook provides a small sample, just twenty inventories made when these people died, were moving house or, in one case, became bankrupt. The appraising work was carried out by the same firm of cabinetmakers; in fact most were compiled by one man, Henry Peat. These circumstances invite comparisons to be made and certain assumptions are possible that would be less justified in isolated examples. The Peat inventories were professionally made lists that employed uniform terms and that followed a set procedure. For example, Henry Peat always referred to 'window curtains' when a room had one window and to two or three 'sets of window curtains' when there were a number of windows. It has been possible to test Henry Peat's system of inventory making in one instance: the home of Alithia Newland. The substantial property occupied by her could be identified from the 1851 census, and as the ground-floor rooms remain unchanged the listing of rooms in the inventory was matched satisfactorily against the disposition of rooms in the house. In addition, the junior member of the firm, Samuel Peat, kept a notebook of his cabinetmaking work for Chichester's wealthier inhabitants.[27] Most of the people for whom an inventory was made also used Samuel for their household and furniture repairs, thus his daybook contributes further evidence of their homemaking.

Household lists were also made for the sale of the contents of a house. These lists were generally less detailed than inventories although they sometimes followed an inventory format, often beginning with the bedrooms, followed by the main rooms and ending with the kitchen and service areas. Although these lists missed out much of the detail found in inventories, their composition indicates what the compiler considered particularly desirable at the time. They tell us the best that a house had to offer. For poorer households the items in a kitchen were listed, but in a grander house such objects were taken for granted with a general comment. Appraisers also used adjectives such as fine, elegant and fashionable to grade objects. Such words were not used indiscriminately but seem to have been used judiciously in accordance with the quality of the goods on offer. Thus some household goods were described as merely clean and neat.

All household lists, in their different ways, can be seen as fairly reliable evidence of what homes contained. Inventories were often legal documents where accuracy was required even when made by ordinary citizens.[28] In the case of house sale particulars, professional auctioneers and appraisers would have been good judges of the goods in which they dealt.

Using lists of house contents offers only a 'snapshot' of a home; indeed one of the criticisms of using inventories is that they only provide knowledge about a particular moment in the history of a household. So much of homemaking is transitory. Objects were moved around in daily use providing cluttered, and sometimes untidy, interiors. Rarely does this survive in the inventory descriptions. Summer and winter may have affected which goods were in use and which stored away. Homes also changed during a person's life, with the addition of children, the loss of a spouse, and sometimes the contraction of a household to a few rooms in old age. To counter the difficulty of retrieving the changing nature of interiors the home and its inhabitants can be placed in context. The reasons for making the inventory, the location of the house, and the occupation, sex and social position of the owner of the goods all help to gauge whether this makes their home exceptional in some way and whether this suggests interesting levels of consumption for the home or unusual ways of organizing the house. Further research can reveal information about the lives of individuals, particularly after the census of 1841.[29] A picture of the lived experience of the inhabitants of a home begins to emerge and suggests ways of reading the home, its contents and organization. Individual homes are thrown into relief distinct from the general and ideal homes described in advice literature. It is through observing the differences between the ideals and reality that allows the use of the home and its symbolic values to be explored.

The Focus of Time and Place

The book deals with the period 1750 to 1850 and predominantly considers homemakers who occupied the middle stratum of society. During this time enormous changes occurred in Britain, not least within the furnishing, use and meanings attached to the home. Society, too, was changing due to industrialization and urbanization. The middle stratum of society evolved from the 'middlemen' of craftspeople and merchants to the business and commercially based sector who avoided getting their hands dirty. This change is signalled by the middle stratum being designated 'middling sort' for the earlier time period and 'middle class' for the later. The middling sort comprised about 20–25 per cent of the population of most towns and formed the polite and respectable contingent, and was a driving force in the move towards urban renewal. However they were not exclusively urban since they included yeoman farmers. By the late eighteenth and early nineteenth century a middle class with a distinct culture and their own set of values had emerged. They distinguished themselves from rural life and the poor in both towns and country, since a polite and respectable lifestyle was central to their aspirations. They also strove to be distinct from the gentry and aristocracy. While they might be ambitious they did not want to emulate what they saw as the lax morals that were associated with people of high social status. The middle class built on the polite society that had evolved amongst the middling sort and shaped the social and commercial urban society. Although at times they might present a unified front the middle class were made up of numerous occupations and degrees of wealth and importance, and should more properly be referred to as the middle classes.[30] They were also central to the evolution of the home. The middle classes invested the home and its furnishings with monetary value and material comforts but they also believed that it expressed social, cultural, emotional and religious attitudes. Their influence on the home extended to the sections of society above and below them, through the nineteenth and into the twentieth century.

Since the changes outlined occurred throughout Britain their impact would be discernable in examples of homes throughout the country, although some time differences would have been evident in the areas more remote from centres of fashion, especially from London. The areas of the West Midlands and West Sussex provide the majority of examples drawn on here. Both areas were provincial, although Birmingham was gradually becoming more metropolitan during the period. However, neither area was adversely affected by geographical remoteness since both had good lines of communication with London. The West Midlands was strongly affected by industrialization but even so some towns continued to display the characteristics of an earlier period, and extensive areas of farmland existed within easy reach of busy centres of industry and commerce. Homes from a variety of towns, villages and rural locations are used, as well as homemakers from a variety of occupations, of high and low status, although middling sort/middle class predominate. A similar mixture of examples is used from West Sussex, especially from the cathedral city of Chichester. This area was slower to change but was still in touch with fashionable developments through its close proximity to centres of fashion. These two areas therefore provide a cross-section of English life for a great number of its people. While London is so often the focus of studies of change and fashionable development, by contrast this book deals with the slower and more circumspect take-up of ideas that operated throughout most of the country.[31]

Organization

The book is divided into two parts. The first and longer part examines homes from a number of perspectives in order that the circumstances that prevailed and the influences on homemaking for particular individuals can be explored. The chapters build on each other to provide separate but related viewpoints for understanding historic interiors. Several of these aspects, but to differing degrees, would have influenced each interior. This is highlighted by some homes featuring in a number of chapters. The source material is revisited several times to interrogate it from different angles. An appendix lists the homemakers and tradespeople dealing in goods for the home which feature in the text. All of these names are included in the index so that their various appearances can be cross-referenced.

The second part examines homes of the past but using entirely different source material. The focus here is on historic houses and their interiors that have survived into the present. Whereas the previous chapters used documentary sources that offer fragmentary evidence that is open to interpretation, historic interiors appear to offer an unproblematic view of homes in the past through their material culture. However, before a house is opened to the public it has gone through extensive interpretation that has added and subtracted objects and even changed their physical nature through the conservation process. These changes mean that the house becomes a representation of an historic interior. Interpretation can reveal the stories of homes and their inhabitants but it may also impose a sanitized narrative based on generic rooms. This reduces homes to a simplistic reflection of period and country. Historic houses open to the public are therefore used in

Chapter 6 to reconsider how the ideas explored in Chapters 1–5 can be used to inform the interpretation.

Part I

Chapter 1 deals with taste and identity through the conflict that people faced in their homemaking strategies over how fashionable a home should be. It was more acceptable, and less costly, for clothing to follow fashion, although even here some caution was needed. Home furnishings were a big investment and were expected to last for many years which prevented a rapid turnover or the choice of styles likely to be ephemeral. In addition, it was necessary to make the home appropriate for a consumer's position within a provincial community. Projecting an image that was in line with expectations for your status and your occupation was a moral duty as well as benefiting your business dealings.

'Provincial' has become a byword for old-fashioned and unsophisticated. Note that both definitions are negative, putting provincial in relation to London and finding the provinces wanting. But homemakers in the provinces responded to their position rather differently. While London might have a central position so far as fashion was concerned the city was also seen as a dirty,[32] corrupt and frivolous place in contrast to the industrious and sensible provincial towns.

The gap between fashionable production of furniture in London and what was available outside the city was huge in the seventeenth century. The majority of homes had the most basic of furniture made in local timber.[33] Fashionable textiles were expensive. Apart from linen tablecloths, napkins and towels the only textiles were often the hangings around the best bed and perhaps a few cushions on wooden-seated chairs. Carpenters and joiners made some furniture along with their other work. Much of it was rough and ready if solid. Styles followed regional forms, although they sometimes borrowed motifs from more fashionable furniture.[34] But even fashionable furniture was evolving and becoming more refined as the seventeenth century ended. The basic chair design, for example, of a square stool with extended back legs became more delicate with the introduction of cabinetry skills; dovetail joints, shaped legs and separate shaped back rails.[35]

Craftsmen, who had trained as cabinetmakers, became more widespread as the eighteenth century progressed. Their work was far more sophisticated than that produced by carpenters and joiners. Therefore the spread of specialist furniture makers to even small towns was directly linked to the spread of fashionable home furnishings. The designs for fashionable furniture were spread from London to the provinces through pattern books as well as other influences such as workmen relocating from the capital, and provincial consumers going to London and viewing goods even if not making purchases. But the idea that provincial homemakers wanted simply to copy, or emulate, London ignores the complexity of the relationship between provincial towns and the metropolis.[36]

The period is particularly interesting for examining the spread of fashionable furniture due to the changes in furniture making, and the increased knowledge of fashion because of printed sources. Added to this was the better provision for shopping in provincial towns along with the improvements to the urban environment.[37] Consumers too felt proud of their towns and developed self-confidence in their identity.[38] Before the period provincial homemakers were somewhat disadvantaged in their access to fashionable commodities for the home; by the end of the period the production and retailing of goods had changed immeasurably and a homogenized market that followed standardized designs was beginning to take shape.[39] In between provincial homemakers were faced with choices in their consumption practices. How provincial makers responded to demand and the choices that consumers made is the subject of this chapter.

Chapters 2 and 3 explore various aspects of the visual and material qualities of the home. Although the sources used do not provide physical evidence of actual objects that furnished the home they do hint at how homemakers reacted to the tangible qualities of their possessions. The emotional value of belongings and how this related to the process of creating a home was governed during the period by the growth of concepts described as a domestic ideology.[40] In the process of homemaking people manipulated the qualities inherent in objects; to shape, improve, discard or preserve the furnishings of the home. The value placed on goods dictated their treatment, and through observing this process the meanings attached to homemaking are revealed.

In Chapter 2 the transient nature of many homes and many of the objects that they contained is examined. Changing the place of abode and losing home contents were common either due to economic necessity or accident. To some extent homemakers anticipated such losses and took practical measures to deal with them. In this way many objects were less valued because they could be easily replaced. Emotions were therefore channelled into a minority of possessions that were retained in all but the direst of circumstances. In work that deals with current attitudes to emotional investment in and the subsequent loss of objects, the anthropologist David Parkin has looked at how people deal with the threat of losing their possessions in times of danger. He claims that as well as practical things or items of monetary value people also saved personal items. In 'rare instances these take precedence: thus, one man is reported as carrying nothing more than a bible, as if to indicate its importance as being greater than that of other property.'[41] Most of the examples looked at in this chapter were in less immediate danger than those examined by Parkin. Quick decisions about what to save may illicit particular responses in individuals. But even in less severe situations it has been found that people value some objects more than others in a way that is not connected with their practical or rational value, but rather with their symbolic value.[42] It is difficult to replicate the methodologies of anthropology and cultural studies, and to gauge the emotional investment in objects from documentary sources for the period. But this chapter seeks to do so by looking at the subject in reverse: what was most easily disposed of from the home. Gradually what is revealed are the possessions that hold special meaning for homemakers, that they were especially attached to, objects in which resided the meaning of home and family, as well as 'selfhood'.[43] Evidence is used in this chapter that shows how people graded possessions, between what was most easy to replace, what was retained if at all possible and those objects that were least likely to be relinquished.

Marcia Pointon has looked at personal possessions left in wills, and paintings that were retained rather than included in house sales; this chapter seeks to complete the picture by looking at household possessions as a whole.[44]

If Chapter 2 looked at the subject of loss in relation to household possessions, Chapter 3 deals with how homemakers retained objects and continued to invest them with meaning. The fashion system dictated that furnishings should be replaced with the latest goods. In contrast, homemaking was more about looking after objects to show your skills, whether as practical housewives and husbands, or as people able to construct and sustain a home with all that that implies.

The maintenance of the home is looked at as a process of homemaking both by individual homemakers and by their employment of tradespeople to do the work. The retention of minor objects by wealthy people demonstrates that they did not simply discard objects that were no longer in fashion.[45] Cabinetmakers and upholsterers, both male and female, all had a particular part to play beyond the work of painters, plumbers and builders in preserving the fabric of a house and its contents.

Beyond retaining objects, homemakers also actively sought out used goods to purchase. These should not be confused with antiques which had a limited appeal before the later-nineteenth century, and even then remained an expensive minority pursuit. Purchasing second-hand goods that were slightly old-fashioned but in good condition was a legitimate means of furnishing the home, and there were good practical reasons for their purchase in the eighteenth century.[46] However, there was a huge trade in second-hand furniture throughout the period that was not simply to cater for people unable to purchase new goods. Although it might be supposed that the increased availability, by the nineteenth century, of fashionable and more reasonably priced furniture would have discouraged wealthier middle-class customers from purchasing used goods, this was not the case.

The final section of the chapter looks at the possible emotional meaning attached to older and used furniture. This is achieved first by looking at how furniture figured in bequests in wills, although it was not the most obvious type of object for singling out.[47] But, as Vickery has shown, furniture was seen as an investment that should last a lifetime and then be passed on to the next generation.[48] By the time it was inherited fashions would inevitably have changed but by then the acquisition of associations with the testator gave added value. Lastly, the predicament of the newly middle class in the early- to mid-nineteenth century is examined to look for motives for purchasing second-hand furniture to suggest that it may have had particular values beyond the practical and economic ones.

Chapters 4 and 5 deal with how the different members of a household used the space within the home, and how varying kinds of households shaped the home to suit their needs and taste. Chapter 4 explores the notion of the extended household; the diverse components that might make up one household. Many homes needed to accommodate more than a nuclear family; commonly other members of the extended family lived with relatives, particularly mothers or fathers lived with one of their children. In addition lodgers, a tutor or a governess, servants and visitors all needed to be housed within middle-class family homes.

During the period the accommodation of additional people was complicated by certain expectations for the middle-class home. By the mid- to late-eighteenth century it was thought desirable for particular rooms to have clear uses rather than multi-functional rooms that had previously been normal. Increasingly distinctions were commonly made between the public and private spaces within the house and between work and the home. These developments put pressure on homemakers to articulate areas of the home quite precisely. A general living room and kitchen, that had commonly been called a houseplace, was not only old-fashioned but seemed to suggest a lack of gentility. While a separate parlour was desirable at the outset of the period, by its close even more precise usage was thought desirable for the better-off middle-class house. A dining room should, it was thought, look different to a drawing room and the difference should be expressed through the choice of furnishings. These differences, moreover, were given gendered characteristics to express whether male or female activities would predominate in the use of the room.[49] Inevitably many homes were not able to put into practice the new ideas for the organization of the home. This chapter looks at examples of people who made compromises due to living in older properties, or ones that were too small fully to embrace the distinctions desired. Common too was the continuation of work-related activities within some homes, and these combined the life of the home alongside the uncouth public world of trade and manufacturing.

The home was increasingly expected to be a haven of domesticity; in particular it should be the woman's role to create a home for her family. This development went hand in hand with the exclusion of middle-class women from the workplace and has come to be known as separate spheres. The extent to which women were relegated to a domestic role has been much debated.[50] Certainly, it needs to be taken into account that leisure activities increasingly took place within the home rather than in public, so that women continued to play a role and took on more onerous duties entertaining at home. There was the expectation that homes should be able to provide a semi-public space for entertaining guests, especially for dinner parties. The chapter ends with a detailed examination of how one home could have accommodated a dinner party for a dozen people and how the whole house and all the members of the household had their part to play for the event to be a success.

The detailed look at what was involved in putting on an elegant dinner party in Chapter 4 also demonstrates the shortcomings that would have been experienced by many householders due to economic constraints. Chapter 5 deals with what I am terming 'incomplete' households due to their consisting of a widow, widower, spinster or bachelor, and therefore not containing the idealized family. During the period it was generally thought desirable for a woman to marry. Her position socially would have been enhanced and she would usually have been better off financially. A widow might have a more secure position in both respects than a spinster. However, judging by the attitudes expressed in novels the difficult social position of single women was beginning to be challenged by the mid-nineteenth century.[51] Throughout the period a significant number of households were headed by an independent individual, whether male or female. The effect of marital status on homemaking decisions and the possible gender bias of these homes are the main themes of the chapter. The reduced household was often at a disadvantage, due to the retrenchment needed after the death of a spouse, and spinsters were likewise often managing on a small income. However, the householder was also sometimes in a position to express individual taste that broke away, slightly or dramatically, from what was considered normal for the time. Some debate exists as to whether women consumed in a different way to men, producing a separate consumer practice of their own.[52] Recently the debate has extended to looking at individual male consumption.[53] The debate is considered here in relation to consumption for the home, and for creating individual gender-specific homes.

A section of the chapter deals with the particular circumstances pertaining to the homes of independent women. These householders were able to maintain a home, sometimes with a lodger to increase income, but many others were supported by invested money, such as an annuity. To what extent such homes and their individual female heads were able to sustain a public role for their homes is intriguing. The chapter ends with an examination of a particular set of inventories for independent women living in Chichester in the 1840s. They are examined for clues as to how the space of the home was used as both private and public space, and the role of furnishings, china and cooking utensils for entertaining.

Chapters 1 to 5 use documentary sources to examine domestic interiors from 1750 to 1850 to establish what homes contained, to see how they might vary one from another, and to establish what might have influenced a homemaker to have produced a particular kind of home. The chapters place the documentary sources into the contexts of time and place, and take into account the influences of status and gender. While the trends of a particular period might produce the strongest influence on homemaking practice still each home conveys narratives about the homemaking strategies of the individuals who lived in them.

Part II

The final chapter takes a different course in order to examine historic interiors. The chapter looks at historic houses that are open to the public. These structures take a number of forms whether preserved or restored. Some have been moved to a different location, some have objects and furnishings that are original to the house, others have period artefacts introduced to furnish them, yet others have replica objects and furniture. Ownership of historic houses also varies from state and local authorities, to large charitable organizations and small societies or trusts that own just one property. This variety produces different kinds of historic interiors for the public to consume. Each house is interpreted whether the methodology is made clear or not. Choices have been made as to how the interiors will look and what they will contain. Apart from academic decisions there are limitations for health and safety reasons as to how realistic a restoration can be of historic living conditions.[54] The use of open fires and candles is not permitted in most National Trust houses for example. In addition there are decisions to be made about the style of presentation and extent of interpretive material to be made available: a guided tour, room stewards, books and panels to read in each room. In this way historic interiors bring the past into the present but each one represents the past differently. Although an extensive literature deals with historic houses and with heritage and preservation issues there is comparatively little on the philosophical decisions behind the presentation methods that they employ. In particular there is little that compares British methods with those of the United States. There are good reasons for this comparison since the methods used are usually different although there has been a long tradition of close associations between the two countries for the study of decorative arts and historic interiors.[55] In England it has been usual to preserve layers of successive occupation, whereas in the United States restoration to a particular date or period in the past is invariably carried out.[56]

The chronology present in Chapters 1–5 is not continued into Chapter 6 although the history of historic house preservation began just at the date that ends Part 1. In England the decision to save Aston Hall, near Birmingham, was taken by the city council in 1850, with the intention of preserving the house and its grounds for the people of Birmingham.[57] The first historic house museum in the US was the Hasbrouck house in Newburgh, New York. This had been George Washington's headquarters on the Hudson River during the Revolution. It was opened to the public in 1850.[58] It might seem that the chronology could have been preserved into Chapter 6 by looking only at houses that date from the period 1750–1850. While many of the examples dealt with in this chapter were indeed built during this time frame it is not when they were built that governs their treatment in the present. A medieval house could be interpreted using the preserved or restored methods. Since there is no direct link between the style of house and the period it was built, with the kind of interpretation it receives, the date of the house is not used as the criterion for examination but rather the contexts that appear to influence the decision-making: namely, the owners of the house at the time it was interpreted and the message they wished to convey through the house. In this way the historic house becomes a representation of the past, serving a particular role for its owners.[59] As Gaynor Kavangh has observed, while museums attempt 'to find or construe a form of lived reality' in how they present the experience of people in the past, the historians and curators involved can never be free of their own 'cultural baggage'.[60]

Historic house interpretation has undergone a series of changes in both England and the US. By examining these changes the nature of interpretation becomes apparent. Rather than producing a 'text' that is historically accurate they reflected current concerns and interests. Indeed, historical accuracy is largely accepted as an impossible goal, and notions of authenticity are widely debated.[61] In the recent past such concerns did not unduly worry the owners of historic houses when decisions were taken as to their contents and methods of presentation. Historic interiors were used to promote political viewpoints and national identity[62] or prevailing notions of aesthetics.[63] Although attitudes have changed the old methods of interpretation continue to be felt. This is partly because some houses that were interpreted for public consumption 50 years ago remain largely unaltered, but also because we have inherited some preconceptions from past methods and these are difficult to shake off, both by the museum professionals and by the visiting public who come to visit houses with certain expectations.

Large country houses are visited by the public to see how the wealthy and aristocratic inhabitants lived; more humble houses provide a glimpse of a different kind of domestic life. But to what extent do they show the lived experience of people's home life? Are the kind of narratives about individual homemakers and their idiosyncratic choices that were explored in Chapters 1 to 5 possible to incorporate in static displays? Chapter 6 concludes with some examples of historic houses where particular aspects of the interiors are portrayed, the lives of their past occupants and how the space of the house was utilized by them. The physical shaping of objects and decorative schemes through conservation and restoration are sometimes permanent and if not they are extremely expensive to change. This creates historic interiors that remain unchanged for many years. However, there are strategies for recent academic research to be incorporated into house displays. These provide opportunities to focus attention on various aspects of a building's history and to explore the ways that people used domestic interiors. Such methods are far more reflexive than they were in the past. Present-day interpretation involves the public and invites them to reflect on the version of history that they are consuming. In this way, when we visit historic houses, we make sense of the meaning that homes had for people and this becomes part of our sense of the past.

Notes

[1]   A few celebrated individuals are included, but they are known for their achievements rather than details of their domestic life, which is the focus here.

[2]   June Philipp quoted in Gaynor Kavangh (1990), *History Curatorship*, Washington DC: Smithsonian, p. 64.

[3]   One example of this use of general trends in a television programme was 'Number 57: the history of a house' on Channel 4 in 2003. See also Maxwell Hutchinson (2003), *Number 57: The History of a House*, London: Headline. The history of just one house, its various inhabitants and how they might have furnished their home were traced. But since they had no evidence of what furniture and furnishings were present in the past the makers of the programmes relied on what had been typical at any period for reconstructing the interiors.

[4]   Claire Walsh (1995), 'Shop Design and the Display of Goods in Eighteenth-Century London', *Journal of Design History*, volume 8, number 3, pp. 157–176.

[5]   Joseph van Aken, 'Saying Grace', c. 1725, in the Ashmolean Museum, Oxford, reproduced in Charles Saumarez Smith (1993), *Eighteenth-Century Decoration*, London: Weidenfeld and Nicolson.

[6]   For an account of this literature see Robert B. Shoemaker (1998), *Gender in English Society, 1650–1850*, London and New York: Longman.

[7]   The linking of the home to religious and moral ideas increased throughout Europe and North America in Catholic as well as Protestant countries.

[8]   Rozsika Parker (1984), *The Subversive Stitch: Embroidery and the Making of the Feminine*, London: The Women's Press.

[9]   Norbert Elias (1978), *The Civilising Process*, Oxford: Basil Blackwell.

[10] Mrs Isabella Beeton (1861), *The Book of Household Management*, London: Ward, Lock & Co.

[11] For how this advice literature may have been received see Patricia Branca (1974), 'Image and Reality: The Myth of the Idle Victorian Woman' in Mary S. Hartman and Lois Banner (eds), *Clio's Consciousness Raised*, New York: Harper.

[12] For example Dan Cruikshank and Neil Burton (1990), *Life in the Georgian City*, London: Viking; Peter Guillery (2004), *The Small House in Nineteenth-Century London*, New York and London: Yale University Press.

[13] Mark Girouard (1978), *Life in the English Country House*, New York and London: Yale University Press. See also Gervase Jackson-Stops (ed.) (1989), *The Fashioning and Functioning of the British Country House*, Washington DC: National Gallery and University of New England.

[14] James Ayres (2003), *Domestic Interiors: The British Tradition 1500–1850*, London and New York: Yale University Press.

[15] Lorna Weatherill (1988), *Consumer Behaviour and Material Culture in Britain 1660–1760*, London: Routledge. See also Carole Shammas (1990), *The Pre-Industrial Consumer in England and America*, Oxford: Oxford University Press.

[16] Amanda Vickery (1998), *The Gentleman's Daughter: Women's Lives in Georgian England*, New Haven and London: Yale University Press.

[17] Leonore Davidoff and Catherine Hall (1987), *Family Fortunes: Men and Women of the English Middle Class 1780–1850*, London: Routledge; Peter Earle (1989), *The Making of the English Middle Class*, London: Methuen; Dror Wahrman (1995), *Imagining the Middle Class*, London: Cambridge University Press; Margaret Hunt (1996), *The Middling Sort: Commerce, Gender and the Family in England, 1680–1780*, Berkeley: University of California Press; Alan Kidd and David Nicholls (eds) (1999), *Gender, Civic Culture and Consumerism: Middle-Class Identity in Britain, 1800–1940*, Manchester: Manchester University Press.

[18] See for example Sandra Burman (ed.) (1979), *Fit Work for Women*, London: Croom Helm. A full account of the literature is given in Amanda Vickery (1993), 'Golden Age to Separate Spheres? A review of the categories and chronology of English women's history', *The Historical Review*, volume 36, number 2, pp. 383–414.

[19] See for example Penny Sparke (1995), *As Long As It's Pink*, London: Harper Collins; I. Bryden and J. Floyd (eds) (1999), *Domestic Space: Reading the Nineteenth-Century Interior*, Manchester: Manchester University Press.

[20] This literature is extensive, see in particular Katherine C. Grier (1988), *Culture and Comfort: People, Parlors, and Upholstery 1850–1930*, Rochester NY: The Strong Museum and Massachusetts University Press; Jane C. Nylander (1994), *Our Own Snug Fireside: Images of the New England Home, 1760–1860*, New Haven and London: Yale University Press; Laurel Thatcher Ulrich (2001*), The Age of Homespun: Objects and Stories in the Creation of an American Myth*, New York: Alfred A. Knopf.

[21] Judy Attfield and Pat Kirkham (eds) (1995), *A View from the Interior*, London: The Women's Press; Irene Cieraad (1999), *At Home: An Anthropology of Domestic Space*, Syracuse University Press; Daniel Miller (1998), *Material Culture: Why Some Things Matter*, London: UCL.

[22] Jeff Cox and Nancy Cox (2000), 'Probate 1500–1800: a System in Transition', in Tom Arkell, Nesta Evans and Nigel Goose, *When Death Do Us part: Understanding the Probate Records of Early Modern England*, Oxford: Leopards Press.

[23] Weatherill's sampling method was to take every tenth inventory 'unseen' from the box, but if this record was unusable because incomplete in some way it was rejected and another taken. Weatherill (1988), *Consumer Behaviour*, p. 202.

[24] Pat Hudson (2000), *History By Numbers: An Introduction to Quantitative Approaches*, London: Arnold, p. 170.

[25] John Styles (2000), 'Product Innovation in Early Modern London', *Past and Present*, number 168, pp. 124–169, p. 126.

[26] West Sussex Record Office, Add Mss 2245.

[27] West Sussex Record Office, Add Mss 2239.

[28] See Jeff Cox and Nancy Cox (1984), 'Probate Inventories: the Legal Background', Part 1, *The Local Historian*, volume 16, number 1, pp. 133–145; Part 2, volume 16, number 2, pp. 217–228.

[29] This was the first census to contain reasonably full information.

[30] See Davidoff and Hall (1987), *Family Fortunes*, p. 24 for a useful table setting out the differences.

[31] The circumstances of the northern industrial towns, more remote rural locations, and the particular circumstances of ports are not represented.

[32] Bed bugs were often known as 'London bugs'.

[33] Christopher Gilbert (1991), *English Vernacular Furniture*, New Haven and London: Yale University Press; Ayres (2003), *Domestic Interiors*.

[34] Gilbert (1991), *English Vernacular Furniture*.

[35] Clive D. Edwards (1996), *Eighteenth-Century Furniture*, Manchester: Manchester University Press.

[36] John Brewer (1997), *The Pleasures of the Imagination: English Culture in the Eighteenth Century*, Chicago: University of Chicago Press, p. 493.

[37] Peter Borsay (1989), *The English Urban Renaissance: Culture and Society in the Provincial Town, 1660–1770*, Oxford: Clarendon Press; Rosemary Sweet (1999), *The English Town, 1680–1840*, London: Longman; Nancy Cox (2000), The *Complete Tradesman: a Study of Retailing 1550–1820*, Aldershot: Ashgate.

[38] Sweet (1999), *The English Town*.

[39] Pat Kirkham, Rodney Mace and Julia Porter (1987), *Furnishing the World: the East London Furniture Trade 1830–1980*, London: Journeyman.

[40] Catherine Hall (1979), 'The Early Formation of Victorian Domestic Ideology', in Sandra Burman (ed.), *Fit Work for Women*, London: Croom Helm.

[41] He is concerned with refugees in Africa. David Parkin (1999), 'Mementoes as Transitional Objects in Human Displacement', *Journal of Material Culture*, volume 4, number 3, pp. 303–320, p. 313.

[42] Kevin Hetherington (2004), 'Secondhandness: Consumption, Disposal and Absent Presence', *Environment and Planning, D: Society and Space*, volume 22, pp. 157–173, p. 169.

[43] Parkin (1999), 'Mementoes as Transitional Objects'.

[44] Marcia Pointon (1997), *Strategies for Showing: Women, Possession, and Representation in English Visual Culture 1665–1800*, Oxford: Oxford University Press.

[45] Margaret Ponsonby (1994), 'Samuel Peat: Chichester Cabinet Maker', *Regional Furniture*, volume 3, pp. 64–72.

[46] Stana Nenadic (1994), 'Middle Rank Consumers and Domestic Culture in Edinburgh and Glasgow 1720–1840', *Past and Present*, number 145, pp. 122–156.

[47] Maxine Berg (1996), 'Women's Consumption and the Industrial Classes of Eighteenth-Century England', *Journal of Social History*, volume 30, number 2, pp. 415–434; Pointon (1997), *Strategies for Showing*.

[48] Vickery (1998), *The Gentleman's Daughter*.

[49] Juliet Kinchin (1996), 'Interiors: Nineteenth-Century Essays on the "Masculine" and the "Feminine" Room', in Pat Kirkham (ed.), *The Gendered Object*, Manchester: Manchester University Press.

[50] Burman (1979), *Fit Work for Women*; Vickery (1993), 'Golden Age'.

[51] The heroines of several of Anthony Trollope's novels, for example, debate whether or not to marry and then regret it when they do.

[52] Lorna Weatherill (1986), 'A Possession of One's Own: Women and Consumer Behaviour in England, 1660–1740', *Journal of British Studies*, volume 25, pp. 131–156; Berg (1996), 'Women's Consumption'.

[53] Margot Finn (2000), 'Men's Things: Masculine Possession in the Consumer Revolution', *Social History*, volume 25, number 2, pp. 133–155.

[54] These issues affect historic houses but have particularly been discussed with reference to open-air museums. See Richard Handler and Eric Gable (1997), *The New History in an Old Museum: Creating the Past at Colonial Williamsburg*, Durham and London: Duke University Press.

[55] The Attingham Society for the Study of the English Country House was founded in 1952 specifically to arrange study courses for Americans.

[56] The emphasis here is on England rather than the whole of the UK as slight differences exist in heritage practice.

[57] *Guide to Aston Hall* (1973), Birmingham: City of Birmingham Museum and Art Gallery, p. 4.

[58] Charles B. Hosmer (1965), *Presence of the Past: a History of the Preservation Movement in the United States Before Williamsburg*, New York: G.P. Putnam, p. 36.

[59] Stuart Hall (ed.) (1997), *Representation: Cultural Representations and Signifying Practices*, London: Sage in Association with Open University.

[60] Kavangh (1990), *History Curatorship*, p. 65–66.

[61] David Phillips (1997), *Exhibiting Authenticity*, Manchester: Manchester University Press.

[62] Diane Barthel (1996), *Historic Preservation: Collective Memory and Historical Identity*, New Brunswick, NJ: Rutgers University Press; Handler and Gable (1997), *The New History*; Patricia West (1999), *Domesticating History: the Political Origins of America's House Museums*, Washington DC: Smithsonian Institute Press.

[63] Louise Ward (1996), 'Chintz, Swags and Bows; the Myth of the English Country-House Style', *Things*, number 5, pp. 7–37; Peter Mandler (1997), *The Fall and Rise of the Stately Home*, New York: Yale University Press.

PART I

Chapter 1

Provincial Homes

In an oil painting, by Joseph Francis Gilbert,[1] of Chichester, painted in 1813, the viewer looks down the middle of East Street towards the butter cross, which was then, and had been since medieval times, the junction of the four main streets of Chichester. On either side of the street are smart Georgian buildings, although their various heights and designs betray that they are merely facades on older structures. Elegantly dressed ladies and gentleman stroll along the pavements and contemplate the wares on display in the shop windows that line the street. Although none of these wares are visible, East Street had a number of fashionable shops that included, by 1828, booksellers and stationers, a confectioner, a glass and china dealer, perfumers, cabinetmakers, milliners and ten drapers.[2] The main focus of Gilbert's painting is, however, the cattle market that is in progress in the foreground and along most of the street.[3] Thus a number of conflicting elements are here brought together. The medieval and traditional nature of the built environment of many provincial towns contrasted with the awareness of fashion expressed in the newer architectural additions, the clothes people wore and many of the commodities for sale. There was the intrusion too of the sights, sounds and smells of rural life, especially on market days. It is this mixture of diverse elements that make provincial towns difficult to evaluate in terms of fashionable taste.

The conflicting regional and metropolitan influences that affected the choice of furnishings for provincial homes will be addressed in this chapter. London exerted an increasingly strong influence. In a minority of cases, provincial tradespeople made goods to London standards, usually where there was aristocratic patronage. Generally though, if one uses connoisseurship to evaluate its worth, then provincial production was a poor imitation. But this evaluation does not do justice to the many good producers in provincial towns, or to the taste and requirements of their customers. Taste in furnishings needs to be seen in the context of the cultural life of provincial towns. As John Brewer has observed, while provincial people were shaping culture that 'bore more than a passing resemblance to the refined entertainments of London, [it] was nevertheless quite distinct from them.'[4] While this comment is specifically referring to literary and visual culture it also applies to the material culture of domestic interiors and the choices that people made about the design of their home furnishings.

Contemporary Perceptions of Metropolitan and Provincial Taste

To establish the intricacies of the relationship between London and the provinces, it is useful to consider the various meanings, during the period, of the words 'metropolitan' and 'provincial'. The definition of provincial as countrified and of narrow outlook was already established by the mid-eighteenth century and was applied in a negative way.[5] However, at the same time metropolitan could also be used negatively: it could mean over-sophisticated and corrupt. Indeed the word fashion itself could be used with both approval and disapproval, its negative application was to designate something or someone as fickle, shallow and ephemeral. So, certainly at the outset of the period there were good reasons not to rush to embrace metropolitan fashions. For some provincial consumers it would have been desirable to distinguish themselves from metropolitan styles.

By the nineteenth century the word provincial was increasingly used to describe things that were lacking in sophistication. At the same time, though, the urban centres in the provinces were becoming increasingly aware of their own worth in economic terms. This expressed itself through their demand for greater political autonomy and an awareness of the distinct nature of life and culture in the provinces.[6] Thus, urban centres such as Birmingham and Manchester saw themselves on an equal footing with London. However, they also distinguished themselves from rural areas, which were designated as countrified and uncouth. So, by the close of the period, tastes were formed in relation to these two or three positions. For many urban dwellers their provincial taste was part of their cultural identity that distinguished them from London ideas and from rural traditions. Expressing cultural identity through the choice of home furnishings was not something to be apologetic about. To appreciate the production and consumption of home furnishings in the provinces thus demands the careful consideration of these choices and acknowledging the existence of a distinct provincial taste.

Non-metropolitan production had long followed 'vernacular' styles that had been influenced by changes in fashion while still reflecting regional diversity. During the eighteenth century, regional forms were slowly being replaced by more fashion-conscious styles, and by the nineteenth century such furniture was seen as distinctly rural. But the change from regional to metropolitan fashion was not a simple one. While knowledge of new fashions spread to the provinces, not all consumers wanted to adopt them outright; but conversely, most were not content with regional items made in traditional ways. To understand provincial taste during this period of transition, it is crucial to evaluate provincial production and consumption in home furnishings rather than judge it by London standards. Four aspects will be considered. Firstly, the nature of regional or vernacular production is investigated and how it was changing in the late-eighteenth and the early-nineteenth century. In the second section the relationship between provincial and metropolitan goods is explored. Provincial consumers had a particular relationship to metropolitan taste. Just as trickle down and emulation theories have been problematized in relation to class or status so they also need to be revised in respect of provincial taste emulating London fashions.[7]

In the third section the effects of urban development and the spread of fashionable ideas to the provinces are examined. The awareness and reactions to fashionable ideas by makers and retailers of furnishings are explored through a consideration of their retailing establishments, their advertisements and their incorporation of fashionable ideas in the goods they made and sold. This section discusses how people perceived the fashionable elements in the design of furnishings, and how they chose to translate those elements into something appropriate for provincial lives.

In the final section of this chapter it will be shown how traditional rural homemaking that was coming under threat in the early-nineteenth century was portrayed in a fictional account while purporting to be reality. The author of the story reveals that she was reluctant to accept fashionable taste in a rural setting since she saw it as an immoral influence on the 'purity' of traditional styles. Thus the author made plain, to contemporary readers, the complex tensions between choosing fashionable and unfashionable goods for the home.

Regional Traditions in Domestic Furniture

Provincial furniture was not the same as regional, sometimes described as vernacular, furniture. But defining these categories is not straightforward. Regional furniture might be defined as 'common' furniture. Its production was usually anonymous and it was made with local timber using methods of production peculiar to particular areas of the country. By the eighteenth century simple lathes were often used for turned elements. Peg construction and seats of rush or wicker were typical features.[8] Oak was the most popular timber, only losing its importance in the nineteenth century, when cheap imported deal became readily available due to better transportation by canals, and later by the railways.[9] Regional makers were carpenters and joiners by trade who made furniture as part of a wider repertoire that included ploughs, mangers, fences and gates.

It might be thought that vernacular-style production indicated unchanging methods of production, but regional goods had always evolved and, to some extent, responded to changes in fashion. But the awareness of fashion filtered down to the makers and then had to be adapted to fit whatever regional form was practised. This resulted in what might be termed hybrid forms. James Ayres defines vernacular as designs that were not drawn on paper but were evolved by the carpenter.[10] Christopher Gilbert refers to vernacular production as unselfconscious. Both of these definitions mark out vernacular as different to provincial production which was consciously fashionable.[11] As Gilbert has observed, 'while many grades of sophistication existed it would be misleading to suggest that vernacular furniture had a complex interrelationship with London taste.'[12] It is this point that perhaps marks the divergence between regional or vernacular production and furniture produced in the provinces that embraced fashionable ideas while still retaining a provincial status.

Increasingly regional wares became associated with rural and rougher ways of life that did not fit in with urban dwellers' expectations for the home, its appearance, how it functioned and how it was perceived by outsiders. During the period, not only was knowledge of fashion increasing but also the awareness of what constituted genteel construction. So, generally, consumers had begun to prefer the use of refined cabinetmaking over the work of the joiner, and imported 'smart' timbers, particularly mahogany, over local timber. Bernard Cotton suggests that some makers in urban areas adapted to making the fancy designs that were wanted, the 'cabinet makers in the major regional towns utilised the work of local turners in producing their own repertoire of chair styles based more on nationally changing fashion than on the native regional styles.'[13] However, some regional-style production continued, and this furniture was consumed in urban centres throughout the period, but was used in the service areas of middle-class homes rather than the rooms where higher levels of comfort and gentility were expected.[14] Large quantities of painted, cheap, pine case-furniture, such as chests of drawers, continued to be made, as well as chairs. However, regional forms were being diluted by nationally recognised styles. The Windsor-type chair was the most frequently made common chair, due to the increased production methods used in High Wycombe. Other types of regional chair continued in greatly reduced numbers.[15]

From inventory evidence it is rare to find regional items still in use in the main living rooms of middle-class houses by the early-nineteenth century. Examples that are found can usually be explained by the prevailing circumstances: rural location or the age of the home owner. James Mullock, a farmer in Shropshire, for example, had several turned chairs in his parlour in 1804.[16] Mullock was not only a farmer living in an isolated position, but he was also a rather old-fashioned bachelor, reflected in his kitchen being referred to as a houseplace – an archaic term by that period. Another example is Miss Drinkwater, who had a comfortable home in Chichester. She had an income of about £200 a year and had been able to furnish her house in some style. But when she died in the early 1840s, she had a settle amongst the furniture in her dining room.[17] This item was certainly a regional piece and would have been at odds with her mahogany dining table and chairs. The reason for its retention was probably that it served a practical purpose, and at 85 Miss Drinkwater did not feel obliged to be completely fashionable.

So, by the early-nineteenth century most middle-class people in urban centres were moving away from regional furniture. It is time now to consider the relationship between the provinces and the metropolis. Although fashionable styles were wanted, in preference to regional style production, it was not a simple shift to a desire for goods that proclaimed a London style of manufacture.

Mediating the Consumption of London-Bought Furnishings

London attracted wealthier people from the provinces for visits of either short duration or for the season. This practice was most prevalent in the counties nearest to the metropolis.[18] London shops provided luxury items, exotic imports and a wider choice of design than could be found anywhere else in the country.[19]

Some provincial homemakers had a close connection with, and inclination to purchase from, London. One such family was that of Matthew Boulton, the metalware manufacturer in Birmingham. He and his children used London makers to furnish their homes.[20] Matthew Boulton began homemaking in 1768 on his marriage to Anne Robinson. During the next three decades he patronized a number of Birmingham cabinetmakers and upholsterers, ordering items of furniture and having numerous pieces repaired over the years. However, when he remodelled Soho House in the 1790s, he demanded a higher level of style and quality. In two years he spent four times as much as he had over 35 years in Birmingham, and from just two cabinetmakers. Boulton ordered complete rooms, rather than individual items. He used fashionable and exclusive suppliers – he was James Newton's only recorded non-aristocratic customer.[21] With the help of these élite tradespeople, Boulton created a splendid interior at Soho House. The dining room was particularly grand. It was this room that hosted the Lunar Society dinners on the Sunday nearest the full moon, with discussions ranging from the latest mechanical inventions to philosophy and botany. This room had pillars painted in cream and yellow to simulate marble. The curtains of a heavy canvas fabric were painted to match. Boulton seems to have consulted an interior decorator on this scheme, Cornelius Dixon, who also painted the pillars using the then fashionable technique of scagliola. Dixon did some of the buying on Boulton's behalf and chose the colours for the curtains.[22] Boulton had plenty of other advice, in the form of pattern books, dealings with designers and architects for his business and mixing with the very best in society in London, again for furthering his business. These connections with London were essential for creating fashionable goods and for finding suitable wealthy patrons. Boulton, however, did not embrace London society and manners. Instead he remained a proud provincial businessman and hated going to the metropolis, which he referred to as 'the great & Debauched Capital'.[23]

For Boulton's unmarried and semi-invalid daughter, Anne, her homemaking chance came after her father's death and when her brother married, allowing her to set up home for herself a short distance away from Soho House. Anne moved into Thornhill House in about 1819 and launched into a whirl of house furnishing. (Illustration 1:1) She used London makers, including the London branch of Gillow. She also used the architect and designer Richard Bridgens to produce designs for her home in the early 1820s (Illustration 1:2). He also arranged for some curtains to be made in London. The curtains were accompanied by a drawing and instructions for the local upholsterer to follow in order that they were hung correctly. The drawing showed how wires were to be inserted to give some of the fancy swags just the right shape.[24] Without this drawing there was the danger that a provincial craftsman might have been unaware of the intricacies of upholstery techniques then in practice. Without this knowledge the extra expense of London production would have been entirely wasted.

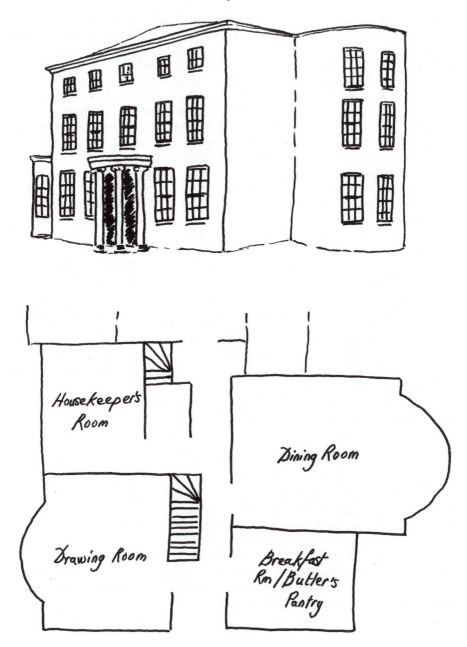

1:1 Thornhill was the home of Anne Boulton from 1819 to her death in 1829.

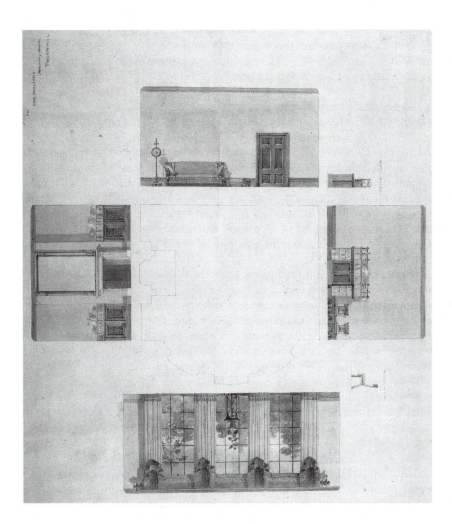

1:2 The design for Anne Boulton's drawing room was produced by the architect Richard Bridgens in the early 1820s.

Anne Boulton was employing an innovative designer at the outset of a promising career. Bridgens had set up his architectural practice in Birmingham in 1818, after the death of his employer, George Bullock. Bridgens had worked closely with the prestigious cabinetmaker and through him had become acquainted with the Boultons and James Watt junior.[25] When the latter began renting Aston Hall, a large seventeenth-century mansion on the outskirts of Birmingham, Bridgens was employed to refurnish the house and this was reason enough to relocate to Birmingham.[26] No doubt he expected other commissions to follow. However, he could not find sufficient work and had to return to London in 1825. Bridgens was cutting edge and this was either too expensive or his designs were too rarefied for Birmingham residents. Either reason would indicate sensible middle-class attitudes or a conservative provincialism.

Despite his personal antipathy to London, Boulton and his daughter were creating homes that were largely metropolitan in nature: London-made and London-inspired furnishings and frequented by national and international figures of their day. But they were exceptional.

Many provincial consumers who had access to the shops and tradespeople of London avoided the extremes of metropolitan fashions. Instead they mediated what was on offer, so that goods would fit in with their provincial lives. In most cases too the metropolitan wares were not purchased unquestioningly. Amanda Vickery found, in the diaries and letters of the Lancashire gentry in the later-eighteenth century, evidence of rather mixed reactions to metropolitan fashions.[27] Striking a balance between extremes was part of middling sort/middle class and provincial tastes.

This was the case with the Staunton family, although since the evidence of their shopping trip to London comes from an account book, their preferences must be surmised. In June 1803 John Staunton, a wealthy gentleman from Kenilworth, Warwickshire, took his wife to London for two weeks. They stayed with his eldest son from his first marriage, William, who was a lieutenant in the First Life Guards. John and Anne (whom he called Nanny) had married in c. 1800, and this was the only trip to London that John recorded in his account book, kept from 1800 to 1811.[28] Whilst there, the Staunton's enjoyed the delights that London had to offer: they went to an exhibition, to see a panorama and paid two shillings to see Canary birds. Luxury food and items of clothing were purchased: a pair of shoes, a suit of clothes, two pairs of stockings, essence of anchovies and, for his son Edmund, some black stockings and six sticks of red chalk; and a bonnet and scissors for Nanny, who was also given 15 guineas to make her own purchases. John treated his grandchildren with wax dolls, a wagon and 'toys'. For their house in Kenilworth, John purchased a Turkey carpet, flower jars, a gridiron, knives and forks, a muffineer and a nutmeg grater. Apart from the carpet, costing, £20 12s 0d, and the suit of clothes, costing five guineas, these were mostly small purchases and offered the Stauntons the pleasure of choosing items in fashionable London shops. They did, however, make another substantial purchase: yellow printed cotton fabric for some bed hangings and matching curtains, costing £12 4s 0d. Changing the textiles in a bedchamber would have dramatically changed the room's appearance.[29] Purchasing fabric in London gave them the opportunity to acquire a more fashionable design than might have been available in Warwick or Coventry, where they usually did their shopping. However, to achieve a truly fashionable scheme for this bedroom John Staunton should have had the bed hangings made up by a London firm, but this he did not do. Instead, he sent the fabric to a local upholsterer, Mr Herbert, to make up into bed hangings and curtains. They were finished in August and Mr Herbert's bill amounted to a mere 18s 9d. John Staunton went to the expense of a new furnishing scheme for his and Nanny's room with London-bought textiles, but he did not go to the additional expense of having them made up in London. This may have been simply to save money. But some customers wanted to avoid the over-fussy and showy designs of London-made draperies, of the kind that Anne Boulton had sent from London with instructions for inserting wires to support sophisticated swags. So, instead, they purchased the textiles in London but had furnishings made up locally, knowing that local tradespeople could be relied upon to produce what was appropriate.

If a personal visit was not possible then provincial consumers often asked family and friends to make purchases for them, particularly for articles of clothing, dress fabrics and accessories. Evidence for these practices exists in diaries and account books, and was clearly considered worth noting down. One such example was Mary Ann Mason, from Brighton, who had married a man from Chichester, and kept a diary of her day-to-day life, recording a round of visiting, going for walks, doing embroidery and singing. Although she frequently mentioned shopping the only purchase of furnishings that she recorded was in December 1836 when 'a large glass came today from London'.[30] The arrival of a looking glass, perhaps carved and gilded, was a special occasion in her household, and unusual.[31]

While many provincial consumers visited London and made purchases or ordered items from makers or through friends and relatives, most of such goods constituted the minority of their homemaking purchases and probably they were more concerned to buy items of clothing and personal attire, for which a different code of consumption operated. Most provincial people had provincial homes.

Fashion, Consumption and Urban Renewal

To ascertain the conditions for purchasing fashionable goods in the provinces requires an understanding of how towns were developing during the period, and how urban circumstances varied between towns, resulting in different levels of provision.

From the later-seventeenth to the mid-eighteenth century, English towns underwent what historians have termed an urban renaissance due to the renewal of the fabric of the towns and the resurgence of building, or at least re-fronting houses, and the growth of amenities.[32] Many towns made improvements to their roads and water supplies and acquired additional leisure facilities such as race courses and theatres. Public buildings were erected in the form of market houses and town halls, built in brick and stone in the style of architecture that was prevalent, rather than regional forms. Jon Stobart suggests that there was generally an emulation of London, including the move towards 'polite architecture' rather than regional, and tradesmen were becoming more aware of London tastes.[33] Shops were affected by both the changes to the built environment and the expectations of the wealthier shoppers who visited provincial towns. Nancy Cox says that 'by the late-seventeenth century the urban renaissance had provided the foundation for the establishment of provincial shopping areas serving a social elite.'[34] The number of towns with such facilities increased during the eighteenth century.

Various arguments have been proposed for the reason for urban renewal and the driving force behind it. These arguments are closely connected with the development of taste in provincial towns during the period 1750–1850 since the predominant attitudes were also forming taste in the private sphere of the home as well as the built environment. One argument is that towns were becoming 'gentrified'; that the gentry influenced the changes and they in turn had been influenced by metropolitan ideas, and therefore provincial towns were simply importing London ideas and tastes. But this ignores the role played by the middling sort in provincial towns. Historians have invented the term pseudo-gentry or town gentry to explain cultural developments within the middling sort in some towns which goes some way to explain the nature of their influence. Pseudo-gentry were a 'class of leisured and predominantly urban families who, by their manner of life, were commonly regarded as gentry, though they were not supported by a landed estate.'[35] Town gentry comprised gentlemen who had taken up residence in towns rather than live on their rural estates, but in addition it included the élite of the professional and mercantile classes who had prospered sufficiently to adopt the lifestyle of gentlemen, while still residing in towns.[36] It is claimed that the pseudo-gentry had close links with London, made frequent visits and used London as a pattern for their behaviour.[37]

Estimates vary as to how large this contingent was and it varied from one town to another: anything from 4 to 14 per cent in the second half of the eighteenth century. In the smaller county towns, the cathedral cities and the 'leisure towns', whose economies were largely dependent upon providing services, there was a high proportion of 'pseudo-gentry' and their influence was most noticeable. Shrewsbury and Chichester were both affected in this way, with the result that luxury trades expanded disproportionately to the size of population. Although both towns also lost some of their importance as neighbouring towns grew, due to industrial and commercial development, the advantages they had gained meant that they continued to attract wealthy residents. An early-nineteenth-century trade directory stated that 'Chichester is one of those favoured towns selected in England for residence, by respectable families of moderate incomes and unconnected with trade; the society of the place is consequently select, yet not unsocial.'[38] The directory of tradespeople in the town was headed by a list of 'Nobility, Gentry and Clergy' consisting of 93 names. At this time the population of Chichester was just 7362 but was able to support a large number of tradespeople catering to the luxury end of home furnishing. The same directory listed ten cabinetmakers, and two carvers and gilders.

It is important to bear in mind that 'pseudo-gentry' is a modern term and it is not clear whether people who have been designated as such would have identified with the gentry. Other historians have pursued a rather different interpretation of the role of the middling sort in initiating urban renewal. They claim that this section of society had a clear idea of what they wanted for their towns, and that they were even rejecting the dominance of the gentry. Beckett and Smith for example suggest that the urban renaissance was caused by the middling sort since they were the element of society most concerned with consumption.[39] Similarly, Rosemary Sweet argues that; 'By the late-eighteenth century not only were the gentry being challenged as consumers, but their influence was being questioned more generally, not just on political grounds, but more covertly, in the cultural sphere, as the proponents of urban culture became more self-conscious and self-confident in their own value.'[40]

The middling sort was different to the middle class that developed in the late-eighteenth and early-nineteenth centuries. The former were not exclusively urban since they included yeoman farmers. They were generally buyers and sellers and therefore 'middlemen'. The middling sort comprised about 20–25 per cent of the population of most towns, but boundaries were not rigid. Some occupations carried more status than others. It was easier for professionals to mix with the country gentry. Shopkeeping had become a new method of acquiring wealth and middling status. This was particularly true in towns that were higher up the urban hierarchy, and in retailing luxury commodities, such as silver and cabinetry wares.[41] It was within this section of society in provincial towns that consumption was increasing.[42] They were also the section of society most concerned with the creation of a polite society, and for whom the home and the private sphere was becoming ever more important; a place to demonstrate social status and family values. It was this middling sort then that played a crucial role in forming provincial taste in the second half of the eighteenth century.

With the later-eighteenth century came further urbanization and growth in towns that had not previously been important but became so due to industrialization. It was here in particular that the middle class emerged as dominant. And here the break with the gentry was most keenly apparent. Even towns that had once been dominated by the gentry were becoming dominated by the middle class. The formation of a middle-class culture and identity grew out of the urban society 'of the eighteenth-century polite and commercial citizen'.[43] The middle-class virtues of thrift, economy, independence and opposition to privilege thrived in the growing industrial towns where the gentry had little influence. For the middle class even more than the middling sort, the home and its furnishings were important not only for material comfort but to express social, cultural, emotional and religious attitudes. It was this middle class that became the taste makers within provincial towns in the first half of the nineteenth century.

Levels of Provision in the Provinces – Fashionable Streets and Retailers of Home Furnishings

All towns, even those at the bottom of the urban hierarchy, had fixed shops long before the mid-eighteenth century. The size of the town and its position within the hierarchy influenced the level of specialization that occurred in shops and the degree of choice that was provided.[44] Furniture and furnishings required specialist cabinetmakers and upholsterers for these goods to be fashionable. Carvers and gilders were more specialized still, although many cabinetmakers often employed craftspeople to perform these aspects of furniture making. The size, but also the type of town, influenced the number of specialized craftspeople present, and the quality of what was available.[45] Quite small towns could claim some importance even if they were losing ground to industrializing towns in the later-eighteenth century. Such towns could often compete in terms of retail provision due to relatively high numbers of middling sort and gentry. One example is Bridgnorth in Shropshire. It had long been important due to its position on the River Severn. Although it was becoming less important as a port, still the High Street in High Town could boast fashionable shops in the later-eighteenth century for the residents of the better-quality housing in that part of the town.[46] Furniture provision did exist, if somewhat limited: a cabinetmaker was working there in 1743,[47] and between two and four cabinetmakers, and one chairmaker, were practising during the first half of the nineteenth century.[48]

The county town of Shrewsbury retained its position through much of the period despite the huge growth of Birmingham and Wolverhampton.[49] As a regional centre it benefited from good schools and provided entertainment with a theatre and race course.[50] These attributes attracted high-status middling and gentry residents as well as people from a considerable area to use its shopping facilities. Large numbers of shops catered for house furnishing requisites, with some well-established firms providing a high level of expertise. Shrewsbury was well provided for with furniture trades in terms of quantity and quality, with specialist firms clearly able to offer fashionable goods made to order. The earliest surviving trade directory, from 1783, included an upholsterer, and there were 20 cabinetmakers, 15 of whom were also able to offer upholstery work, in 1850. Even more specialized was the work of carvers and gilders, and Shrewsbury had three by 1850.[51] One firm of carvers and gilders, Donaldson, who had a shop in the High Street in the early-nineteenth century, had provided Lord Berwick with some highly decorative work when he refurnished nearby Attingham Hall.[52] However, Shrewsbury had retained its medieval buildings and street plan, with many narrow alleyways and inadequate street lighting. Although individual shops had fashionable new fronts, the streets themselves were slow to improve.

The situation in Shrewsbury closely resembled that of Chichester, another regional centre, albeit rather smaller, with the added attraction of the cathedral, but the fortnightly cattle market was not removed from the central streets until the 1870s.[53] There were ten cabinetmakers and upholsterers in 1828.[54] Cabinetmakers were, with just one exception, situated in East Street and North Street, fashionable shopping streets that were lit by gas lights from 1823.[55] Whereas carpenters and chairmakers, at the lower end of the furniture making trade, were further out, and most were in the St Pancras area, noted for poorer dwellings, and liable to flood.

Smaller rural towns did not have specialist cabinetmakers and therefore had to make do with a carpenter or joiner to do repair work on furniture or to make modest items. In Stone, in Staffordshire, for example, John Foden did some of the work of a cabinetmaker but he had probably trained as a wheelwright.[56] According to the account book that Foden kept, he was working in Stone from 1822 and on and off until 1867, although by this time, aged 74, he was only doing occasional jobs.[57] During his early years Foden took on all manner of work: making and repairing wooden furniture, some upholstery work such as putting up or taking down window curtains and bed hangings, house repairs, painting and decorating, shopfitting, and making wheels and carts.[58] The wide range of work and its nature suggests that Foden had not served an apprenticeship in cabinetmaking or upholstery. Most work was in deal, apart from a few repairs to mahogany furniture. Throughout the first half of the nineteenth century no cabinetmakers and upholsterers were recorded in trade directories for Stone; just a couple of chair makers, probably making regional items. When Foden worked in Longton, in the Potteries district, during the 1830s and 1840s, he almost exclusively made wheels and carts for people employed in the pottery trade. Unlike Stone, Longton did have a modest number of furniture makers: three cabinetmakers in 1834 and four cabinetmakers and upholsterers in 1850.[59] Therefore it seems that the small market town of Stone could not support specialist furniture making skills. Foden was found adequate for a wide range of customers, mostly middle-class tradesmen, with a few gentlemen employing him to do joinery and repair work. By the time Foden was back in Stone in the 1860s the consumption of fashionable furnishings had probably increased slightly. Foden mentioned rather more mahogany furniture being repaired and several entries to repairing 'sheffineers' which was his name for chiffoniers, then fashionable items in a parlour or drawing room.

The circumstances were rather different in industrializing towns, although they had other difficulties to contend with: larger numbers of lower-status residents, large areas of poor-quality housing, and filthy rivers and a smoky atmosphere all contributing to dirty and smelly, unsanitary conditions. One such town was Wolverhampton. It was growing fast, particularly in the early-nineteenth century.[60] The better-quality houses and their residents were situated out of the centre. What had formerly been the fashionable residential areas became commercial premises. A few streets such as Snow Hill, St John's and Worcester Street attracted the better-quality shops, including a number of cabinetmakers, while the lower kind of retailers congregated on the eastern side of the town. There were four cabinetmakers in 1809 but this had grown to twelve by 1850, along with seven carvers and gilders offering looking-glass and picture frames.[61] Although not featuring in any trade directories the upholsterer James Eykyn was well established in Wolverhampton by 1780, selling furniture made on the premises and a wide range of other furnishing goods such as Dutch tiles and wallpaper.[62] But, unlike Shrewsbury, where a number of firms stayed in business for 20 or more years, there was a bigger turnover in Wolverhampton. This suggests that gentry customers provided a continuous demand; whereas a town like Wolverhampton, that had a fast-growing population but with fewer wealthy residents, was affected more by downturns in trade.

By the middle of the eighteenth century, Birmingham had succeeded Shrewsbury and Coventry as the highest town in the urban hierarchy in the West Midlands area, and its growth continued into the next century.[63] Birmingham had become large enough by the later-eighteenth century for a number of distinct retailing areas to exist.[64] The fashionable streets were on the higher ground, with New Street as the most prominent. Digbeth, once a separate village but swallowed up in Birmingham's growth, was a low-lying area and liable to flood. It attracted shops selling less fashionable and less expensive goods. It was also an area where larger firms had their factories and wholesale premises. Some firms had two addresses; Kendall and Son, makers of toilet cases, gave their retail address as New Street but their wholesale address was Lombard Street, in the Digbeth area.[65]

Birmingham had a few streets where the most fashionable furnishing shops were found. In New Street in particular a number of high-quality firms had their premises; Hensman, Smallwood and Apletree all had elegant showrooms for their customers. On his trade card Hensman had two windows, with attractive wares on display, on either side of the steps up to the front door.[66] Fashionably dressed ladies and gentlemen walk outside, some alighting from a carriage. When such customers approached the shop Mr Hensman or an assistant would have greeted them and given them every attention. Clearly only smart middle-class people could shop here (Illustration 1:3).

Other parts of Birmingham grew and took on a particular character as the town spread. So, the area around Worcester Street had a great many firms making or selling furniture. Increasingly however this had become a rather low-status retail area and many shops dealt with second-hand merchandise. The mid-nineteenth century growth of suburbs, beginning with Edgbaston, resulted in retail establishments specifically to cater for this middle-class market, on the streets leading out from the centre of town towards the housing developments. The central streets in Birmingham benefited from improvements from the late-eighteenth century onwards, with the cattle market removed and several narrow alleyways widened to give better access to the streets, and street lighting by the 1820s.[67] However, Birmingham still retained much of its old character despite the piecemeal road widening and smart shop fronts. The drastic modernization of New Street and other central locations did not happen until Joseph Chamberlain became mayor in the 1870s and introduced a sweeping rebuilding programme.[68]

So, each town that could provide cabinetmakers and upholsterers also was able to provide a fashionable ambience for its customers. Although some towns were losing importance, still enough wealthy customers patronized their businesses to keep trade buoyant. It was in these towns that firms stayed in business for many years, 20 and more, demonstrating that they could depend on a steady trade with many loyal customers. In other towns that were growing rapidly the better-quality

1:3 The premises of Thomas Hensman, cabinetmaker and upholsterer, New Street, Birmingham in 1812.

furniture retailers were situated in smart streets where the wealthier inhabitants could shop in comfort.

Sources of Influence for the Fashionable Provincial Home

Peter Borsay suggests that London was a 'melting pot' of ideas from many sources, abroad and from the provinces.[69] So, in the provinces the sources of ideas were also diverse. London was only the 'benchmark' for provincial towns up to a point.[70] London goods and ideas were desirable but not exclusively. The dynamics of influence were more complex. Provincial newspaper advertisements for goods often employed phrases to suggest that London goods were on sale or that a tradesmen had 'lately arrived from London' as a selling point. In 1750, for example, an advertisement appeared in Aris's *Birmingham Gazette* for the sale of goods at the Spread Eagle in Birmingham of 'A large Collection of Cabinet Maker's Goods from London'.[71] But this was not the only source of goods. The following year a Birmingham upholsterer was making much of 'a large fresh stock' that would be on sale for a few days in Wolverhampton, which he had just purchased at Bristol Fair.[72] Advertisements might claim that highly fashionable items, such as wallpaper, were lately arrived from Paris, and foreign china and art works were clearly desirable: for example, in 1770 Aris's *Birmingham Gazette* carried an advertisement stating that Italian and French paintings and ornaments were 'Just arrived from ABROAD – To be sold, by Mr Campione, Italian'.[73]

As well as importing ideas from abroad or other urban centres towns in the provinces were capable of generating their 'own indigenous culture'.[74] Part of this self-sufficiency extended to the products for which particular towns were renowned. By the early-nineteenth century advertisements were just as likely to stipulate that a commodity, such as ironmongery goods, were the best produce of Birmingham or Sheffield.

Good-value rather than extravagant commodities were a selling point for local retailers. An independent spirit is clear from an advertisement for household furnishings placed in 1851 in a trade directory by the Birmingham cabinetmaker and upholsterer Thomas Harris. He declared that 'Families about to furnish are invited to inspect the showrooms' in New Street in which they would find 'every article of furniture suited to the mansion or the cottage, of appropriate designs and superior workmanship, in great variety and at cheaper rates than any establishment in the kingdom.'[75] This full-page advertisement was a clear boast by this cabinetmaker in Birmingham that his stock was equal to any in the land. It also drew attention to Harris's understanding of what was appropriate for different households, in terms of price and of design.

While provincial tradespeople might boast of London goods and styles, their customers undoubtedly relied on them to have chosen from the fashions available and to carry 'appropriate' styles. Many aspects of cultural life in the provinces took ideas from elsewhere, from London perhaps especially, but then translated them into appropriate forms for local consumption. Hannah Barker suggests that newspapers reflected local attitudes and opinions, rather than blindly following the metropolitan lead. The choice of news items and the way they were treated all demonstrated an awareness of the 'distinctiveness of provincial culture'.[76] While discussing provincial taste it is important to note that the word taste was defined at this time as discernment and a sense of what was appropriate. Provincial makers and retailers provided a desirable source of goods for their customers because they could provide what was appropriate. The complexity of cultural exchange meant that provincial towns could look to London for some ideas and elsewhere for others; but all the time the importation of goods and ideas went through a filtering system that appropriated, rejected and modified the style of goods to suit local taste. While a bespoke trade in furniture production continued it was possible for cabinetmakers to produce fashionable items that suited the taste of their individual customers in provincial towns.

The Influence of Pattern Books on Provincial Makers

Undiluted fashionable ideas spread to the provinces through printed publications. They were almost always produced in London and were becoming more plentiful during the eighteenth century. Pattern books illustrated fashionable designs and were consulted in the provinces, although evidence is fragmentary. One example was a Shrewsbury joiner, Robert Urwick, who had an inventory made of his goods when he died in 1744 and among his possessions were '4 Books of Articheture' [sic].[77] The inventory of his workshop included a number of items for carving, so it is possible that his work extended to producing architectural details for rooms, for which the pattern books would be useful. Thomas Shakeshaft, a carpenter and joiner who lived in Middleton, halfway between Sutton Coldfield and Tamworth in rural Warwickshire, appears to fit Gilbert's description of a maker of regional furniture since he clearly concentrated on joinery work, just making occasional items of furniture. However, in his notebook, kept between 1751 and 1764, he revealed his awareness of pattern books.[78] Shakeshaft included a few drawings of furniture; one was of a writing cabinet that closely resembled items found in Chippendale's *Gentleman's and Cabinet Maker's Director*, published in 1754[79] (Illustration 1:4). It seems unlikely that Shakeshaft made such goods for his customers; all the lists of work that he carried out required the skills of a joiner rather than a cabinetmaker, and he had, like his father before him, been trained as a carpenter and joiner. Shakeshaft specialized in making gates and fences, window frames and doors. His notebook recorded his work for various customers, including Lord Middleton; but an unprofessional note is struck by his lists of joinery work being interspersed by such additions as lists of clothing bought at Tamworth and Fazeley Fairs and a recipe for a remedy for 'the ague'. However, Shakeshaft also made drawings of what he termed a 'hatch' or gate. These drawings were similar in design to the many Chinese gates and palings, sometimes called hatches, that were a feature of pattern books around the mid-eighteenth century, and found in for example Paul Decker's *Chinese Architecture*, published in 1759.[80] Shakeshaft thus

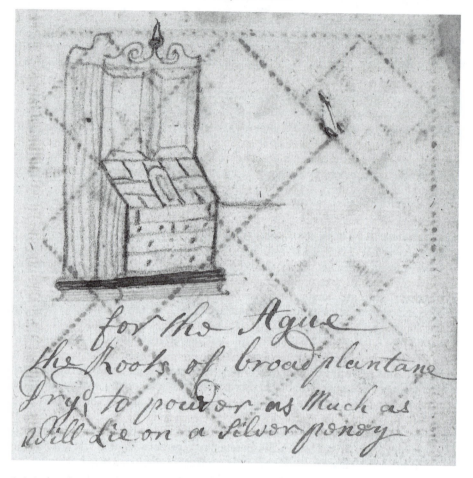

1:4 A drawing for a bureau, from the notebook of carpenter and joiner Thomas Shakeshaft, kept between 1751 and 1764.

demonstrates that in the provinces the lines of demarcation between trades was far from fixed and, together with Urwick, that knowledge of fashion infiltrated the joinery trade as well as that of cabinetmaking.

Despite this spread of ideas, the early pattern books did not include details for making the furniture and needed to be interpreted by the maker. Throughout the eighteenth and first half of the nineteenth century, a bespoke trade in cabinetmaking and upholstery continued, with only minor changes to furniture making methods influenced by new technology.[81] Thus, a degree of interpretation on the maker's side, and space for the customer to negotiate with the maker, influenced what was produced and consumed. Customers could view images in pattern books, examples of ready-made furniture, and samples of materials. In addition, the cabinetmaker might provide drawings of the item to be made. In Chichester in the 1840s the cabinetmaker Samuel Peat practised drawing furniture in his notebooks with mathematical solutions for producing particular shapes.[82] One drawing is of a cabinet with projecting lower cupboards below. Although the level of expertise is not great, it demonstrates Peat's ability to convey reasonably well the details of a piece of furniture for a customer, and his own knowledge of fashionable designs. A very similar design appears in Thomas King's pattern book of 1839.[83] However, when the Peat drawing is studied it is clear that he has not understood the application of the classical orders since he has placed the Corinthian columns at the bottom of the cabinet and the Ionic columns above.

A clear influence of pattern books is shown in the fine trade card produced by Tanner, a Birmingham cabinetmaker, and used as an advertisement in a trade directory in 1815[84] (Illustration 1:5). The trade card was a detailed depiction of a section of a room with upholstered furniture and draperies at a window through which can be seen an attractive garden. To display objects in an interior was still a relatively new idea. Hepplewhite had first employed the device of room settings for his pattern book *The Cabinet-Maker and Upholsterer's Guide* in 1788, and the method was further exploited in the monthly publication Ackermann's *The Repository of Arts* which was published between 1809 and 1828. However, just like Samuel Peat's drawing the Tanner trade card displayed an imperfect knowledge of fashionable practice. The interior had a couch placed against the pier, that is, between the windows. This arrangement of furniture was never used in fashionable pattern books. Although this might seem a minor point, in the eighteenth and nineteenth centuries furniture had prescribed uses, and it was important to observe the appropriate use.

To some extent then, provincial makers misinterpreted metropolitan fashions but they were aware of the latest fashions and were expected to mediate them for their customers. For their part consumers recognized the fashionable elements of both the advertising images and the goods made and retailed by the better class of provincial tradesperson. Through his trade card Tanner showed his prospective customers his ability to provide beautiful furniture and window draperies, and perhaps even advice on furnishing.[85]

The level of fashionability of provincial makers and retailers depended on the place of an individual town within the urban hierarchy. But what was on offer

1:5 The elegant advertisement for the Birmingham cabinetmaking and upholstery business of Tanner in 1815.

also corresponded to the tastes of provincial consumers. While looking to the metropolis for new ideas they, and the retailers who served them, filtered the current fashions to retain acceptable aspects and reject extravagant and outrageous elements. Thus makers/retailers such as Tanner were able to boast, in words or pictures, that they could provide for a fashionable *provincial* interior and their customers understood the message. Penny Sparke has commented on the notion of the middle class emulating the gentry. She suggests that while this was the case to some extent: 'Seldom did emulation mean exact copying but resulted rather in an approximation of what was being copied. In this way the language of material goods acquired dialects which communicated, at a glance, the social standing of their owner.'[86] This is a useful way of thinking about emulation that could also be applied to the relationship between provincial consumers and the metropolis during this period. Provincial taste was a hybrid and separate version of London taste. To some extent, however, this began to change by the end of the period due to changes in the way that furnishings were produced and retailed.

The Homogenization of Taste

The spread of fashionable ideas to the provinces was aided by developments within the furniture trade which occurred in the early-nineteenth century, and which influenced, to some degree, consumption patterns in provincial towns, and led to greater homogeneity in household furnishings. One development was tighter instructions to the trade on pricing their work, through the Cabinet Makers' Union. The *Price Books* gave the trade exact formulas for arriving at a price for cabinet work. These publications began in 1788 in the London trade but quickly spread to provincial towns, including Birmingham.[87] The *Birmingham Price Book* was published in 1803 and included items that were particularly made in Birmingham such as gun cases and Venetian folding blinds, items which complemented other trades in Birmingham.[88] Since the *Price Books* were aimed at the trade, they were utilitarian in format and style of illustration, and were revised or had supplements to keep them up to date. From the early-nineteenth century they had reached a fairly tight set of rules that the trade fought hard to adhere to, in order that their piece-rates might be protected.[89] Since the trade of cabinetmaking involved numerous small processes that had almost endless variations, it was difficult to establish rules for every application and craftsmen were meant to negotiate individual jobs based on the general guidelines. However, it was perhaps inevitable that the jobs already priced up should be preferred since they were already agreed. The *Price Books* therefore had the effect of standardizing the trade: what was made as well as how much was charged.[90] This also, to some extent, helped to eliminate differences between London and the provinces.

Furniture was particularly difficult to produce for a national market due to the continued dependence on craft skills. Few aspects of the trade leant themselves to mechanized manufacture, except the preparation of timber and cutting veneers. Pat Kirkham et al. suggest that during the nineteenth century the trade in London

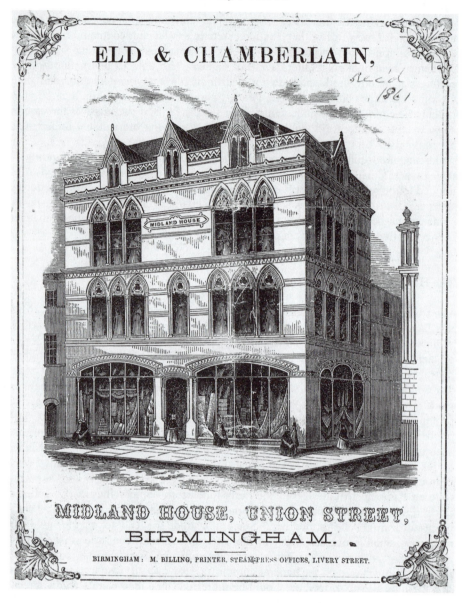

1:6 The front cover of Eld and Chamberlain's catalogue for their furnishing drapery shop in Birmingham in 1860 shows the grand new building that replaced their more humble premises on the same site in the 1850s.

was increasingly made up of firms that specialized in particular aspects of furniture making, and through these subdivisions output was hugely increased and prices were brought down.[91] It thus became harder for small independent cabinetmakers producing bespoke goods to compete, whether they were in London or the provinces. By the later-nineteenth century the national market for producing furniture became largely dominated by London goods and methods. Large quantities of furniture were made to the same designs or with slight variations, and most of the producers were situated in London. By centralizing production furniture producers, or the middlemen who distributed the goods, were able to engage in large-scale production for a national market and exploit the economies of scale that resulted.[92]

How furniture was sold was also changing. Cabinetmakers and upholsterers had traditionally sold their own goods in a showroom attached to their premises but by the early-nineteenth century furnishing drapers existed who sold furniture that they bought in. By the 1850s and 1860s, many middle-class people acquired their furniture and household furnishings from furnishing drapers.[93] These firms were able to offer a wide range of wooden and upholstered furniture, most of which they bought in when required, having only samples in their showrooms. Some of these goods came from London or else big manufacturers in the provinces. The furnishing drapers also produced printed catalogues from which customers could make their selection. The catalogues gave the appearance of a wide choice, but much of it was accomplished by swapping components that could all be made in advance and assembled when the customer placed the order.

In 1861 the Birmingham furnishing draper Eld and Chamberlain sent out a catalogue to a solicitor, Henry Wace, in Shrewsbury. From the catalogue Mr Wace chose a carpet that was sent to him through the post (Illustration 1:6). He commented favourably on some walnut furniture, but generally found the wares 'very dear'.[94] A furnishing draper, like Eld and Chamberlain, offered a safer, more homogenized choice than dealing with a quality cabinetmaker that provided a bespoke service. Merely by producing a printed catalogue, Eld and Chamberlain demonstrated their homogenization of choice. By the end of the period, consumers were able to travel more easily to different towns and knowledge of fashion was spread through printed media. Middle-class homemakers typically purchased their furniture from shops that produced catalogues illustrating their wares but that did not produce their own furniture on the premises. Instead furniture was made in larger firms, many in the East End of London, and supplied to shops throughout the country. Furniture was cheaper, more uniformly fashionable.

The Changing Consumption of Regional Furniture

In 1825, Catherine Hutton wrote an article for the ladies' magazine *La Belle Assemblé* in which she described the changing tastes and homemaking preferences of different generations of a family. Although the article was written in the first person, the family she described did not correspond with her own family's history.[95] She related how 'her' father's family were farmers in Derbyshire with a farmhouse in a small village. Catherine Hutton describes how her grandfather took his bride to live at his parents' home, and how she meekly accepted the domestic arrangements. Despite all her accomplishments she suggested no improvements to the running of the household or the arrangement of its furnishings. Here is the central theme of Catherine Hutton's article (every time she used the word improvements it was underlined). Her grandmother waited until she was mistress of the house, and then she made some changes to modernize the farmhouse, which was obviously a vernacular building.

> The house was composed of wood and plaster, and covered with thatch. It contained five rooms on the ground floor, ranged along the farm-yard like a rank of soldiers; the left-hand ran next to the 'town street' and from the right ran an excrescence called the buttery. Stairs there were, which led to chambers above; but some were ill lighted; others quite dark; and all were open to the beams and the thatch, these were in the several occupation of men servants and maid servants, pigeons and cheese, wheat, malt and apples.

> My grandmother added a handsome parlour to the family mansion, with a handsome chamber over it and placed beds in both; in the former for the accommodation of her husband and herself; in the latter for that of a guest. For the first time, in that house, beds had four posts, and were wholly surrounded by curtains.[96]

Catherine Hutton established that the modernization to the farmhouse was to add comfort and to aid the public role of the house, but the traditional arrangements were not overly interfered with. The next generation followed a similar pattern, and her mother, as a young bride, went to live at the farmhouse with her mother-in-law still in residence. Her mother wanted to make some changes, but:

> her proceedings were regulated by due respect for the feelings of my grandmother. In what was called 'the house' that is the spacious room in which the family lived throughout the day, my mother left the dresser with drawers and the rows of pewter, from the dish which held the sirloin, to the plates from which it was eaten and shone above it. She left the four-legged oaken table, from which the servants dined in the presence of their master and mistress; each continuing to eat his broth from a wooden noggin, or little pail and cutting his meat on a wooden trencher with a clasp knife taken from his pocket.

Also in this room vernacular furniture, in the form of an old oak settle, was retained in its old position. Having made these compromises for the sake of her mother-in-law, Catherine's mother then made some changes.

> She took the scanty curtains, of thick and ancient woollen, from her bed, converted them into carpet and supplied their place with curtains of blue and white striped linen, spun by her own hand. She had a screen in the house formed into a closet in which she placed her tea china, her silver

cream jug, and her plates and dishes of earthenware. My father, however, set his face manfully against the earthen plates, so far as regarded himself, and it was many years before he could be persuaded to part with his trencher.

An old armchair was also transformed with the addition of upholstery using fabric that she had embroidered. So once again, the new daughter-in-law made changes but also preserved some elements, and retained some of the traditional ways of running the house. Both her grandmother and mother made their own textile furnishings, demonstrating their good housewifery.

With the next generation the changes were extensive and by implication the nature of the farmhouse was ruined. When Catherine visited her brother and his wife she was overwhelmed by the changes in 'the house'.

> 'Yes' said my sister-in-law, with an air of triumph, 'I knew I would surprise you. There have been great <u>improvements</u> made since you were here; the old lumber is all gone into the kitchen, or into the fire.' There it was, I could recognise nothing but the windows and clock. The dresser and pewter had given way to prints, framed and glazed; the ancient chairs and table were exchanged for modern and the bright grate, with its knobs as large as warming pans, had been dismissed for a Bath stove…When we rose from table, she proposed our removal into 'the other room' and led the way into what had been the bedchamber of my father and mother. At last thought I, my passion for old times will be gratified, for I reckoned on seeing the blue and white striped curtains of my mother's spinning, and the bed on which she reposed during her married life and her widowhood; but I reckoned without my hostess; for she had sent the bed upstairs for the accommodation of maids. The plaster floor was covered with carpet; the white-washed walls were covered with paper; the tables and chairs were of mahogany; the valances of the window curtains being in graceful drapery…

In fact, all the necessary elements were there of a fashionable parlour. The fictitious character that Catherine Hutton had created was distressed, not only by the changes to the physical appearance and arrangements of the house, but also by the contingent changes in how life was lived in the farmhouse. It might have been fashionable, but it was no longer a home. Visitors were shown meagre hospitality, the children were sent away to school, the husband turned to drink and died an early death. Finally, the farm was sold and 'the farm house is now occupied by a stranger.'

Conclusion

During the period provincial taste in home furnishings was distinct from metropolitan taste. Consumers and producers in provincial towns looked to London fashions but did not want to follow them slavishly. Instead they filtered and modified them to produce appropriate furnishings in what might be termed a hybrid style. By the nineteenth century regional goods were no longer acceptable; but already by the 1820s, as evidenced by Catherine Hutton's story just quoted, there were signs of nostalgia for rural objects and the way of life that was felt to accompany them. This feeling found full expression through the Arts and Crafts Movement in the later part of the century.[97] By that time even fashionable provincial production by independent cabinetmakers had largely given way to metropolitan-inspired large-scale production and taste became more homogenized.

But during the period towns at different levels in the urban hierarchy, in all their variety, offered homemakers plentiful choices to suit provincial middling/middle-class taste as well as the multiplicity of individual homemaking needs that will be considered in the next four chapters.

Notes

[1]   West Sussex Record Office.

[2]   *Sussex Directory* (1828), London: Pigot.

[3]   The cattle market was held fortnightly and extended the length of East Street and North Street. In summer when more animals were sold the market spilled into West Street too. A cattle market, on the outskirts of Chichester, was not erected until 1872. *Trade and Industry* leaflet, Chichester District Museums, n.d.

[4]   John Brewer (1997), *The Pleasures of the Imagination: English Culture in the Eighteenth Century*, Chicago: University of Chicago Press, p. 493.

[5]   Johnson's dictionary gives the definition 'rude and unpolished'.

[6]   See Donald Read (1964), *The English Provinces c. 1760–1960: a Study in Influence*, London: Edward Arnold; Rosemary Sweet (1999*)*, *The English Town, 1680–1840: Government, Society and Culture*, London: Longman.

[7]   Peter Borsay, for example, suggests that trickle-down theory is too simplistic for explaining London's influence on the built environment of the provinces in Peter Borsay (1994), 'The London Connection: cultural Diffusion and the Eighteenth-Century Provincial Town', *London Journal*, 19, pp. 21–35. Trickle-down theory suggests that fashionable ideas began amongst the wealthiest in society and gradually filtered down the layers to the poorest. This theory first emerged in the early-20th century in the work of Simmel. Along with Veblen's theories that the motives for consumption were emulation, trickle-down has been problematized in recent years. For a discussion of these theories see Grant McCracken (1990), *Culture and Consumption*, Bloomington and Indianapolis: Indiana University Press.

[8]   Christopher Gilbert (1991), *English Vernacular Furniture 1750–1900*, New Haven and London: Yale University Press.

[9]   Gilbert (1991), *English Vernacular Furniture*, p. 11.

[10] James Ayres (2003), *Domestic Interiors: The British Tradition 1500–1850*, New Haven and London: Yale University Press.

[11] Although by the later-19th century the Arts and Crafts Movement's use of vernacular methods was certainly self-conscious. See Gilbert (1991), *English Vernacular Furniture*, p. 2.

[12] Gilbert (1991), *English Vernacular Furniture*, p. 2.

[13] Bernard D. Cotton (1990), *The English Regional Chair*, Woodbridge: Antique Collectors' Club, p. 289.

[14] See also the exhibition catalogue Christopher Gilbert (1977), *Backstairs Furniture from Country Houses*, Leeds: Temple Newsam.

[15] Variations on the Windsor-type chair were originally made in the South West, North East and East Midlands areas of England, Cotton (1990), *The English Regional Chair*. See also Ivan Sparkes (1973), *The English Country Chair*, Buckinghamshire: Spur.

[16] Shropshire Record Office, inventory and will, 6000/12167.

[17] West Sussex Record Office, inventory, Add Mss 2245.

[18] For an examination of earlier-18th -century examples of customers going to London for goods see Nancy Cox (2000), *The Complete Tradesman: A Study of Retailing, 1550–1820*, Aldershot: Ashgate, p. 121–2.

[19] Talking of the period 1650–1750 Wrigley suggests that one adult in six had direct experience of London. This number would have increased during the next 100 years, especially after the introduction of the railways from the 1840s. E.A. Wrigley (1967), 'A Simple Model of London's Importance in Changing English Society and economy 1650–1750', *Past and Present*, number 37, pp. 44–70, p. 50.

[20] Matthew Boulton was a successful entrepreneur with a manufactory, called Soho, for metal goods. He was in partnership with James Watt for the development of steam engines. See Jenny Uglow (2002), *The Lunar Men: The Friends Who Made the Future*, London: Faber and Faber.

[21] Giles Ellwood (1995), 'James Newton', *Furniture History*, volume 31, pp. 129–205, p. 136.

[22] Birmingham City Archives, MBP Correspondence Box 'N', number 74.

[23] Uglow (2002), *The Lunar Men*, p. 200.

[24] Birmingham City Archives, MBP 282/13.

[25] Clive Wainwright (1988), *George Bullock Cabinet Maker*, London: John Murray. James Watt junior was the son of James Watt who developed steam engines in partnership with Matthew Boulton.

[26] Virginia Glenn (1979), 'George Bullock, Richard Bridgens and James Watt's Regency Furnishing Schemes', *Furniture History*, volume 15, pp. 54–67.

[27] Amanda Vickery (1993), 'Women and the World of Goods: a Lancashire Consumer and her Possessions, 1751–81'; John Brewer and Roy Porter (eds), *Consumption and the World of Goods*, London: Routledge, pp. 290–291.

[28] Birmingham City Archives, Account book 397971, inventory 397968, cuttings about the Staunton family (IIR 63) 73128.

[29] Only the main bedchamber in John Staunton's house had matching bed hangings and window curtains. Birmingham Archives, inventory 397968.

[30] West Sussex Record Office, Diary of Mary Ann Mason, Add Mss 29,830.

[31] Ordering goods from London required the services of a carrier. Nancy Cox (2000) comments on carriers, *The Complete Tradesman*, p. 123. The safe arrival of furniture was worth commenting on in diaries. See Amanda Vickery (1998), *The Gentleman's Daughter. Women's Lives in Georgian England*, New Haven and London: Yale University Press, p. 165.

[32] See C.W. Chalklin (1974), *The Provincial Towns of Georgian England: a Sstudy of the Building Process, 1740–1820*, London: Edward Arnold; Penelope Corfield (1982), *The Impact of English Towns 1700–1800*, Oxford: Oxford University Press; P. Clarke (ed.) (1984), *The Transformation of English Towns 1600–1800*, London: Hutchinson; Peter Borsay, (1989), *The English Urban Renaissance: Culture and Society in the Provincial Towns, 1660–1770*, Oxford: Clarendon Press; Peter Borsay (ed.) (1990), *The*

Eighteenth-Century Town 1688–1820, London: Longman; Rosemary Sweet (1999), *The English Town, 1680–1840*, London: Longman.

33 Jon Stobart (1998), 'Shopping Streets as Social Space: Leisure, Consumerism and Improvement in an Eighteenth-Century Town', *Urban History*, volume 25, number 1, pp. 3–21, p. 4.

34 Cox (2000), *The Complete Tradesman*, p. 75.

35 A. Everitt (1966), 'Social Mobility in Early Modern England', *Past and Present*, number 33, pp. 56–73, p. 71. See also Susan Wright (1990), 'Sojourners and Lodgers in a Provincial Town: The evidence from Eighteenth-Century Ludlow', *Urban History*, volume 17, pp. 14–35.

36 Sweet (1999), *The English Town*, p. 191.

37 Wrigley (1967), 'A Simple Model of London's Importance', p. 54.

38 *Sussex Directory* (1828), London: Pigot.

39 John Beckett and Catherine Smith (2000), 'Urban Renaissance and Consumer Revolution in Nottingham, 1688–1750', *Urban History*, 27, pp. 31–50.

40 Sweet (1999), *The English Town*, p. 197.

41 It is estimated that around 20 per cent of London shops provided luxury goods and services, whereas in the country as a whole it was about 8 per cent. Sweet (1999), *The English Town*, p. 181–182.

42 See Lorna Weatherill (1988), *Consumer Behaviour and Material Culture in Britain, 1660–1760*, London: Routledge, p. 189.

43 Sweet (1999), *The English Town*, p. 179.

44 Most of the examples in this section refer to the West Midlands; other areas would have developed slightly differently and would require individual consideration.

45 Apart from furniture makers who resided in the town there were also occasional sales of goods, often at a local inn. These sales were advertised in the local press, see for example Aris's *Birmingham Gazette*, 1 September 1760, when the Birmingham upholsterer, Isaac Tipping, advertised the sale of furnishings to take place for one day in Walsall and one in Wolverhampton.

46 A grocer with a substantial business in Bridgnorth in 1741 is commented on in Cox (2000), *The Complete Tradesman*. See also Malcolm Wanklyn (1993), 'Urban Revival in Early Modern England: Bridgnorth and the River Trade, 1660–1800', *Midland History*, volume 28, pp. 37–64. Population figures for Bridgnorth were 4408 in 1801 and 6172 in 1851.

47 The belongings of William Adams, cabinetmaker of Bridgnorth, were advertised in Aris's *Birmingham Gazette*, 12 November 1743. He was perhaps retiring or going out of business.

48 *Directory of Shropshire* (1822), London: Pigot; *Royal National and Commercial Directory and Topography of Shropshire* (1850), Manchester and London: Slater.

49 Census figures give the population of Shrewsbury as 14,739 in 1801 and 19,681 in 1851.

50 See Angus McInnes (1988), 'The Emergence of a Leisure Town: Shrewsbury 1660–1760', *Past and Present*, number 120, pp. 53–87.

51 Western and Midland Directory (1783), Birmingham: Bailey; *Royal National and Commercial Directory and Topography of Shropshire* (1850), Manchester and London: Slater.

52 See Geoffrey Beard & Christopher Gilbert (eds) (1986), *Dictionary of English Furniture Makers 1660–1840*, Leeds: Furniture History Society and W.S. Maney and Sons Ltd; *National Trust Guide to Attingham Park, Shropshire* (1998), London: National Trust.

53   Population figures for Chichester were 7362 in 1821 and 8662 in 1851.

54   *Sussex Directory* (1828) London: Pigot.

55   West Sussex Record Office, *Chronology of Chichester*, Add Mss 29,710.

56   Census figures show that the population of Stone rose from about 5,000 in 1801 to 8,700 in 1851. Also see A.F. Denholm (1988), 'The Impact of the Canal System on Three Staffordshire Market Towns 1760–1850', *Midland History*, volume 13, pp. 59–76.

57   Staffordshire Record Office, John Foden account book, 3161. Inside the front cover Foden recorded his own date of birth together with those of his brothers and sisters.

58   The only time he appeared in a trade directory was in 1854, the entry listed him as a wheelwright in Market Street, Stone. *Post Office Directory of Birmingham with Warwickshire, Worcestershire and Staffordshire* (1854), London: Kelly.

59   *History, Gazetteer and Directory of Staffordshire* (1834), London: White; *Directory of Staffordshire* (1850), London: Slater.

60   Population figures for Wolverhampton were 12,565 in 1801 and 49,985 in 1851.

61   *Triennial Directory of Shropshire* (1809–1811), London: Holden; *Royal National and Commercial Directory and Topography of Shropshire* (1850), Manchester and London: Slater.

62   Public Record Office, Kew, James Eykyn probate inventory, 1780, PROB 31/678/155.

63   Population figures for Birmingham were 71,000 in 1801 and 233,000 in 1851.

64   Numbers of furniture makers were: 19 cabinet makers and 11 upholsterers/upholders in 1770; 39 cabinetmakers (19 were also upholsterers) in 1816; 146 cabinetmakers with 61 upholsterers (most of whom combined the two trades) in 1849. *Directory of Birmingham* (1770), Birmingham: Sketchley; *Commercial Directory of Birmingham* (1816), Manchester: Wardle and Pratt; *History and General Directory of Birmingham* (1849), Sheffield: White.

65   *General and Commercial Directory of Birmingham* (1858), Birmingham: Dix. For further comments about the role of showrooms in Birmingham see Eric Hopkins (1989), *Birmingham: the First Manufacturing Town in the World 1760–1840*, London: Weidenfeld and Nicolson, p. 69.

66   *New Triennial Directory of Birmingham* (1812), Birmingham: Thomson and Wrightson.

67   Robert K. Dent (1973 first published 1878), *Old and New Birmingham: A History of the Town and Its People*, London: EP Publishing, pp. 206 and 368. See also Gordon E. Cherry (1994), *Birmingham: A Study in Geography, History and Planning*, Chichester: Wiley.

68   Dent (1973), *Old and New Birmingham*, p. 525.

69   Borsay (1994), 'The London Connection', p. 31.

70   Borsay (1994), 'The London Connection', p. 24.

71   Aris's *Birmingham Gazette*, 22 October 1750.

72   Aris's *Birmingham Gazette*, 18 February 1751.

73   Aris's *Birmingham Gazette*, 20 August 1770.

74   Peter Borsay (1994), 'The London Connection', p. 31.

75   *Directory of Wolverhampton* (1851), Worcester: Melville and Sibury.

76   Hannah Barker (1996), 'Catering for Provincial Tastes: Newspapers, Readership and Profit in Late-Eighteenth Century England', *Historical Research*, volume 69, number 168, pp. 42–61, p. 61.

77   Lichfield Joint Record Office, probate inventory. I am grateful to Nancy Cox for bringing this inventory to my attention.

[78] Birmingham Archives. Notebook of Thomas Shakshaft, MSS 556647 (IIR41). R.W. Whorwood, a descendent of Thomas Shakeshaft, has demonstrated that the name should be spelt with the middle 'e'. Whorwood has pointed out that Shakeshaft was continuing in the same line of work as his father but that he travelled to London in 1755 and stayed for about a year. During this time Shakeshaft perhaps gained employment with a cabinetmaker and thereby increased his knowledge of cabinetmaking skills and of fashionable taste. See R.W. Whorwood (2001), *The Notebook of Thomas Shakeshaft 1751–1764*, Ashbourne, Derbyshire: published by the author. A corner cupboard and a small carved box, made by Shakeshaft, have remained in the family; photographs are reproduced in R.W. Whorwood (2004), 'The Notebook (1751–1764) of Thomas Shakeshaft Carpenter and Cabinetmaker of Middleton, Warwickshire', *Furniture History Society Newsletter*, number 155, August 2004, pp. 4–5.

[79] Thomas Chippendale (1754), *The Gentleman and Cabinet Maker's Director*, London: published by the author.

[80] Paul Decker (1759), *Chinese Architecture*, London: printed for the author and sold by Henry Parker.

[81] See Clive Edwards (1993), *Victorian Furniture: Technology and Design*, Manchester: Manchester University Press; Clive Edwards (1996), *Eighteenth-Century Furniture*, Manchester: Manchester University Press.

[82] West Sussex Record Office, Add Mss 2238.

[83] Thomas King (1839), *The Modern Style of Cabinet Work Exemplified*, London: Architectural Library.

[84] *New Triennial Directory of Birmingham* (1815), Birmingham: Wrightson.

[85] Upholsterers were employed much as interior decorators are now and stocked all manner of interior requirements, far beyond what they made on the premises.

[86] Penny Sparke (1995), *As Long As It's Pink*, London: HarperCollins, p. 28.

[87] For a list of Price Books see C. Gilbert and P. Kirkham (eds) (1982), 'London and Provincial Books of Prices: Comment and Bibliography', *Furniture History*, volume 18, pp. 1–266, pp. 16–19.

[88] *A Supplement to the London Cabinet Makers' Price Book of 1797 As Agreed in Birmingham January 1 1803* (1803), Birmingham: Printed by M. Swinney. Local Studies and History, Birmingham Central Library, MS 108061.

[89] Details of these transactions were recorded in the Society of London Cabinetmakers Job Settling Committee Book, Winterthur Library, Winterthur, Delaware, MSS 742.

[90] Gilbert and Kirkham claim that details of the pricing reveal that 'batch production' and the use of 'standard decorative elements ready-made from a specialist supplier' were common, all pointing to greater standardization of the trade. Gilbert and Kirkham (1982), 'London and Provincial', p. 11.

[91] Pat Kirkham, Rodney Mace and Julia Porter (1987), *Furnishing the World: the East London Furniture Trade 1830–1980*, London; Journeyman, p. 10.

[92] This trend never completely ousted the smaller makers. See Judy Attfield (1996), '"Give 'em something dark and heavy": The Role of Design in the Material Culture of Popular British Furniture 1939–1965', *Journal of Design History*, volume 9, number 3, pp. 185–201.

[93] Pat Kirkham has shown how furnishing drapers came to dominate the retailing of furniture in London. Pat Kirkham (1988), 'The London Furniture Trade 1700–1870', *Journal of the Furniture History Society*, volume 24, pp. 1–219, p. 66. Similar

developments in the provinces can be observed through the numbers of furnishing drapers recorded in trade directories by the mid-19th century.

94 Birmingham Archives, MS 1081/1–8.

95 Sections are quoted by kind permission of Birmingham City Archives, Hutton Beale Papers 106/12.

96 It was still common in the later-18th century for rural properties to have beds in parlours.

97 See Sarah Medlam (1993), 'The Decorative Arts Approach: Furniture', David Flemming, *Social History in Museums: a Handbook for Professionals*, London: HMSO, p. 39.

Chapter 2

Transient Homes

Mr Thomas Farnel of Sutton Coldfield, brickmaker and farmer, was in debt when Aris's *Birmingham Gazette* announced, in August 1830, a sale of his 'household Furniture, Farm Stock and Effects under an assignment for the Benefit of creditors'.[1] A short list followed to give a flavour of what might be expected but the descriptions did not attempt to embellish what was on offer; the bedsteads had 'suitable' hangings and the culinary articles were merely 'clean and useful'. It is clear from the wording that Thomas Farnel had little of any value; this may have always been the case or perhaps he had previously sold off items as his position worsened. Bankruptcy could provide a public humiliation as well as resulting in the loss of material goods and livelihood.

The physical components of a home were not fixed or secure. Even on a superficial level homes were constantly changing. Objects that were in use produced an ever-changing clutter in interiors. Protective covers on furniture and carpets were only removed when visitors were expected. But these transitory elements are almost impossible to gauge from documentary sources.[2] On a deeper level homes did not always offer continuity for their occupants. Many people had to change homes frequently due to economic retrenchment, changes in employment necessitating a move, the death of a spouse and old age. Employment and income were all precarious. Seasonal work and periods of unemployment could not always be avoided and there was little by way of legislation to protect employees or pensions when old age, accident or ill health resulted in lack of income. Even the middling sort could lose their money due to bad investments, or from giving too much credit to customers. Most of the sources that have been used for this book were recorded because of change. Wills were often drawn up shortly before someone died and probate inventories were made soon after the death of someone with assets. A home needing to be sold up to meet debts or when the owner had died sometimes required inventories to be made and these survive either as handwritten lists or as printed catalogues. The house sales that appeared in newspaper advertisements occurred for the same reasons. The challenge for homemakers was to achieve some sense of permanence and security in their home environment against a backdrop of changing circumstances.

Advice literature of the later-eighteenth century, and throughout the nineteenth, celebrated the notion that a home was an emotional construct not dependent on the quantity or quality of material possessions.[3] As *The Family Economist* put it, in 1851, a host of 'things have been called household gods; but though we may respect and admire we are not to worship them. They are some of the amenities of existence, the adornments and refinements of home, but not the home itself.'[4] Still, physical comfort and day-to-day subsistence required household furnishings to be somewhat more than basic. For middling-sort and then middle-class households the furnishings of the home had multiple uses beyond the obvious practical ones. As the last chapter demonstrated, material goods in the home were also a means of communicating to others in your sphere your taste and position in society, even your moral attitudes. Home furnishings could also have attributed to them personal associations, with family and friends, both alive and dead. Then again, some objects might be valued as a means of saving with the intention of selling or pawning them if necessary.[5] Therefore selling your household possessions was to be resisted.

The anthropologist, David Parkin, has examined how people who are forced to move from their homes use objects as mementoes of their home and their life there. The people that Parkin is concerned with are refugees who have to flee their homes with little or no notice, often in fear of their lives. 'Even under these conditions of immediate flight or departure, people do, if they can, seek minimal reminders of who they are and where they come from…family photos, letters and personal effects of little or no utilitarian or market value.'[6] The reason for this, Parkin theorizes, is because such 'personal mementoes taken by people in flight may indeed re-articulate socio-cultural identity if and when suitable conditions of resettlement allow for the retelling of the stories that they contain.'[7] Although the people dealt with here were in less immediate peril than those examined by Parkin, still the loss of possessions was a common experience that demonstrated the transient nature of the home. Since household belongings carried emotional meanings, then their loss for economic reasons or due to some disaster was distressing and even traumatic.

This chapter contrasts transience and continuity in household possessions and identifies the objects that people most valued in their home furnishings. This is not an easy task to accomplish since, beyond occasional comments in diaries and wills, evidence is scarce. Probate inventories, usually one of the best means of knowing what was in a home, tell us little about what was most valued. In many cases these very items would have been omitted from the list, since if the home was to be sold up, or when their owner died, it was these goods that would previously have been given away, or left as a bequest in a will. To some extent this problem can be overcome by observing the kind of items that people most readily parted with. By reversing the inquiry and exploring how people parted with the most temporary aspects, followed by the relatively temporary parts of the home, then gradually the most permanent parts will be revealed. The occasional inclusion of objects that were usually omitted from inventories and house sales offers fragmentary evidence from which can be surmised the nature of the things that were particularly valued and which people most wanted to retain as symbolic elements of the home.

This chapter will look for clues of people revealing the value they placed on domestic objects when their home was threatened or their belongings lost. The most common reason for losing a home was the need to move from one temporary rented home to another requiring the furniture to be sold because it was too difficult or expensive to move. Older people often gave up their homes and moved into a few rented rooms or in with relatives. Homes were also lost when the inhabitants needed to sell up their belongings to pay debts, especially when someone was declared bankrupt. Most dramatic of all was when a disaster of some kind destroyed the homes and its contents. While the poorer in society no doubt suffered the most in these circumstances still, as the examples in this chapter will demonstrate, people throughout society were affected and in some cases the loss was severe and life changing. The chapter will end with an example of a family needing to retrench. This they did over several moves, from a grand manor house to a smaller but comfortable and elegant country house. Finally, they were forced to flee to France where the patriarch of the family died three years later.

Temporary Homes: Rented Homes and Hired Furniture

Renting a home was extremely common during the period. Few people inherited a property or were able to save enough to buy one. And purchasing a house in instalments was not the common practice it is now. It was perhaps more common to purchase a freehold in rural areas than in urban districts, and the building of suburbs also gradually led to more middle-rank people purchasing properties.[8] Therefore relatively wealthy and respectable people resorted to renting a house. Middle-rank and poorer people often rented a house or just a few rooms on a short contract, of three to six months, to enable them to move on when they needed to. Many properties on this level would have been rented complete with furniture. S.J. Wright has found, that in eighteenth-century Ludlow, the most mobile part of the renting population was people who took rented rooms or were lodgers; many people only staying in one place for a matter of weeks or months. People who were able to rent a whole house were more stable. Half of her sample stayed for over five years and between a third and a quarter for a decade or more.[9] A town like Ludlow attracted wealthier people for the season as well as poorer people in search of work. The frequency of people taking in lodgers was higher in Shrewsbury than in Ludlow; about a quarter of its households contained a lodger.[10]

Moving from one home to another required the assistance of a firm to carry out the work. Cabinetmakers were often involved in removals. One example was Samuel Pearson, a cabinetmaker in Worcester Street, Birmingham, who claimed on his letterhead that furniture would be 'Carefully Packed & Removed'.[11] Similarly, the joiner John Foden who worked in Stone in Staffordshire throughout the first half of the nineteenth century not only helped people to move – he referred to the process as 'flitting' – he also repaired furniture and carried out decorating work on numerous properties that were let furnished.[12]

The many domestic advice books published in the first half of the nineteenth century always assumed that their readers would be in rented houses. They therefore devoted many pages to giving advice on the subject. Finding suitable accommodation was always a difficult task especially where income was limited. Frequent moves just compounded the problem. Advice literature often gave instructions on how to judge a good house to rent. In 1829 in *The Home Book* the list of things to check included looking for signs of damp, of smoking fireplaces, unpleasant smells from drains, 'annoying trades' carried on in nearby streets, and whether the house had a supply of 'good water.'[13] About 40 years later *The Book of the Household* had a similar list warning against a 'low situation' since this was usually unhealthy, likewise 'anything likely to produce unwholesome effluvia'.[14] Noisy streets and smoking fireplaces were again to be avoided, and a good water supply was essential. *The Book of the Household* went into more detail on each point than *The Home Book*, warning of all the problems in detail; and yet this section of the book began with the suggestion that since the perfect residence was impossible to find it was desirable that people should take a positive and cheerful view since in this way they would 'see all things that cannot be avoided in a pleasant light, and turn to good account what others would mourn over in despair.'[15]

Some practical advice was offered by *Cassell's Household Guide*, a periodical aimed mainly at the lower-middle class. It gave estimates for household expenses, including how much it was prudent to pay in rent. The lowest annual income it gave was £150 – the lowest that was thought could sustain a middle-class lifestyle. The formula most books gave was one-tenth of the annual income; one-eighth was the most that should be paid and this should include local taxes and rates.[16] This publication also detailed the legal side of renting premises and gave sample agreements of various kinds, including the legal position of tenants being evicted or if they were unable to keep up payment of rent.[17] In such cases the landlord could issue a 'distress for rent' and under this law if the rent was not paid then goods could be seized:

> The landlord or the bailiff may call in a policeman, if violence is offered or threatened by a tenant.

> When the seizure had been made, an inventory of as many of the goods as will make up the amount of the debt and of the costs of the distress, must be drawn up. A copy of the inventory was then made with a notice at the foot stating that the distress has been made, that the goods mentioned have been taken, and mentioning the day on which the rent and cost must be paid. This inventory and notice must be served upon the tenant, and if he is not there, must be fixed in a conspicuous place on the premises. A witness should be in attendance to be able to prove that all the proceedings were strictly regular.[18]

Cassell's Household Guide gave advice on suiting a house to your means and not taking on more than one's income could cope with. It began the article with the warning that 'Far too often an appearance of luxury, but with real wretchedness exists in the same habitation. Living in a fine house with very straitened means frequently entails great discomfort, and it is in most cases excessively imprudent…' However, it also concedes that there are circumstances when people have good reasons for renting expensive houses:

> A respectable-looking house, in a desirable locality, is to a profession or trade absolutely necessary to future success, even though the tenants be poor. The style of the house in a degree determines the respectability, class,

credit, or means of its occupier, even though he be without fixed income, and living to the extent or beyond his means.

Where there is a fixed income, derivable from whatever source, it is a positive dishonesty to live in a finer house than the means honestly permit.[19]

The *Household Guide* article is thus making a connection between how people lived and the image that they presented to the outside world. It suggested that outsiders needed to be aware of a person's status regardless of their income. It is perhaps for similar reasons that some people hired furniture. The obvious reasons for this were to acquire items that they could not afford to buy. Again *Cassell's Household Guide* had advice to give. It suggested that when 'people cannot be sure of permanent employment in the same place, it may be advisable to hire, not purchase, furniture.'[20] The reason was a practical one as if the furniture had been bought and then had to be resold when the homemaker relocated then they would inevitably lose money. The guide also suggested that it was better to hire and then gradually replace items when you could afford to rather than buy everything and run up large debts.

Both cabinetmakers and furniture brokers rented furniture. The diary kept by James Hopkinson while he was a journeyman cabinetmaker in Nottingham in the first half of the nineteenth century provides some insight into this process. One of his jobs was delivering hired furniture and in some cases reclaiming it when the rent due was not paid.[21] His description of one such episode shows that he and his fellow workmen were aware of the legal situation as stipulated in the laws governing distress that the *Household Guide* outlined. A clergyman in rural Nottinghamshire was more than a year behind in the rent for the hire of a quantity of furniture and carpets. After letters requesting payment had gone unanswered, the master cabinetmaker directed his men to call on the clergyman, early in the morning, when the servants were just up. They were instructed not to open the door themselves but as soon as a servant opened it they were to 'take possession'. Hopkinson began his description of this event in the manner of an adventure. It was a cold morning with snow falling, and the men set out at three a.m. after a breakfast of bacon, bread and coffee. The journey there took them three hours. Only the foreman and one other man went to knock at the door, and while the servant went to inform the clergyman of their intention of taking the goods if the bill was not settled, the rest of the men crowded into the kitchen and began removing goods. The clergyman came downstairs with a gun and swore at them but fortunately did not shoot anyone. He also directed a servant to ride to the nearby town to send a policeman to stop them. Hopkinson and the other men worked quickly and cleared the house before this plan was effected. However, he says how sorry he was for the family, especially the two young frightened daughters who were forced to leave their beds. When Hopkinson helped to carry the beds out of the house they were 'still quite warm', and he felt ashamed to be part of such an 'unpleasant business'.

The following morning the clergyman called at the shop and 'paid up what he owed like a man, and was very civil'. The goods were to be polished and sent back again in a week 'before his boarders who were gone home for their Christmas holidays, should return to school.' This clergyman was clearly using his home to make a good impression and it was an important part of his means of making a living. He would not have attracted wealthy parents to entrust him with the education of their sons without a comfortable and genteel house in which they could board. Just as the *Household Guide* suggested that renting a nice house was important to project the right image so renting furniture could also be justified if it was a necessary outlay for ensuring a continued income.

Moving to a Distance or Giving up Housekeeping

A common reason, given in newspaper advertisements, for the sale of someone's household furniture was that they were moving to a distance. So, for example, in 1770 all the neat and clean household furniture of Mr Joseph Hunt, gunsmith, in Colemore Row, Birmingham, was advertised to be sold on the premises. Joseph Hunt, the advertisement stated, was 'going to reside in London'.[22]

The same reason was given when gentlemen were selling up their goods. It seems likely that this frequently used excuse was to obscure the real reason.[23] So, for example, in 1794 a sale took place at the Vicarage House in Shifnal of 'All the genuine and elegant Household Furniture of the Rev. Mr Huntley' who, it was claimed, was going to reside in Oxfordshire. The long list of goods described items of good quality. As well as the moveable furniture two marble chimney pieces and some mortise locks were to be included in the sale.[24] Similarly, Aris's *Birmingham Gazette* advertised the sale of what they described as 'Superior Household Furniture' belonging to 'a Gentleman who is changing his Residence to a Distance'. Included was furniture made in mahogany and rosewood, curtains were in chintz, and elegant looking glasses were in gilded frames.[25]

Even grander was the Lichfield home of Fairfax Moresby Esq. who, the 1816 advertisement claimed, was 'changing his residence'.[26] This 'Superb Household Furniture of exquisite wood and workmanship, the greatest part of which is London made', included a 'fine toned piano forte', china and glass. A long and detailed list followed with numerous articles that justified the description of 'superb'. Moving to another residence may have been the reason for selling everything, but in many cases it was probably a convenient excuse for someone who needed to retrench.

Shopkeepers and tradesmen retiring from trade was another reason frequently given for the sale of household goods. In 1815 the stock in trade of a cabinetmaker and upholsterer in Kidderminster (no name was given) was to be sold along with his household furniture; the latter, not surprisingly given his occupation, was described as best quality and of modern construction and design.[27]

Another commonly given reason for selling household goods was 'declining housekeeping'. Moving into a few rented rooms, perhaps furnished, or in with relatives was a common economic measure for people when they were elderly and their income was diminishing. This cut down on their living expenses and the need for extensive home furnishings. Perhaps this was the case in 1834, when a sale took place, on the premises of his tannery at Balsall Heath, of 'the genteel Household Furniture and effects of Mr Avery Homer, Tanner (who is relinquishing the trade and declining housekeeping)'.[28]

So, there were many reasons for selling up the contents of a home and these were experienced by a large proportion of the population. These circumstances, together with renting a furnished house or rooms, prevented many people getting attached to the bulk of the home furnishings with which they were surrounded. Purchased furniture often had to be sold by homemakers when they next needed to move and the alternative was to rent furniture from a cabinetmaker or furniture broker; both methods discouraged any sentimental attachment. This then constitutes the first layer of loss: the items that could easily be replaced, providing the money was available. But all these householders would have owned some possessions that were not rented or included in the sale; personal items connected with the body and personal adornment: clothing, shaving and hair care items, jewellery and so on.[29] Their close connection with the owner meant that they would not normally be sold. A few items such as a favourite piece of furniture, some linen, paintings or silver would be retained if possible, not necessarily because they were of great monetary value but due to their associations with the family, past and present. These items would have been taken from house to house, however temporary those homes were.

Lost Homes: Debts and Bankruptcy

More serious reasons than those outlined above for selling up the home threatened even the most treasured of possessions. This was the case when a notice of distress was served on Richard Evason, a farmer in Cardington, Shropshire, and his goods were inventoried and sold in 1777.[30] The items were of poor quality and old. The appraisers, Thomas Norris and Richard Pool, included small items of little or no value, such as a pail, an old bench, two sheep shears and a broom hook in the kitchen, and a small wooden bottle and an old half-barrel in the adjoining room. Despite their efforts to raise the value of the household goods they were all sold for just £3 15s 7½d. Goods outdoors and corn in the field raised the total by another £25. Thomas Evason and his wife, Joan, were probably left with little or nothing.

In the case of Mary Young, a milliner and dressmaker in Coventry, her goods were to be sold, in 1841, to discharge debts. However, the document stipulated that she could retain some household furniture; how much was not specified but presumably just enough to get by with.[31]

An inventory of the Chichester home of Ann Burge was made in 1841 by the appraiser, Henry Peat. The goods were to be sold for the benefit of her creditors.[32] The Peat firm of cabinetmakers made inventories of the homes of deceased middle-class people who invariably had employed them to do work in their homes, during their lifetime.[33] Ann Burge seems to have no other connections with the firm apart from the inventory. Perhaps her landlord was a customer. Her home had four rooms together with a cellar and wash house. Although containing a few luxuries, such as a mahogany dining table and tent bedstead with calico hangings, most items seem to have been of poor quality. For example, the mattress was only filled with straw, and a number of items were described as 'old'. Her back sitting room appears to have been a work room; its contents consisted of six black chairs, a deal ironing board, a copper warming pan, three trays, snuffers and stand, and a flat iron. The items for ironing clothes suggest that she took in laundry work, especially when these items are placed alongside those listed in the wash house. This outbuilding had a few cooking implements, and a wash stool, a water tub, a six-gallon brass furnace and brick work, and an iron ironing stove. If Ann Burge was about to lose her home and belongings, then it seems she was also about to lose her source of income.

Probate inventories sometimes reveal that the goods listed were to be sold for the benefit of the deceased's creditors. An inventory was made of goods in the home of Bridgnorth widow, Mrs Ann Devey, in August 1767.[34] The maker of the inventory began with the feather bed, bolster and blankets and then proceeded to kitchen items. Further down the list were a further two beds, one filled with feathers and the other with only flock. A few more items were listed and then finally came the '3 pair of bedsteads'. This ordering of goods obscures how many rooms were in her home, although with three beds it seems likely that Ann Devey lived in more than one general-purpose room.[35] The value of her goods amounted to £19 6s 2d despite including a few luxury items. These were a dresser with frame and nine pewter dishes, four brass candlesticks and a brass kettle, a clock and case, a small quantity of china, some delft plates, a teakettle and a frying pan. Some of these items had an intrinsic value: the pewter and brass, and the clock which was worth £4 2s 0d, the largest amount for anything on the list. The other luxury items were connected with new ways of preparing food and novel consumer goods. The majority of the items that Ann Devey owned, as listed in her inventory, were connected with kitchen utensils for preparing food and serving meals and beverages. Apart from the beds and dresser the only other furniture was an oak table, a further small table and six chairs. Perhaps, then, other substantial pieces of furniture had already been sold. Ann Devey was in debt when she died and all her belongings were to be sold for her principal creditors. While some people incurred debts due to extravagant living this was not always the case; prolonged illness or the death of a spouse could also be factors. In the case of Ann Devey, the administration document states that her principal creditors were Thomas Pass, a cheesefactor, and Benjamin Yates, a Grocer, both of Bridgnorth. So the majority of Ann Devey's debts were for food, and had perhaps been merely the necessities of life rather than extravagant delicacies.

Hannah and Catherine Poyner by contrast lived in some comfort in Bridgnorth, at the same period as Ann Devey; indeed the same person, John Bartholomew, compiled both inventories.[36] These two sisters, both spinsters, shared a house in Bridgnorth until their deaths, in quick succession in 1765. The sisters enjoyed a comfortable income derived from the rents on properties that they owned. They had a high status within Bridgnorth. Their father had been a successful timber merchant and had been a burgess and churchwarden in the town in the early-eighteenth century. The family had enjoyed a respectable position in the community. However, their late brother John ran up debts and their goods were to be sold for the benefit of his creditors.[37] The sisters lived in a house with three main rooms on each floor and a cellar and garrets. The inventory was very full, with particularly long lists of china and linen. While their servant was to have their wearing apparel for her work looking after them in their last illness, the sisters left everything else to their nephew. But he perhaps inherited little after the debts were settled. Probate inventories do not always reveal the financial situation of the deceased. An apparent wealth of material goods to be inherited by the family may have soon been dispersed due to debts.

A higher level of wealth than that of the Poyners prevailed in the home of Richard Grevis, whose inventory was made on his death in 1759.[38] But again, not all was as it seemed. Richard Grevis lived at Moseley Hall near King's Norton in Worcestershire. He was a Justice of the Peace and a deputy lieutenant for Worcestershire, and Aris's *Birmingham Gazette* published a glowing obituary. Moseley Hall had extensive service areas, a Great Parlour, Best Parlour, Little Parlour and a study. There were 12 bedchambers, with garrets above, for servants. The room in the inventory with the most goods, and that were worth the most money, was Mr Grevis's 'Chamber Dressing Room and Closet'. This room contained:

> One bed, bedsteads and appurtenances, seven chairs, a fire screen, four cushions, two grates, fender, fire shovel, tongs and poker, one plate, one chest of drawers, two looking glasses, one beaurow, and one ditto table, one little broom, three dressing boxes, two waiters, one stand, one tea table, one warming pan, one pair of bellows, one deal stand, one table, seven small boxes, two saucepans, a parcel of books, one flasket, some china and plate, and window curtins.

These items alone amounted to £25 15s 0d. However, other rooms in the house seem rather empty and somewhat lacking in furniture. The items in the Great Parlour only amounted to £4 and in the Best Parlour they came to £5 13s. The 27 pictures on the Best Stair Case were valued at just two shillings and sixpence. Perhaps Richard Grevis had already disposed of some of his household goods. The very last item in the inventory was 'Cash received since testators death on account of arrears in rent…£105 3s 6d'. But this sum was not nearly enough. Richard and his wife Jane were so much in debt that their land and belongings all had to be sold soon after this inventory was made. So, their son inherited nothing and was forced to become a labourer in a gravel pit.[39]

Public humiliation was involved for a homemaker after the auctioneer, John Fallow, had placed two advertisements, printed side by side, in Aris's *Birmingham Gazette* in 1849. They both began with the announcement 'RE Thomas Francis, A Bankrupt'.[40] One advertisement was for his home in the middle-class suburb of Edgbaston and the other was for his furniture.[41] The house was described as a 'pleasantly situated and convenient cottage' although the description made it clear that it was substantial enough to suit to a large family. Thomas Francis had lived there for some years and the house had 'every requisite for domestic comfort'. The garden was laid out 'with great taste'. The house was let on a lease which had 20 years still to run. The advertisement for the household furniture and other effects made clear that the Francis family enjoyed every comfort in their home. The bedroom furniture was in mahogany with 'rich draperies' and the beds filled with goose feathers. The dining room was furnished in mahogany while the drawing room was in rosewood, exactly as advice books dictated.[42] There were Brussels carpets, plate and plated goods, framed oil paintings and china dinner, dessert, tea and coffee services. A carriage, phaeton, cart and a pony were also to be sold. Thomas Francis had gone from being a well-established resident of Edgbaston with a comfortable and fashionable home to a bankrupt. He then had to suffer the shame of his bankruptcy being advertised in the newspaper, and his home could be inspected by ticket, and catalogues of his possessions could be purchased. Everything listed was to be sold for whatever was bid for them at the auction; the advertisement stipulated that there were no reservations on the prices.

Lost Homes: Disasters

During the riots in Birmingham in 1791, brought about by a group of Dissenters holding a dinner to celebrate the fall of the Bastille, their three places of worship and a number of houses were broken into, their contents smashed or stolen, and the buildings in some cases set on fire. Both Joseph Priestley's and William Hutton's homes were among those targeted by the mob.[43] Contemporary accounts state that when the mob arrived at Priestley's house, he and his wife had already fled, and the doors were broken down and furniture was thrown out of the windows. The library had its contents 'scattered to the winds' and the rioters then found the wine cellar and drank until they were senseless. It was hoped that they would then disperse, but instead they returned to their work and destroyed the laboratory.[44] In a letter to the newspaper after this event it was the laboratory that Priestley was most upset about since it was his life's work and had taken many years to assemble.[45]

Priestley had appraisers make a list together with valuations of all his household possessions that were lost in the riot. The inventory was 34 pages long.[46] It began with the costs of rebuilding and reinstating the dwelling house, the surveyor's fees and rent for two years while the work was done. All this came to £1267. The inventory of the contents of the house was minutely detailed for the three attic rooms, the four bedchambers and on the ground floor, the two parlours, the library, the kitchen, back kitchen and laundry, various store rooms for china, plate and glass, and the cellar with its store of wine, beer, cider and preserves. There was then a list of miscellaneous items, clothing and 'trinkets' and lastly, the laboratory, that was built adjoining the main house. The appraiser's final sum for replacing the contents of Priestley's home came to £1307 8s 0d. Just £20 18s was deducted as the value of articles that had been saved and returned to Priestley. The inventory ended with a comment from the appraiser:

> The above Schedule and Appraisement hath been made and taken by Mr J. Phillips Sworn Broker and Appraiser 134 Fenchurch Street in the City of London and by other eminent Brokers and Appraisers as will be proved in

the Tryal of this Cause if necessary and all these Valuations are made at the price and sums it will cost the plaintiff to replace and reinstate every Article.

The reason for the inventory was unusual. The house had been completely furnished when it was destroyed in the riot. Every item needing to be replaced, the appraisers therefore needed to be very thorough in their work. The result is an inventory that is particularly full and detailed with many items described quite precisely. For example in the best bedchamber there was listed 'A large four post Bedstead 5ft 6 wide Lath Bottom compleat and furniture of fine printed calico lined and fringed compleat £10 12s'. The size of the bedstead and its construction and the nature of the bed hangings, good quality but not the best, all help in constructing a picture of this home and in appreciating the care and expense with which the furnishings had been chosen. Also in this room were listed items for treating the family during illness: 'A Quantity of medicines, Apparatus Medicines scales and Weights £4 4s; A vessel to steam the throat 7s 6d; A Patent Glystor Machine 8s.' Each of these details had meaning for their owners who came into daily contact with them.

Every room in Priestley's home was listed with the same detail: the precise nature of its contents, their materials and construction. In this manner the inventory clearly shows how this list of goods was peculiar to this household. In the Large Back Parlour was 'A Sofa Mahogany frame Stuff in Canvas One Cotton Window Curtain lined a Sofa Cover to correspond and 14 yards of new Cotton same as the window Curtains and three Japan'd Cornishes £6 3s', along with three irreplaceable portraits in frames valued at £9 9s. So the list continued. In the Kitchen the items included 'Four Japan'd Spoon and Knife Trays new and an Oak Knife Tray 9s 6d; Two Tea urns plated Cocks and Heater Compleat £2 10s; Two mahogany Tea Boards one fret Border and the other oval £2 7s 6d; Two small Tea Boards a Japan'd Tea Board and Waiter and a new Japan'd Waiter £1 13s; Twelve Window and Door Bells 15s'. Here is evidence of differentiation in design long before the Victorian period when it became common: a total of seven trays for carrying food and china but of different design, materials and construction.[47]

Towards the end of the inventory was a list titled Miscellaneous and it contained a mixture of objects that presumably had been forgotten during the room-by-room inventory. The list of items included 'An Umbrella bought the Christmas preceding the Riots 5s; A new Elegant shaving Green Morocco apparatus £3 3s; Two phials of Reeve's water colour 2s; About a Dozen of painting brushes 1s'. Many objects were of little value and many would not necessarily have needed to be replaced for Priestley and his family to feel that their home was complete; still the listing of all these possessions no doubt stimulated the overall sense of loss.

The inventory of Priestley's home shows the nature of consumption in household goods practised by the family: the quality of the furnishings, the sheer scale of items that a house of this size and complexity would have contained at this period. While many objects were stored in furniture or built-in cupboards much must also have been on show, some things displayed for affect, others left negligently on surfaces to be picked up and used. The list suggests that this home, and others on this scale, offered a dense and rich material culture. Clear, too, is the quantity of the detritus of people's lives, the slightly worn shoes, the jars of pickled walnuts maturing in the cellar, and the nearly new umbrella. Although Priestley proclaimed that the destruction of his laboratory was the biggest loss to him, the contents of his home would have been impossible to replicate, even if the full money had been forthcoming.

On the third day of the riots in Birmingham in 1791, it was the turn of William Hutton's two houses to be the focus of the mob's attention. His daughter Catherine described the event in some detail.[48] Whilst at their country home in Bennett's Hill, they heard of the riot. Catherine sent her keys to their servants at their Birmingham residence, to 'secure the plate, linen and clothes'; she then gave orders to dismantle bedsteads and to take down hangings and window curtains. A neighbour had offered to store their furniture. China was packed up ready to be taken when they fled the property. But then the neighbour became afraid of the consequences of harbouring their furniture in his barn, and it was all sent back. By this time Catherine, her mother and their servants were exhausted. A hackney coach arrived to take them to safety and Catherine spread a sheet on the floor and threw into it some of her mother's clothes. That was all they took with them. After staying one night nearby, they went to Sutton and heard that their house in the High Street in Birmingham had been ransacked but not burnt, as that would have destroyed neighbouring houses. At Sutton Catherine found them lodgings at a butcher's with 'a parlour, just decent, and a bedroom far from it-being open to the stairs and roof, and containing two tattered, moth-eaten stuff beds. I then went to purchase muslin for a nightcap, otherwise my pocket-handkerchief must have been the substitute, as it had been the night before.'[49] In such a dreadful situation it is a curious indication of contemporary ideas concerning propriety that a nightcap should concern her to such a degree.

Similarly, when Catherine described the condition at their house in Birmingham, she put emphasis on decency rather than the monetary losses they had incurred. Her father and brother patched up the house so that it could be inhabited by her brother and the servants. 'Curtains are a luxury my brother does not know, except to his windows, and one if these is blue and the other yellow. A piece of oil cloth hung up serves for a door, and but for this, the room would be open to the court, for there is no outer door below.'[50] At this period the main curtains in a bedchamber were round the bed and offered both warmth and privacy. Only servants slept in beds without bed hangings.[51]

The ringleaders of the riots were tried but were dealt with leniently. The Dissenters had lost many thousands of pounds and although their claims were relatively modest they received only a portion.[52] In addition the 15 Dissenters who had brought the claims to trial had to pay the costs, which amounted to £13,000. Apart from the financial disaster brought about by the mob, each family that lost their home faced emotional loss too. Catherine Hutton exclaimed in her diary 'never shall I forget the joy with which I entered our own gates once more. That our house was spared I was grateful beyond measure; it seemed as an old dear friend restored to life from a dangerous disorder.'[53] The Huttons were able to rebuild their business and establish a new home, although Mrs Hutton's health never recovered. The loss was greater for Priestley. Parkin's work on the importance of retaining objects during times of displacement is pertinent here. He claims that:

> the donor of a gift imparts part of their personality in the gift and expects it to be returned. Perhaps in my description we have something of the reverse: persons may withhold selfhood when faced with the possibility of collective annihilation, merging it in the materiality of concrete objects, hoping that in due course it should again be socially presented when and if the threat is lifted.[54]

But in losing everything Priestley was not able to do this. He was utterly crushed by the loss of his laboratory that embodied his life's work. And by losing his home he and his family lost all their possessions with emotional symbolic value. Having lost his investment in life in Birmingham, Priestley lived for a time in London and then emigrated with his family to America where he joined his friend Benjamin Franklin.[55]

Objects with Special Associations: Portraits

Among the possessions that Priestley lost when his home was destroyed were family portraits and other items that depicted close friends and associates, for example in his library Priestley had paintings, medallions and engravings of numerous illustrious people whom he counted amongst his friends. Portraits provided a close connection with the person depicted. They were therefore among the objects that people were least likely to relinquish.

Having a portrait painted in the period before the invention of photography was important for recording the likeness of a person, to mark milestones in their life, and for posterity. It was also important for remembering people.[56] There was a high mortality rate, amongst children in particular, so a portrait was a permanent reminder of someone. When he was about to leave Chichester for America in 1833 the brother of Miss Jupp commissioned the portrait painter John Lush to paint her likeness.[57] Mr Jupp paid two guineas for the portrait that presumably he intended to take with him, to remind him of his sister whom he might never see again.[58]

Portraits were also a favourite item to be named in bequests. The testator intended that the recipient would remember them, hopefully with affection, for years to come. Such was the case when gentlewoman Anne Cave left a detailed will in 1755.[59] She was a spinster and wished to be buried with her mother in Clifton upon Dunsmore, in Warwickshire. Besides various sums of money, she left a portrait of herself to Dr Thomas Burgh of Coventry, and another portrait of herself to her friend Mary King, a spinster. To Sir Thomas Cave, baronet, she bequeathed six family pictures from her dwelling house.

It was not only wealthy families who had family portraits painted, but tradesmen and middle-class families also invested both money and emotions in this way, especially by the early- to mid-nineteenth century. One such was Elizabeth

Goodall, from a family of plumbers and glaziers in Coventry, who died in 1837.[60] In her will she left her clothes to her sister Catherine who was married to a stay maker in London. To her unmarried daughter Charlotte, she left her piano forte, a mahogany chest of drawers, a looking glass and china, and two white counterpanes. To her daughter Mary, who was married to Thomas Jones of Mosely, Birmingham, she left various items of furniture; but enumerated first in the list was 'the portrait of my late husband Jeremiah Goodall'. By passing on the portrait to Mary perhaps Elizabeth Goodall intended that the portrait should pass on to Mary's children and therefore be kept in the family. In this way the portrait would remain meaningful and Jeremiah would be remembered.

A further dimension to the use of portraits as a means of remembering people is demonstrated in the example provided by the conversation piece of the Mynors family. In this picture the artist, James Millar, depicted the family amidst a fictitious domestic scene.[61] The interior is grand. A theatrical element is produced by a red curtain draped across one corner, and with a large archway to one side through which can be seen a view of distant countryside.[62] A large framed picture hangs on a wall depicting an imposing country house set in extensive grounds, as if implying that this was the exterior of the house in which the portrait was set. However, the Mynors lived in a far more modest house, in central Birmingham in Snow Hill, where Robert Mynor was a surgeon and man midwife.[63] Painted in c. 1790 the portrait is a late example of a conversation piece in which stylized scenes with stock elements, like stage props, were commonly used.[64] But still Millar was instructed to include elements that were extremely personal to the Mynors family. Robert Mynor is shown with his wife and three children, one of whom is seated on the floor with a pet cat and dog. Another child lies on the sofa beside his mother, who lifts a gauze fabric that is draped over him. This child had died sometime previously but the family portrait still included him.[65] At their home in Snow Hill this portrait would have been displayed in a public room. There it would serve as a personal reminder to the family and visitors to the house, of the family group, as it existed in 1790, but in addition, the member of the family no longer alive at that date. This was how they wished to be memorialized.

Portrait pictures were common in many middling and middle-class homes. They hung on the wall as part of the decoration of parlours and drawing rooms, the public rooms of the home. Their frames were an additional attraction and were sometimes embellished with fashionable carving and gilding. This was especially the case in the nineteenth century, by which time the cost of decorative frames had come down in price due to cheaper methods of manufacture.[66] But while family pictures were part of the furniture they were also individual objects that carried symbolic meanings for the family. They signified family lineage. Portraits made a link between the past, present and future. Pointon claims that portraits were often left in wills as 'an attempt to govern the behaviour of future generations' and the bequest was accompanied by rules for its retention.[67] Portraits then were symbolic of permanence in the material culture of the home.

Objects with Special Associations: Objects Retained When Homes Were Sold

When John Staunton died in 1811 his house and its contents were sold by auction. As a younger son he had not expected to inherit the family home, Longbridge, in Warwickshire, and had therefore allowed his eldest son William and his family to take possession, while he remained in his home in the centre of Kenilworth.[68] John Staunton lived with his second wife, Anne, and his youngest son, Edmund, who was about to take holy orders. As well as William and Edmund John Staunton had another son, John Grove Staunton, who was a clergyman and lived in a nearby village.

The detailed list of the house contents was made by an auctioneer and appraiser in preparation for a catalogue to be printed. He valued the furniture, plate and carriage at £1279, and the paintings and books at a further £344. The main rooms of the house were furnished in a grand style if perhaps a little old-fashioned. The auctioneer's list had annotations to indicate what was to be omitted from the sale. None of the fine furniture was distinguished in this way. Instead an assortment of goods, some with monetary value others with very little, were singled out. Most of these objects can be explained by the symbolic value that they might be supposed to carry for the family members. Not surprisingly for a gentry family with a long lineage, all the family portraits were to be retained. Most of the other paintings were to be sold with a few exceptions; these were landscapes and portraits mostly attributed to Dutch Old Masters. According to Dianne Sachko MacLeod, these were typical for a gentry family to value.[69] The extensive quantity of silver plate was to be retained and the majority of items in a long list of linen. Silver plate was a traditional item for people to value and pass on within the family. In this instance it would have had a crest engraved on it. Linen also had family associations, made and embroidered by the females of present and previous generations. Likewise, two coats of arms that hung in the family parlour – one worked in paper and another in shell work, and both glazed in black frames – were to be omitted from the sale. These objects were no doubt the work of family members. Apart from personal associations that they might possess for the family, they would not have been valued by anyone attending the public auction. Their inclusion in the sale would therefore have opened the family's private possessions to the public gaze.

The long lists of ceramic wares kept in a china closet were all to be included in the sale with just a couple of exceptions. These consisted of a small tea set of blue and white earthenware and another in red and white china. Presumably William and his wife with their well-established home would have had no particular use for them. But these two tea sets would have been sufficient for a reduced household, perhaps for Edmund or his stepmother Anne, when they were settled in new accommodation.[70]

After the auctioneer had dealt with the rooms downstairs he moved on to the bedchambers, and here he listed many personal items that were to be omitted from the house sale. Under the heading 'Mr J.G. Stanton' was a list of items presumably belonging to John Grove.[71] These included five quadrille boxes, an India tea chest, a razor box with two razors, a small dressing box, a gold watch chain, a gold swing seal and two small steel seals, a magnifying glass and some small shagreen cards tipped with silver, an English Testament and a Latin Bible. A shorter list was headed Mr E. Stanton and consisted of just two gold seals, a small caddy, and four shagreen cases.

A long list was headed by William Stanton's name and the auctioneer commented 'including Longbridge', which seems to suggest that some items had previously been removed to William's new home. All the items were of a personal nature as in the lists for his brothers. These were all objects that the children of John Staunton kept in their own rooms and were used by them in a personal way. These are the items that are often missing from probate inventories because they have already been dispersed. The auction marked them out for distinction and thereby highlighted that they were valued.[72] The chief beneficiary, William the eldest son, was already well established in the ancestral home and had no need for additional furnishings. It was mainly items relating to family pedigree that he wanted to retain. These were the objects that helped to provide 'future continuity...like ancestral memorials encoding continuity between and across the generations'.[73] In addition, William and his brothers kept objects from their childhood home with which they had particularly personal associations.

The Transient Homes of Francis Blythe Harries

The house and estate at Benthall in Shropshire came into the Harries family in the late eighteenth century. Richard Benthall died in 1720 and having no children the estate was inherited by the Browne family, related to the Benthalls by marriage.[74] After the death of Ralph Browne the estate then moved to his wife's niece who was married to the Rev. Edward Harries, and then, in 1812, to his son Francis Blythe Harries.[75] Whilst in his care, the house of Benthall Hall, built in the sixteenth century, with some alterations in the eighteenth century, suffered a fire in which much damage was done. After this event when the house was restored, a new wing was added complete with a large new dining room. A comfortable life in an impressive house and with a fine country estate was not to last long for Francis Blythe Harries, his wife and five children. He ran up debts of £80,000 and was forced to sell the house and estate to a nearby landowner for £60,000.[76] Then followed a few years of successive retrenchment before Harries finally left England for the south of France where he died in c. 1850.[77] The sale of the contents of Benthall Hall, and subsequently Broseley Hall, offer some insight into how Harries and his family parted with their belongings layer by layer.

The evidence of the sale of Harries's household belongings at Benthall Hall comes in the form of a small account book of the 'Particulars of Sale at Benthall as furnished by Mr Smith' and dated the 10, 11, 12 March 1845. Mr Smith was the auctioneer. He charged seven guineas for his time valuing goods, and for attending at the Lion Hotel for the sale of the estate. The sale of the animals and implements was on the first day and then the household goods on days two and three. If the sale of the household effects was at the inn rather than at the premises, it would explain the somewhat random ordering of the list. The sale began with bedchambers and proceeded to living room furniture and effects, such as china. But no clear idea of particular rooms emerges. The second day of the sale ended with such items as dog kennels and saddles. The third day of the sale was concerned wholly with the offices, the kitchen, including a servant's bedroom, and outbuildings. The amount raised by the sale was mostly derived from the animals and farm implements; these came to £413. The household goods came to a mere £115. This low figure was the result of only part of the household furniture being included in the sale, and the prices offered for individual items were extremely low. Perhaps because Harries was bankrupt the goods were sold without reserve, as in the case of Thomas Francis, previously quoted.

Benthall Hall was a large house and contained numerous rooms for both the family and servants to use. Ten bedsteads plus two named as 'servants bedsteads' might account for most of the bedrooms but little other substantial furniture was included. No carpets, silver, paintings, books or clocks were included. Only a couple of items specify that they were made of mahogany. In the mid-nineteenth century this was the fashionable timber for smart furniture, and which might be expected to command a high price. The most expensive items listed in the sale were three pianofortes, sold for £5, £4 and £2 15s. Most other items sold for just a few shillings.[78]

By the time the sale of these household goods took place Francis Blythe Harries and his family had moved to nearby Broseley Hall.[79] This eighteenth-century house was a plain but well-proportioned dwelling spread over three floor with grounds laid out with a summer house by local architect Thomas Farnolls Pritchard, who had also designed a number of cast-iron chimney pieces for the house.[80] But the comforts of Broseley Hall were not long enjoyed by the Harries family. Debts were still bearing down on Francis Blythe Harries. The contents of Broseley Hall were sold up in 1848 (Illustration 2:1).

The evidence of the house sale at Broseley Hall takes the form of an inventory and appraisement made in July 1848. This document followed a logical perambulation around the house with the names of rooms and their contents listed in some detail. The main rooms on the ground floor were the breakfast parlour and dining room with matching curtains, and a combined drawing room and library. Three bedchambers and a dressing room were listed, together with four attic rooms, one of which was for the manservant. Also on the ground floor were the kitchen and scullery, as well as a small housekeeper's room and butler's pantry. The valuation came to £330, twice that produced by the sale at Benthall.

A number of points can be deduced from the inventory of Broseley Hall. The living rooms followed the ideal pattern as recommended by advice books.[81] There was a formal dining room, a family breakfast room and a smart drawing room. The descriptions of the furniture suggest that the rooms were appropriately furnished in items that were fashionable in design and were probably reasonably new. In the breakfast parlour, for example, there were '8 imitation rosewood trafalga chairs brass ornaments cane seats loose cushions in chintz en suite'. The chintz cushions matched the cover on the square sofa, both being decorated with crimson flowers. This chintz picked up the colour of the crimson flowers, on drab ground, in the Brussels carpet and no doubt harmonized with the damask moreen

2:1 Broseley Hall was the temporary home of the Harries family in the 1840s after money problems forced them to sell Benthall Hall.

window curtains trimmed with amber gimp and fringe. These curtains matched those in the dining room, which had all mahogany furniture, a table, 12 chairs with hair seats, a beer cooler, a celleret to hold six bottles of wine, and a 'sweep front sideboard'.

Presumably Thomas Blythe Harries brought some furniture from Benthall Hall. It seems likely that he bought new and fashionable items during the refurbishment following the fire in 1818. Certainly the new wing with large dining room would have occasioned new furniture. Perhaps then, in the first sale, he sold off some older items that were not fashionable, including some of the old Benthall family furniture. These items would have no particular resonance for Harries who needed suitable furnishings for a smaller house with fewer rooms.

When further retrenchment was required, the sale at Broseley included all the newer furniture since its removal to France was out of the question. So, too, was the transportation of extensive quantities of china. Numerous small items of an individual nature such as embroidered workboxes, antimacassars and lace edged tablecloths were to be relinquished. However, as at Benthall, no silver, paintings or books were included in the sale probably because of their specialized and valuable nature they were sold separately. The other group of objects missing from the sale were precisely the same kind that was retained by William Staunton and his brothers in the sale of their father's home. This time the Harries family was only taking with them their most personal possessions, items that were relatively easy to transport. These items could be accommodated in furnished rented rooms in France, which would have offered the Harries family a temporary and impersonal home, which, as we have seen, so many other homemakers experienced during the period.

Conclusion

In this exploration of the transient nature of homes, it was established that temporary rented houses or rooms were common. The majority of household goods in many homes came with the accommodation or might be rented or sold up each time a move was effected. But some objects had special associations for homemakers and these were not given up lightly.

These circumstances affected people throughout the period. By the nineteenth century homes contained an increasing number of possessions, which resulted in more money being involved in their setting up and the cost of replacing them, should that prove necessary; although lower prices for many consumer goods helped to mitigate the expense. However, the emotional investment in special objects was a constant element in homemaking.

The loss of the entire home was emotionally damaging and people tried to retain or rescue special things. As with the likeness of the beloved relative when far from home or the image of the dead child in a family portrait, personal objects carried remembrance of family and friends. Other objects carried 'selfhood'. These were the objects that provided continuity despite the transient nature of most physical aspects of the home.

Notes

[1]   Aris's *Birmingham Gazette* 16 August 1830.

[2]   Paintings of interiors often show a clutter of objects on mantelpieces rather than a few choice things displayed. Similarly pans and vegetables are shown on the floor of kitchens. See Charles Saumarez Smith (1993), *Eighteenth-Century Decoration*, London: Weidenfeld and Nicolson.

[3]   Advice literature on homemaking had always blended practical instruction with moral and religious comments. For seventeenth-century examples see Kathleen M. Davies (1981), 'Continuity and change in literary advice on marriage', in R.B. Outhwaite (ed.), *Marriage and Society: the Social History of Marriage*, London: Europa. For a general account of advice literature and its link with early nineteenth-century Evangelical thinking see Robert B. Shoemaker (1998), *Gender in English Society 1650–1850: the Emergence of Separate Spheres?*, London: Longman.

[4]   *The Family Economist: a Penny Monthly Magazine for the Industrious Classes* (1851), London: Groombridge and Sons, volume 5, p. 182.

[5]   John Benson (1996), 'Working-Class Consumption, Saving, and Investment in England and Wales, 1851–1911', *Journal of Design History*, volume 9, number 2, pp. 87–99.

[6]   David Parkin (1999), 'Mementoes as Transitional Objects in Human Displacement', *Journal of Material Culture*, volume 4, number 3, pp. 303–320, p. 313.

[7]   Parkin (1999), 'Mementoes as Transitional Objects', p. 314.

[8]   John Burnett (1978), *A Social History of Housing 1815–1970*, Newton Abbot: David and Charles, p. 97.

[9]   S.J. Wright (1990), 'Sojourners and lodgers in a provincial town: the evidence from Eighteenth-century Ludlow', *Urban History*, volume 17, pp. 14–35, p. 19.

[10] S.J. Wright (1990), 'Sojourners and lodgers', p. 35, note 65.

[11] Birmingham Archives, MBP 479, bill dated 1824.

[12] Staffordshire Record Office, Account book of John Foden, 1827–1866, 3161.

[13] A Lady (1829), *The Home Book: or Young Housekeeper's Assistant*, London: Smith, Elder and Co., p. 106.

[14] *The Book of the Household* (c. 1870), London: The London Printing and Publishing Company, pp. 47–49.

[15] *The Book of the Household* (c. 1870), p. 47.

[16] Annual income of £100 - £17 for rent, taxes and water rates; £200 - £35; £400 - £50; £500 - £62. *Cassell's Household Guide* (1870–74), London: Cassell, Petter, and Galpin, volume 1, p.3. See also Burnett (1978), p. 96.

[17] *Cassell's Household Guide* (1870–74), volume 1, pp. 38–39, volume 2, pp. 258–259, 338–339, volume 3, pp. 10–11.

[18] *Cassell's Household Guide* (1870–74), volume 3, p. 11.

[19] *Cassell's Household Guide* (1870–74), volume 1, p. 2.

[20] *Cassell's Household Guide* (1870–74), volume 1, p. 312.

[21] Jocelyne Baty Goodman (ed.) (1968), *Victorian Cabinet Maker: The Memoirs of James Hopkinson 1819–1894*, Routledge and Kegan Paul, pp. 33–36. No date was given for the incident recounted but it would have been in the 1840s before Hopkinson moved to Liverpool in 1851 and set up in business there as a cabinetmaker.

[22] Aris's *Birmingham Gazette*, 18 June 1770.

[23] Cynthia Wall (1997), 'The English Auction: Narratives of Dismantlings', *Eighteenth-Century Studies*, volume 31, number 1, pp. 1–25.

[24] Aris's *Birmingham Gazette*, 16 July 1794.

[25] Aris's *Birmingham Gazette*, 5 January 1818.

[26] Aris's *Birmingham Gazette*, 13 March 1815.

[27] Aris's *Birmingham Gazette*, 3 July 1815.

[28] Aris's *Birmingham Gazette*, 10 February 1834.

[29] Marcia Pointon comments on these kinds of objects being carried to temporary habitations in spa towns or from town to country homes. Marcia Pointon (1997), *Strategies for Showing: Women, Possession, and Representation in English Visual Culture 1665–1800*, London: Oxford University Press, p. 31.

[30] Shropshire Record Office, inventory, 6000/17750, Notice of Distress, 6000/17751.

[31] Coventry Archives, Assignment of goods for creditors, 101/118/1.

[32] West Sussex Record Office, Henry and William Peat notebook, Add Mss 2245.

[33] West Sussex Record Office, Samuel Peat account book, Add Mss 2239.

[34] Lichfield Joint Record Office, probate inventory and administration.

[35] Probate inventories sometimes grouped things together for convenience – although that does not seem to have been the reason in this case.

[36] Lichfield Joint Record Office, Probate inventory and will.

[37] Lichfield Joint Record Office, Probate inventory and will. Family details for the Poyners can be found at Shropshire Record Office, St Leonard, Bridgnorth parish records.

[38] Inventory for Richard Grevis transcribed with notes in Malcolm Wanklyn (ed.) (1998), *Inventories of Worcestershire Landed Gentry 1537–1786*, Worcestershire Historical Society New Series, volume 16, Worcester: Worcestershire Historical Society.

[39] W.S. Brassington (1894), *Historic Worcestershire*, Birmingham: The Midland Education Co. and Simpkin, Marshall, Hamilton and Kent, pp. 296–298.

[40] Aris's *Birmingham Gazette* 1 October 1849.

[41] Edgbaston was well established by the mid-nineteenth century and was exclusively middle class.

[42] See for example J.C. Loudon (1833), *Encyclopaedia of Cottage, Farm and Villa Architecture*, London: Longman, Orme, Brown, Green and Longman.

[43] Joseph Preistley was a Presbyterian minister. He also conducted research into the chemistry of gases and discovered oxygen. He was a friend of Matthew Boulton and a fellow member of the Lunar Society. See Jenny Uglow (2002), *The Lunar Men: The Friends Who Made the Future*, London: Faber and Faber. William Hutton was a successful bookseller and stationer who wrote a history of Birmingham. See Carl Chinn (1998), Introduction to *The Life of William Hutton*, Studley, Warwickshire: Brewin Books.

[44] Robert K. Dent (1973 originally published 1878–80), *Old and New Birmingham*, volume III, Birmingham: EP Publishing Ltd., p. 229.

[45] Quoted in Dent (1973), *Old and New*, p. 248.

[46] Birmingham City Archives, (IIR30) 399801.

[47] Adrian Forty (1987), *Objects of Desire: Design and Society 1750–1980*, London: Thames and Hudson.

[48] Dent (1973), *Old and New*, pp. 235–243, 250–2.

[49] Catherine was appalled at the bedroom being 'open' to the stairs and roof and yet by the 1820s, in a story she wrote for *La Belle Assemblé*, she could write nostalgically about just such a dwelling, although in her story the rooms in the attic were used by servants. See Birmingham Archives, Hutton Beale Family Papers 106/12, and quoted in Chapter 1.

[50] Dent, (1973), *Old and New*, p. 252.

51 Susan Prendergast Schoelwer (1979), 'Form, Function and Meaning in the Use of Fabric Furnishings: a Philadelphia Case Study, 1700–1775', *Winterthur Portfolio*, volume 4, number 1, pp. 25–40.

52 William Hutton claimed £6736 3s 8d and received £5390 17s 0d. Joseph Priestley claimed £3628 8s 9d and received £2502 18s 0d.

53 Dent (1973), *Old and New*, p. 230.

54 Parkin (1999), 'Mementoes as Transitional Objects', p. 318.

55 Benjamin Franklin was a US statesman, writer and scientist. He conducted research into electricity. He had been on a number of diplomatic missions to Britain during which he had met Priestley.

56 It has already been noted that David Parkin has found that photographs are amongst the most treasured possessions of displaced people. Parkin (1999), 'Mementoes as Transitional Objects', p. 313.

57 West Sussex Record Office, Diary of John Lush, Add Mss 19026.

58 Portraits could be relatively cheap from a 'jobbing' artist. Marcia Pointon suggests that a fee of 3–8 guineas was usual. Marcia Pointon (1993), *Hanging the Head: Portraiture and Social Formation in Eighteenth-Century England*, Paul Mellon Centre for Studies in British Art and Yale University Press, p. 3.

59 Coventry Archives, will of Anne Cave 1 January 1755, 487/1.

60 Coventry Archives, will of Elizabeth Goodall 13 February 1837, 101/8/658.

61 The portrait hangs at Soho House, the Birmingham home of Matthew Boulton although the Mynors were unrelated to the Boultons.

62 Pointon (1993), *Hanging the Head*, suggests that Conversation Piece paintings were specifically about family lineage and property, p. 159, and 'articulation of family continuity', p.175.

63 *Western and Midland Directory* (1783), Birmingham: Bailey; *Birmingham Directory* (1801), Birmingham: Chapman.

64 Another portrait by Millar of an unnamed Birmingham family makes use of the same curtain, archway and musical instruments. Reproduced in Ellis Waterhouse (1981), *The Dictionary of British 18th Century Painters*, Woodbridge: Antique Collector's Club, p. 241. For an account of this style of portraiture see Saumarez Smith (1993), *Eighteenth-Century Decoration.*

65 Infant mortality rates were high. In 1850 146 infants in every 1000 died in their first year and the same number before they reached the age of five. Burnett (1978), *A Social History*, p. 99.

66 Frames for gilding were made in composition, a mixture of whiting, resin and size, rather than carved wood.

67 Pointon (1993), *Hanging the Head*, p. 161.

68 John Staunton had inherited Longbridge House when his elder brother died in 1795, by which time John was 60 years of age. See John Burke (1837), *A Genealogy and Heraldic History of the Landed Gentry*, volume II, London: Henry Coburn.

69 Dianne Sachko MacLeod (1996), *Art and the Victorian Middle Class: Money and the Making of Cultural Identity*, Cambridge: Cambridge University Press.

70 No will for John Staunton survives but other documents reveal Anne's fate. An account book kept by John and taken over by his son Edmund when he became ill makes a final reference to Mrs Staunton a few days after John's funeral. The expenses were recorded for taking her to Charterhouse, her father's home in Coventry. From her father Anne was set to inherit £1500. John Staunton made provision for her to have an annual

income of £300. Some years later she was recorded residing in London. Coventry Archives, lease and conveyance, 242/2/1 VII.

71   The Staunton name was often written as 'Stanton'.

72   For a further discussion of the value placed on objects with symbolic associations attached to them that outweighs rational decisions see Kevin Hetherington (2004), 'Secondhandness: Consumption, Disposal and Absent Presence', *Environment and Planning, D: Society and Space*, volume 22, pp. 157–173.

73   Parkin (1999), p. 318.

74   *Guide to Benthall Hall* (1997), London: The National Trust. Benthall Hall is now owned by the National Trust and open to the public.

75   Victoria County Histories, *Shropshire*, volume 8, p. 274.

76   Victoria County Histories, *Shropshire*, volume 4, pp. 209–210.

77   Shropshire Record Office, codicil to the will of Thomas Blythe Harries, 6000/1277.

78   An oak table was listed at 2s 6d and the purchaser was Roden. Much later in the list, amongst items in the outbuildings, were three benches. These were also bought by Roden for 6s 3d. Could these items be the 'One Long Table and fformes' valued at £1 in the inventory made on the death of Richard Benthall in 1720? Herefordshire Record Office, probate inventory. A seventeenth-century table that had been in the great hall at Benthall was returned to the house in the twentieth century, one of the few items of furniture now in the house to date from the occupancy of the Benthall family.

79   In the later-18th century this house was owned by members of the Blythe family so possibly Francis Blythe Harries owned Broseley Hall rather than rented it. For details of the house, the work of Thomas Farnolls Pritchard and the ownership of the house see Julia Ionides (1999), *Thomas Farnolls Pritchard of Shrewsbury: an Architect and 'Inventor of Cast Iron Bridges'*, Ludlow: Dog Rose Press, p. 171.

80   See also Veronica West (1982) 'Broseley Hall and Thomas Farnolls Pritchard', *Journal of the Wilkinson Society*, number 10, pp. 10–11, copy at Shropshire Record Office.

81   Loudon (1833), *Encyclopaedia*.

Chapter 3

Recycled Homes

In the 1770s Susannah Whatman wrote directions for her servants on the correct way to maintain her home. She gave precise information about particular items of furniture, including the mahogany cabinet in her dressing room which was 'of very nice workmanship and should be well rubbed occasionally, but it has acquired such a very fine polish by good care that common dusting will keep it in order.'[1] One hundred years later *Cassell's Household Guide* gave directions to male homemakers for repairing furniture, including a method of repairing the legs of 'couches and sofas, the screwed legs of which very frequently become loosened long before the pieces of furniture themselves are half worn out.'[2] The link between these two pieces of advice is common attitudes to maintaining the home that prevailed throughout the period, and encompassed the upper middle-class lady with numerous servants and lower middle-class households where the husband and wife had to do much of the maintenance themselves.

Most middle-class homes were not completely fashionable. Most certainly contained some smart things, and in many cases the majority of the furnishings were in relatively new styles. But still in most homes the overall image was not one of a perfectly fashionable scheme. The economic difficulty of keeping up with rapidly changing styles was not the only reason for this. Rather it was a reflection of the various consumption practices that were associated with furniture and furnishings. Furniture was an investment and often bought to last a lifetime, and it might then be passed on to children. It was certainly expected to last for long periods and accordingly items were serviced, repaired and altered rather than discarded. In addition, to include some second-hand items was a legitimate method of furnishing the home. Such goods were bought from cabinetmakers or specialist dealers and auctioneers, or items were inherited from members of the family. These might be seen as cost-cutting measures that the middle classes would have avoided if possible. However these were widespread and particular structures were developed for middle-class customers, structures that gave them a high level of personal service from tradespeople and enabled them to acquire goods that suited their homemaking needs.

This chapter will deal with the process of maintaining the physical elements of the home and the economies practised in retaining older furniture or purchasing second-hand goods. Keeping furniture and furnishings in good repair was important for the frugally minded middle classes, but also, as the chapter will go on to explore, older furnishings that had acquired the patina of age were valued for their nonmaterial qualities too.

Maintaining the Home

Styles changed less frequently in furniture than they did in clothes but also a different attitude, and cultural values, governed furnishing the home to the contents of the wardrobe. As suggested in Chapter 1 people did not expect their home to be as fashionable as their clothing. Furniture that had become scratched could be polished, hinges and other metalware could be replaced, and upholstered items could be cleaned or given new covers. The habit of 'recycling' furniture and furnishings meant that items were retained in the home long after fashions had changed.

Homemakers, especially female, took a pride in looking after home furnishings and developed their own special recipes, for removing stains and for making floor polish that they used themselves or passed on to their servants. A member of the Morris family in Lewes, East Sussex, kept a notebook with recipes for homemade medicines and for keeping the house clean and free of vermin, particularly 'London Bugs' on bedsteads. Included was this recipe for a furniture polish:

> Oil for furniture which is French polished
> Of fine olive oil two thirds to one of Spirits of wine
> First wash the polish with cold soft water rub it dry and gently use the preparation with very soft cloth or wash leather[3]

Susanna Whatman kept notes on the work she expected of her servants along with detailed comments that applied to the conditions of her house and its contents. She recorded, for example, what time the sun reached particular rooms so that the blinds could be drawn to keep the sun off the furnishings.[4] Textiles were the most vulnerable elements of a furnishing scheme and they were the special province of the women in the household. Every little girl had to learn how to darn linen.[5] Ladies might also produce more ambitious pieces of needlework that an upholsterer could then use for covering or recovering the seats of chairs and stools and so on. Catherine Hutton, the daughter of the stationer and historian of Birmingham, William Hutton, carried out many such projects, including bed hangings, window curtains, counterpanes, and matching chair and sofa covers for her drawing room.[6]

At most levels of the middle classes homes were serviced to a greater or lesser extent by tradespeople. The lowest level, in rented houses or rooms, had to forgo this aspect of homemaking and had to accept poorly maintained homes or else do the work themselves. But servicing was an important part of the work of cabinetmakers and upholsterers as well as carpenters, plumbers and house painters. John Claudius Loudon recommended quarterly or twice-yearly checks of the fabric of the building by carpenters, plumbers and glaziers.[7] But there is plentiful evidence in both customer and tradespeople's accounts to suggest that not only expensive items but quite mundane objects were repaired and generally homes were maintained through a frequent and close involvement by tradespeople.[8]

The carefully preserved bills and receipts for the Boulton household record the many instances of tradespeople performing maintenance work.[9] Matthew Boulton carried out extensive alterations and enlargements to Soho House, in Birmingham, in the 1790s, making it into a genteel residence suitable for a wealthy man and his family. Apart from building work Boulton also purchased large amounts of furniture, incurring additional expense by commissioning the prestigious London cabinetmaker, James Newton. However, Boulton regularly employed local cabinetmakers and upholsterers to do work on the decoration and furnishings at Soho. Thomas Smallwood was a reputable firm who sent in their account to Boulton on a six-monthly basis. In 1795 Boulton had a bedroom repapered and a bed put up in the room.[10] A number of pieces of furniture were recovered, including the loose seats of six chairs that had to be taken to pieces, stuffed with hair and covered in damask, costing seven shillings and six pence. Two elbow chairs likewise were re-covered and the frames repaired, costing nine shillings. At the bottom of the bill someone, perhaps the housekeeper, had summarized the bill under the heading 'Household Expenses, Furniture £2 12s 6d [for a mahogany cellaret], Repairs £10 13s 3d'. Thus highlighting that repair work accounted for the majority of the bill. Presumably also these different aspects of homemaking were listed separately in the household accounts.

In Chichester, the Peat firm of cabinetmakers and upholsterers performed a wide range of furnishing work. In the early years of the nineteenth century Henry Peat recorded, for example, mending a hall chair for the mayor of Chichester, Mr William Newland, adding silk linings to the doors of a bookcase for Mrs Bayley, and making a sofa table in deal for Miss Drinkwater. These examples show the mixture of making and repairing, and also his readiness to take on both cabinet and upholstering work.[11]

Maintenance work by the firm continued into the next generation. Samuel Peat worked as a journeyman cabinetmaker in the family firm, until he set up in business on his own in the 1850s. Servicing and repairs made up the bulk of his work in the early 1840s, many of the families sharing the same names as those in the earlier day book of his uncle, and quite a few households employed him several times a year to carry out mundane tasks.[12] Miss Drinkwater had Peat come to her home to put up a tester bedstead just a few months before she died, then in December 1841 Samuel made her coffin while his uncle, Henry Peat, made an inventory of her home. Similarly, Charles Ridge, who was proprietor of the Chichester Old Bank with his brother, often employed Samuel Peat to carry out repairs and servicing work. In 1839 he had a fire screen repaired and French polished, and a mattress made up. In 1840 he had a number of cushions made and in September the matting in his house was taken up and carpet was laid. It was a common practice for wealthier people to have matting on the floor to keep their rooms cool in summer and then to replace it with carpets in the autumn. The process took Peat a total of four and a half days. To fix the carpet in place was a skilled job if it was done properly. Another regular customer was Miss Livingston who employed Peat 13 times during a three-year period, for such work as papering rooms, putting up window curtains, re-stuffing a sofa, making new cupboard doors and a mattress. As in the example of Miss Drinkwater, the final entry for Miss Livingston was for making her coffin, in February 1842.

The family that employed Samuel Peat on the most regular basis were the Newlands. Branches of this family each employed Peat on various occasions throughout the year. Four branches of the family lived next door to each other in North Street in Chichester, and just a few doors from where Peat was employed. The close proximity adds to the sense of the cabinetmaker's work complementing that of the household servants in maintaining homes to a high standard. William Charles Newland Esq. lived in an eighteenth-century house with an elaborate gothic oriel window.[13] His home was shared with his three adult children and four servants. Two doors away lived his sister-in-law Alithia Newland, who was designated Mrs G. Newland, since her husband had been Gideon, William's younger brother. By the 1840s she was a widow with four adult children living at home, in a large house of some distinction with service wings on either side and set back from the road.[14] Mrs G. Newland had four servants to service her home, including a male servant, with a butler's pantry beside the front door. The two other Newland households consisted of Miss Sarah Newland, a spinster, with just one live-in female servant, and William Newland, son of William Charles, who was married with two children and was a partner in Chichester Old Bank. They had one male and four female servants. Between them the Newlands employed Samuel Peat 43 times during 1839-1843 on small servicing and repair jobs (Illustration 3:1).

The Newland households each replaced wallpaper in one room or another every year. In 1841 Mrs Newland chose new paper for her dining room, a formal room with mahogany furniture and moreen curtains. Some of the textiles in these homes required regular expert attention and Peat was usually employed to do this in the spring and summer, during spring-cleaning and when laundering was most readily carried out. Five times William Newland senior had beds and their textiles taken down and sometimes the bed re-erected in a different room during spring months. Elaborate hangings and curtains were often nailed in place to achieve the professional draperies that were fashionable. Samuel Peat was needed to take down the hangings, clean and repair them and to re-hang them, perhaps with new trimmings. Mrs Newland however, did not use Peat to take down bed hangings but relied instead on her servants to spring-clean her bedrooms. This is explained by Mrs Newland preferring dimity bed hangings. Her choice of this crisp, white cotton fabric was fashionable but also meant that the simple hangings could be dealt with by her servants, and laundered frequently, giving her more hygienic bedrooms.[15]

When the joiner and wheelwright John Foden was working in Stone in Staffordshire he was asked to do work normally carried out by cabinetmakers and upholsterers, since the little market town did not have more specialized tradespeople at that date. His account book[16] detailed the work he did for local gentry, professional people and tradespeople. Foden was certainly versatile, turning his hand to all manner of work in customer's houses or the shops or inns run by them. And no job was too small. For Mr Bradbury in 1823 he repaired a dining table and charged four shillings and six pence. The table was made of deal and presumably had folding leaves, since the cost included the replacement of three hinges. Foden also listed repairing, for Mr Bradbury, a 'Closehorse' with one yard of web for which he was charged just eight pence. Miss Marshall, a milliner in Stone, employed Foden at her shop and her house. In 1825 he made her two forms and altered some bedsteads, and in 1828 he painted her shop and made for it a glass case with drawers. Foden also painted her kitchen. Repair work was not a simple economic measure. Wealthy people too went to great lengths to have this kind of work done. William Dixon, Esq. had an account with Foden and employed him 36 times between 25 October 1825 and 6 December 1826. In April 1826 Foden listed taking down a bedstead, window curtains, blinds and a servant's bed and for all this he charged just three shillings and six pence. In May the same year Foden recorded putting up a bed in Mr Dixon's bedroom, window curtains and blinds, putting up a bed in the servant's room and 'Sundry labour in the house'. This work was all done for two shillings and six pence. Mr Dixon finally settled his bill when it totalled £21 1s 6d.

Further evidence of a wealthy person going to the trouble of repairing an item of furniture is provided by the Boulton family. In 1838, Matthew Robinson Boulton, the son of the entrepreneur, wanted the sofa in his study recovered.[17] This must have been a valued item of furniture to go to the expense of recovering it since his housekeeper, Mrs Wilkinson, estimated that it would require 18-20 yards of fabric, if the cushions were included. In a letter she asked Mr Westley, Boulton's agent in Birmingham, to measure the sofa for her. Letters passed between the two on an almost daily basis to discuss the purchase of items, moving furniture and cleaning rooms as well as what to plant in the garden. At this time the family were in London and so Mrs Wilkinson said they would purchase the requisite fabric there.[18] The sofa would then go to a local upholsterer for the work to be done. This was following a similar pattern of behaviour to his father's, using London makers for prestigious pieces of furniture but also making use of local tradespeople for servicing work.

On an even more intimate level was the work of female upholsterers who worked in homes for long periods of time. They provided a professional level of expertise but were treated in a way that was somewhere between their male counterparts and the servants in the household.

After Anne Boulton, the daughter of Matthew, had established her own home at Thornhill House, in Birmingham, she employed one particular female upholsterer, Elizabeth Cooke, extensively; 21 times between 1819 and 1823.[19] Cooke's premises were situated in Canon Street, just off New Street, the area where the most reputable firms were found. Cooke had a number of employees, mostly female upholsterers, who carried out work both in Canon Street and in the homes of customers. Work for Anne Boulton ranged from making mattresses and cushions, making bed hangings and window curtains for several rooms, making drugget and carpet covers. Not only were these upholsterers employed on numerous occasions but they also spent long periods, up to 17 days at a time, at Thornhill, carrying out work.

3:1 Fernleigh, the Chichester home of Mrs G. Newland and her children, was a house of some distinction. It was built of brick and flint with pieces of flint pressed into the mortar. The service wing was to the left and the stables to the right of the main house.

The employment of female upholsterers is also revealed in the letters between Mrs Wilkinson and Mr Westley on behalf of the Boultons. A misunderstanding arose in 1838 about the employment of Apletree to make a bed for the governess, Miss Burgess's room. Mr Apletree was one of the leading cabinet-making and upholstering firms in Birmingham, with a shop in New Street. Mrs Wilkinson wrote that they did not want Apletree to make the bed. But she declared:

> having a female upholsterer in the house to make up a bed is not like employing any other upholder in preference to Apletree – and if upon consultation with Miss Burgess we agree to let the person you name make up the bed, it is only wanting a note to Apletree to say we defer his order till out return home and employing him upon a new bed for the Pink Room – if we go to the expense it had better be for a best bed.[20]

So, Apletree was too expensive to make a bed for the governess and they did not want to offend him by employing another cabinetmaker. But a female upholsterer, whom Mrs Wilkinson did not even bother to name, was clearly in a different class to the prestigious Apletree. 'Having a female upholsterer in the house' suggests that this was an entirely different process to commissioning a male cabinetmaker and upholsterer.[21]

The Boultons' use of female upholsterers suggests that they worked in homes as an extension of the household; somewhere between the external tradesperson and the internal servant. Through this intermediate person middle-class people were helped in the furnishing and servicing of their homes in a quite intimate manner while achieving a professional finish. The retention and recycling of objects and materials was cost-cutting but it was not simply an economic measure practised by the thrifty middle classes. It also reinforced their status. Professional tradespeople offered a high level of expertise. Therefore the regular employment of them to service the home enhanced its smart ambience and gave distinction to its occupants.

Second-hand Furniture for Middle-class Customers

Furnishing with second-hand furniture was another practical recycling aspect of homemaking used by the middle classes. Stana Nenadic claims that in the later-eighteenth century 'When new, these articles had been produced for a middle-rank market and they were, in effect being recycled within that market.' However, by the 1820s Nenadic says that purchasing second-hand goods reflected a lack of interest in fashion and style content, since 'it was much more likely that working people would be able to purchase second-hand goods that had once belonged to the relatively wealthy'.[22] By this date, she continues, the value of such goods to people of middle rank was only in their content of wood that might be made over into other items. However, there is evidence that middle-rank people continued to purchase second-hand furniture and that traders in such items were specifically aiming their wares at them. And, like servicing the home, practical economic considerations do not fully explain these consumption practices. There were cultural explanations too, and how these operated changed over time, as people's attitude to homemaking also evolved.

Some aspects of the trade in second-hand goods had a bad reputation, particularly pawnbroking and retailing second-hand clothing, suggesting that the trade only catered for the poor. But this only applied to the lower end of the trade.[23] There was a wide range of tradespeople involved in selling second-hand furniture and the goods passing through their hands also varied, encompassing the whole range of what was available, from the most basic and soiled to the best quality, in perfect condition. Second-hand furniture was included in the stock of cabinetmakers and upholsterers, auctioneers, furniture brokers and antique dealers.[24]

Cabinetmakers and upholsters, while they may have concentrated on making new goods, also on occasion, exchanged new for old and then sold the used goods to another customer. Workshops varied but tradespeople made their skills and the quality of their wares, even the nature of their desired customers, apparent through their advertisements. As noted in Chapter 1, cabinetmakers like Hensman in New Street, Birmingham,[25] had smart trade cards that were intended to send a clear message to prospective customers that they were respectable and fashionable. Cabinetmakers of this calibre could be relied upon to be discreet when used furniture was acquired from, or sold, to them.[26] Second-hand furniture acquired from such a source would also be guaranteed to be well made, in good-quality materials and free from vermin.

Part-exchange and selling some old furniture was a useful means of stimulating trade. The cabinetmaker James Hopkinson set up in business in Liverpool in the middle of the nineteenth century.[27] When he was ready to open his shop he did not have sufficient furniture that he had made to fill his showroom, so he went to an auction to bid for some second-hand pieces. He thought that the furniture was good quality but found later that it was newly made 'slop goods', stained to look old. The poor lighting in the auction rooms had concealed this. He had difficulty reselling the furniture. This episode not only shows how cabinetmakers added to their stock with used goods for which there was a ready market, but also shows the pitfalls of bidding in an auction. *The Home Book*, an advice book for people setting up a home, advised its readers that although they might think it was possible to furnish a house 'in a superior style, at a very modest expense' by purchasing goods in auctions, they should also be aware of the dangers. 'Artful dealers' attend such sales and the inexperienced person could be drawn on by them to bid far more for an item than it was worth.[28]

Newspaper advertisements by cabinetmakers occasionally make reference to their work as brokers of second-hand goods. One example was Richard France, cabinetmaker and chairmaker, who traded in old and new wares at his shop in Shrewsbury. He advised his customers that he was moving premises, through an advertisement in the *Salopian Journal* in 1794, and took the opportunity to list the skills and services that he offered, including the fact that he intended to 'open a Repository for second-hand Cabinet and Upholstery Furniture. Gentlemen and ladies who have any Furniture they would wish to dispose of, proper attention shall be paid at his Repository to the sale of them, or if exchanged for new, much more than the common Valuation will be allowed.'[29] Similarly, Thomas Barke of Shifnal in Shropshire advertised in 1835 that he was in future adding the work of appraising and auctioning to his cabinetmaking and upholstering business.[30] As well as extending the list of what he could offer his customers Barke was also moving firmly into the trade in second-hand furniture. Both France and Barke were reaching a largely middle-class market through advertising in newspapers.

The well-established cabinetmaking firm of Richard and Henry Peat in Chichester, during the first half of the nineteenth century, included the work of appraiser and auctioneer.[31] They were employed to value and list goods when a householder had died and their heirs wanted to sell some, or all, of the goods. The other major reason for having an inventory made for a subsequent sale of goods was when a householder was bankrupt. Cabinetmakers were well placed to do this work since their skills in making furniture made them aware of the quality of materials and workmanship. The Peats made lists of house contents in preparation for sales with valuations beside each item (unfortunately in code); from the list a catalogue would have been printed and the house sale advertised.

In London auctioneers had professionalized their business practices and moved into smart premises by the mid-eighteenth century. This encouraged auctions to become part of the social scene with fashionable society attending as much to observe other people and their purchases as to bid for items.[32] These trends were a little slower in the provinces. Auctioneers varied in status, but again, like cabinetmakers, some firms were situated in the main streets where rents were high, with prestigious shops and showrooms and advertised through trade cards and newspapers. Auctioneers offered a more varied means of acquiring second-hand goods than cabinetmakers and upholsterers, since sales were conducted on the premises of homes that were being sold up, or sometimes at nearby inns or hotels, or increasingly, at well-appointed salerooms. Auctions might be a rather public method of buying goods and there is evidence, as in the case of Hopkinson, that some auctioneers were unscrupulous; but they also provided the means of purchasing goods literally at a knock-down price, often with a known provenance and one that might on occasion be from the ranks of the gentry or aristocracy. Most editions of newspapers included advertisements for house sales whether held on the premises or elsewhere. Long and detailed lists gave the main items for sale, often with descriptions to whet the appetite of prospective customers.

The auctioneer Jonathan Perry for example advertised, in 1814, the three-day sale of goods at a property near Shrewsbury:

> The whole of the genteel and most valuable HOUSEHOLD FURNITURE belonging to Col EGERTON, comprising handsome Fourpost and Tent Bedsteads with Rich Moreen and superfine Dimity Hangings of Modern fashion; Prime Danzic Feather Beds of the first Quality, Hair, Flock and Straw Mattrasses, super Whitney Blankets, Marseilles Quilts and Counterpanes, Children's Bedsteads and Bedding complete, Servants Bedsteads and Hangings with seasoned feather Beds,

Mattrasses and Bed Clothes; Spanish Mahogany Chamber Furniture of the finest quality in Wardrobes, Chests of Drawers, Night Tables, Dressing Tables, and Bason Stands, Japanned Washing Tables, Chamber Chairs, Swing Glasses, Bidettes, Bedsteps and other Articles appropriate to Bed Rooms; a Drawing Room Suite of Rich Chintz Curtains, lined, with elegant fringed Draperies, Cornices and Appendages complete; Grecian Commode for Books, ebonized chairs, Chaise Longue, Ottomans; a well toned square PIANO FORTE (by Meyer), Mahogany Card, Pembroke and Quartetto Tables, Dining Parlour Suite of handsome Orange Moreen Curtains and rich Draperies, set of Beautiful Mahogany Dining Tables, on best Castors, 9 feet by 4 feet 8 inches, a Pair of neat sideboards fitted up with Curtains, a handsome Brass Rod and Pillars; twelve Mahogany Grecian parlour Chairs, Wine Celleret, Deception Table, a rich Turkey /carpet, 14 feet by 13 feet 8 inches (perfect, as new), and other articles appropriate to a Dining Room, various miscellaneries including a neat and elegant Hall Lanthorn, Chamber Organ, Dinner Service, Tea China and Glass, Butler's Trays, Knife Boxes, Cheese Wagon, Supper Tray, a capital Lady's Saddle and Bridle (by Whippy), never used, Stair, Room and Bed Carpets, and Hearth Rugs the general routine of Kitchen Furniture and Culinary Vessels &c.
Also 12 dozen of superior Old PORT WINE (vintage 1804) and a valuable milking cow.

The Auctioneer assures genteel families and the Public that during his Experience of more than 20 years he has not had to dispose of by Auction a Property in Furniture so deserving of their notice as the Present, every Article is truly excellent and when seen must be admired. To be viewed on Friday and Saturday the 13th and 14th by Tickets from the Auctioneer, of whom a Catalogue may be had.[33]

At auctions, on the premises or at nearby inns, prospective customers could expect some entertainment along with the chance of a bargain. Warm fires were provided in winter, food and alcohol were readily available at inns but even at house sales some refreshment might be included; one sale advertised that 'A person will attend with a cold Collation, Ale and Liquers for the Accommodation of the Company'.[34] The long descriptive lists of goods in newspapers, along with the detailed catalogues and viewing of furnishings before the sale, were all part of the pleasures of consuming goods through an auction.[35] Customers could also enjoy watching the bidding, observe who bought what and gain the opportunity to see rooms in a house otherwise closed to view, and to see the objects in the correct setting.[36] Time wasters could be excluded by charging an entrance fee, often the price of the catalogue that was then redeemable against a sale. So, whatever the practical benefits of purchasing furniture at a bargain price, auctions also provided entertainment. In the eighteenth and early-nineteenth centuries it was much less common for newly made goods to be bought ready made; therefore, auctions gave access to an exciting array of things available to buy immediately or simply to consume vicariously.

There is some debate about the attractions of purchasing second-hand furniture. Jon Stobart says in the eighteenth century people did not distinguish between first- and second-hand; they considered either to be legitimate means of securing what they wanted.[37] Such practical reasoning was probably behind Matthew Boulton's purchase of some chairs in 1787. He was sent a bill from the auctioneers Thomas Warren for six Upton chairs bought in 'Mr Welshie's sale' for £1 7s. Since Upton chairs probably had rush seats these chairs were not intended for the public rooms of the house and therefore their source was not important.[38]

Both Stobart and Nenadic suggest that purchasing furniture second-hand was mainly due to availability in the period before cabinetmakers were established in any quantity and when smart timbers were only spasmodically available.[39] In addition purchasing second-hand furniture could bring better-quality goods within the reach of middle-class customers than they could otherwise afford. Knowing to whom the goods had belonged provided another dimension to enjoy. Purchasing a table or chest of drawers that had once belonged to a local dignitary might suggest snobbishness at work but perhaps equally there were subtler reasons for purchasing goods with a known provenance. The quality of the goods was assured as well as having associations with a person or family who were wealthy and respected in the community.

Well into the nineteenth century auctions continued to be aimed at middle-class customers. Catalogues remained expensive, advertisements continued in newspapers for their largely middle-class readers. Even in the provinces some auctioneers ceased to hold sales in temporary rooms in inns and instead moved into permanent and quite grand salerooms. The firm of John Rodderick for example moved in c. 1849 from their premises, of three adjacent properties in Temple Row, Birmingham, to the Shakespeare Salerooms in New Street.[40] This gave them a purpose-built four-storeyed building complete with pilasters. Purchasing goods from Rodderick and similar auctioneers was not a homemaking strategy reserved for the poor or even the lower middle class.

Matthew Robinson Boulton was sufficiently wealthy to create a number of homes for his family and for entertaining friends and business associates. The house that his father had created near to his business interests, Soho House, was retained but in addition he acquired a fine country house in Oxfordshire, and the family also rented accommodation in London. Despite his wealth Boulton was not above purchasing used furniture. In mid-September 1837, he and his wife decided they wanted a comfortable sofa for reclining on, in a family room rather than a public room, at Soho House. They conveyed this requirement to Mrs Wilkinson, who travelled with the family and took care of the day-to-day running of their homes. In September Mrs Wilkinson wrote to Mr Westley that the family needed a sofa: 'we will look out for [one] at a sale, and should one be met with in this neighbourhood first we will appraise you – and you must do the same, should you find one that is reasonable. It is wanted for an ordinary room and provided it is a good length to lie on say 6ft, no matter for the fashion of it.'[41] In November Mrs Wilkinson refers to the subject again, saying: 'Don't look out for a sofa – we have just heard of one at Banbury which will answer our purpose and comes over next week.' Although only for an 'ordinary room' rather than one of the main living rooms where guests would be received this was still for the family's use rather than for servants. A second-hand item, and possibly unfashionable, was thought acceptable and worth searching for over several months to find just what was wanted. The Boultons had a good income and with their country house were moving into the gentry class. So if a second-hand sofa was acceptable to them then it was certainly acceptable to the majority of middle-class consumers.

The house sale at Hams Hall in 1837[42] provided the opportunity for a number of middle-class homemakers to view household furnishings in an opulent setting, perhaps to promenade and see other people's purchases as well as to purchase some bargains for their homes. Hams Hall was a large mansion in Warwickshire, just south of Birmingham. The sale occurred because it had for many years been let, furnished, to a number of people, the last being Lady Ross. But in 1837 the owner, Charles Bowyer Adderley, had finally come of age and wanted to take possession of the family home. Among those present at the sale and making purchases were the Reverends Morse and Salmon, Captain Miller, Mr Samuel Hutton, Mrs Chilwell, Mrs Dale and Miss Holbeche. Captain Miller, Mrs Chilwell and the Reverend Salmon all seem to have gone with particular requirements in mind, bought what they wanted and were not tempted by other items. Mrs Chilwell made just two purchases, both textiles: muslin curtains and a piece of Brussels carpet. The Reverend Salmon and Captain Miller both acquired items for fireplaces: a kitchen fender, a polished fender and sets of fire irons. These were practical purchases and ones to which little personal association would have adhered. More interesting are the varied purchases of the other people referred to. Mrs Dale purchased an oblong mahogany loo table that was intended for a public room in her home, since mahogany was a fashionable and expensive wood, and loo tables were a common item in a smart drawing room or parlour. Rev. Morse bought plates and dishes, an ornamental chimney piece, two tea stands, an ash kitchen table, a night convenience, a japanned chest of drawers and three fire grates. Only the chimney piece and the tea stands might have been seen by guests since the table and night convenience were for either the service or private areas of the home. The japanned chest of drawers would also have been used in a bedchamber.

The person making the most purchases at Hams Hall was Mr Samuel Hutton, the great nephew of William Hutton, the stationer and historian of Birmingham. Samuel Hutton had come to Birmingham in 1798, aged 11, to work for William Hutton's son, and since he had no children, Samuel inherited his uncle's business.[43] He was a well-established businessman by 1837. Like Matthew Robinson Boulton he had moved up socially by buying a country residence, Ward End Hall, just north east of Birmingham. But still Hutton was content to satisfy some of his household needs by purchasing goods second-hand. For the bedrooms of his house Hutton purchased a walnut dressing table for £1 14s, an easy chair for £1 5s and a cheaper oak dressing table for just two shillings, no doubt for a servant's room. For his library and dining room Hutton acquired a number of items including library book frames, 12 mahogany chairs, a further 14 chairs with Morocco seats, and a sideboard. Hutton also bought a six-fold papered screen for the rather high cost of £6. Presumably this screen was a luxurious item, perhaps with hand-painted Chinese paper, that would have made a strong statement in the room for which it was intended. The mahogany furniture, and chairs with leather seats were meant to create a good impression in his dining room, an important public room in the home where guests were entertained.

It is clear that furniture of some quality and which remained in good condition was available through cabinetmakers and auctioneers, and aimed at middle-class consumers well into the nineteenth century. However, furniture brokers, who accounted for the least respectable part of the trade in second-hand furniture, increased most in the nineteenth century, particularly in industrializing towns with large populations of working-class people. In contrast to the other sources brokers generally sold poorer quality new furniture, increasingly made in factories in London or the larger cities, much of which was on the level of the slop goods that Hopkinson had bought by mistake. Likewise their trade in second-hand goods was poorer quality and less desirable. The firm of Onions in Birmingham's Worcester Street being a good example, the pencil illustration of their shop displays a poor shop front with mattresses hanging from all the windows, and nearby buildings were in an obvious state of disrepair.[44] (Illustration 3:2) Although Worcester Street was not in the best shopping area of Birmingham still, even here, there were some respectable traders. A bill survives for the purchase of an oak wardrobe, in 1826, from Elizabeth Vowles, broker and saleswoman, at 53 Worcester Street. The purchaser was Matthew Robinson Boulton. And Elizabeth Vowles had a smart printed bill head for her business.[45]

Trade directory entries for furniture brokers reveal that most were situated in the poorer parts of towns and they generally had a lower profile than cabinetmakers and auctioneers; they rarely seem to have produced trade cards or advertised in newspapers or trade directories, beyond an alphabetical entry. However, in Birmingham, some furniture brokers had their premises on the main roads leading out to new areas of housing, including on the western side of the town leading to the firmly middle-class suburb of Edgbaston. It is clear then that even furniture brokers had a hierarchy and some at least were respectable and dealt in reasonably good quality wares.

Purchasing second-hand goods was not the same as collecting antiques. Dealers in antiques were few and far between in the eighteenth and early-nineteenth centuries, since an interest in antiquarian items was a specialized taste.[46] Collectors were not interested in recently made goods of the previous century but rather ancient furniture along with manuscripts and early printed books, maps and prints and paintings, and other items of a curious nature, such as geological specimens, natural history and classical items. A small minority of collectors created antiquarian interiors as described by Clive Wainwright.[47] But more usual was a collection that was restricted to a museum, library or study within an otherwise fashionably-furnished home. Such were the collecting habits of David Parkes, a schoolmaster and artist, who lived in Castle Street, in Shrewsbury. He amassed a huge collection of antiquarian artefacts and books, described in a 72-page catalogue with a separate 31-page catalogue for his pictures.[48] The whole collection was auctioned over six days in 1833. By contrast the sale of the contents of his house took just two days. Unfortunately a catalogue

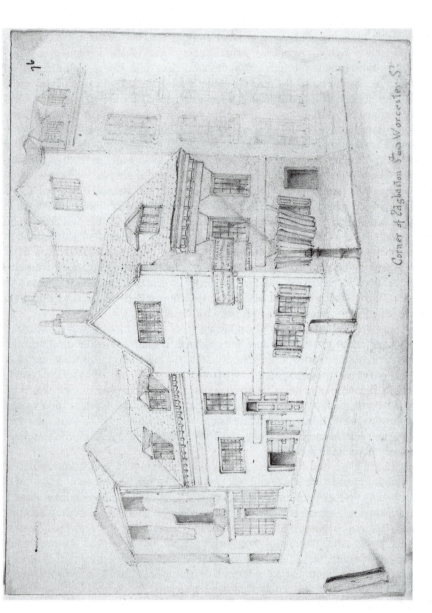

Corner of Eagbaston from Worcester St.

3:2 The shabby street where Onions was situated suggests a downmarket second-hand trade for this furnishing broker in Birmingham.

for the contents of the house has not survived and his home can only be judged from the list in the newspaper advertisement. What does seem clear though is that the home of David Parkes was fashionable and had furniture made in the 20 or so years before his death in 1833. All the furniture listed was mahogany, which was the fashionable wood of the period, and in any case had not been imported much before the mid-eighteenth century.[49] Descriptions of the furniture in the advertisement give some idea of their design, for example a sofa was described as 'on mahogany legs, with scroll ends, hair squab and chintz cover' and the dining chairs were described as 'Trafalga' chairs. These items must all have dated from the Regency period. And the essential item of a fashionable drawing room, a loo table, was also listed. So, David Parkes, with his wife and sons, had a fashionable home in the centre of Shrewsbury where he held an important position in local life, entertaining professional people, other collectors and people connected with his various artistic and publishing ventures.[50] The main public rooms of the house might only have demonstrated his antiquarian interests through the choice of pictures, including some of his own depictions of the ruins of priories and castles in Shropshire and Wales.[51] But his study, or library, no doubt had a stronger antiquarian feel where his collection of books was arrayed on shelves and his coins, cameos, seals, shells and fossils were displayed. After dinner Parkes and his male guests might peruse Richard Jugg's Bible of 1568 or other rare volumes or study geological specimens or enjoy his collection of curiosities that included a piece of the mulberry tree planted by Shakespeare, that had been cut up and sold to tourists visiting his house in Stratford.

David Parkes's huge collection of objects were sold through an auction in Shrewsbury and must have attracted collectors from near and far, but generally dealers that catered for such specialized interests were mainly found in London. In the later-nineteenth century it became fashionable to include a few antiques in interiors and then antique dealers began to operate in the provinces. However, furnishing wholly in antiques remained a specialized manner of furnishing the home and one that was reserved for a wealthy minority. Gregson and Crew, in their examination of present-day consumption practices, suggest that some second-hand merchandise is used to 'capture difference'.[52] This notion certainly applies to antique furniture during the period when it was of limited appeal; limited that is to a few wealthy patrons, and somewhat eccentric or at least scholarly professionals.

Unlike antiquarians homemakers purchasing second-hand furniture from a cabinetmaker, upholsterer, auctioneer or furniture broker wanted goods that would blend with a vaguely fashionable scheme, not make a particular statement about their taste. While the lack of availability of fashionable goods might explain the purchase of second-hand furniture by middle-class customers in the eighteenth century this explanation is inadequate for the nineteenth when cabinetmakers were more widespread. To fully explain this homemaking practice the common physical attribute of second-hand furniture needs to be considered; this was its patina or signs of age.

Patina and Inherited Furniture

In the eighteenth century furniture was, according to Amanda Vickery, associated with the continuity of family life.[53] She suggests that furnishings of good quality 'carried family history down through time [and] were emblems of genteel status'.[54] So, despite the growth in importance of fashion and therefore in replacing goods, there was still a continued expectation that substantial objects, such as furniture, were expected to last, not just a lifetime but several generations. References to furniture in eighteenth-century wills show the attitude that Vickery has noted. There are indications that similar ideas, of furniture as family history, continued into the nineteenth century and for people lower down the social order. Even more intriguing, and elusive, is the implication that furniture could carry emotional reminders of the testator to the recipient. Maxine Berg has argued that using wills rather than inventories tells us about people's relationship with their possessions. 'The goods mentioned in bequests were singled out for attention by the individual, and thus endowed with some emotional, familial or material value.'[55] Although furniture was not detailed in wills to the same extent as jewellery and pictures, objects that had obvious close associations with the testator, still furniture featured in some bequests in significant ways.[56]

Most references to furniture in wills were fairly cursory and reflected practical concerns and family obligations of providing for widows and children. For example, Thomas Robinson, a confectioner in Coventry left everything to his wife in 1853[57] so that she could continue his trade, saying that she was to keep the furniture during her lifetime and then it was to pass to his daughter.[58] Some wills made a distinction between the sources of the furniture. These are perhaps examples of the informal settlements that Margot Finn suggests some women came to with their husbands, to protect their property from before the marriage, despite the laws governing coverture that deprived women of legal rights to such property.[59] So, for example, in 1856 William Pickard of Walgrave in Warwickshire left his wife Mary her premarital furniture whilst the other furniture was to be shared by his children.[60] Similarly, John Alcott, a stonemason, left his son Joseph £100; but to James Thorniwork, the son of his late wife by a former husband, he left £50 and his deceased wife's furniture.[61]

The wills of wealthy people, both male and female, tend to have more detailed bequests, reflecting the greater quantity and monetary value of their belongings. Furniture figures alongside other personal effects, and seems to indicate that these goods had been invested with emotional associations by their owners that they hoped would be reciprocated by family or friends when they inherited these goods.

The gentlewoman Anne Cave left a detailed will in 1755.[62] She was a spinster and wished to be buried with her mother in Clifton upon Dunsmore. She left portraits of herself to several friends. To Sir Thomas Cave, baronet, she left six family pictures from her dwelling house. Portraits were a favourite item for naming in a bequest and had clear associations with the testator and their wish to be remembered. Anne Cave however also left, to a female relative, Cave Cheslin, a spring repeating clock and her favourite armchair.

A similar way of singling out items of furniture is found in the will of John Haines, a silkdyer in Coventry, in 1821.[63] A tenement in Foleshill, Coventry was to go to his unmarried daughter Mary along with the furniture in her room, tea china, a piano and £100 when she reached 21 or on her marriage if sooner. John Haines' bequest provided in monetary terms for Mary as well as securing objects that were familiar and important to her.

In the wills of widows and spinsters the division of goods often took a more personal form with items singled out for mention, whereas in the wills of men a general comment, such as 'all the household goods', was often employed. This disparity was a reflection of the nature of their estates but also of women's relationship to material goods, investing them with emotional meaning.[64] In 1838 Mary Bucknill, a widow, left her sister Martha Bates £100, her best bed to her nephew John Ogden and other beds to another three nieces and a nephew.[65] Elizabeth Parsons a widow of Wolston, Warwickshire, in 1849, left her household goods to her sister but specified that two chests of drawers were to go her son and to Thomas Rogers, a friend or relative.[66] Catherine Wright of Withybrooke, Warwickshire, left her unmarried daughter Mary Wright a bed, bedding and six Windsor chairs.[67] Although the rest of the household goods were to be shared between her three daughters Mary was to have the pick of the 'Household and fancy goods' providing that they were valued and that Mary paid her sisters a third of their value.

In 1858 Fanny Downes, a spinster in Coventry, left two properties to be sold and the money divided between her two brothers after purchasing mourning rings from the proceeds.[68] Fanny also left instructions for hair rings to be made and distributed to her female friends. Throughout the nineteenth century there prevailed a cult of mourning and rituals connected with death. The use of the hair of the deceased for making jewellery to be given to family and friends and worn in remembrance of them is a particularly strong instance of this.[69] Other objects could also have a strong physical association with the deceased: the favourite armchair, the desk used for writing letters every morning, the bed habitually slept in by them. So, Fanny Downes gave attention to objects with strong physical associations by which her friends and relatives could remember her. She left instructions that her brother Henry was to receive her writing desk; surely this was a piece of furniture that had important meanings for her and which she hoped Henry would share.

Throughout the period it is clear that furniture had practical reasons for being mentioned in wills, also a sense of continuity in the form of the household goods being passed on with the house to the next generation. In addition particular items of furniture could be ascribed emotional meanings by their owners which they wished to convey or transfer to a relative or friend.

Patina and the Home as Domestic Ideology

There were, however, changes during the period in the expectations of middling-sort homemakers. A new middle class was growing in numbers by the early-nineteenth century, particularly in urban areas. This section of society placed great importance on family and home,[70] as delineated by the domestic ideology of the day, thus making inherited goods valued for more than their monetary worth. As *The Family Economist: a Penny Monthly Magazine for the Industrious Classes* stated in 1851: 'We may keep with fondest care some article of furniture, some piece of silver plate which belonged to our fathers and grandfathers, which brings memories of former homes and old familiar faces to *consecrate* the homes of the present.'[71] [my italics]

The early- to mid-nineteenth century domestic ideology placed a moral obligation on people to make a good home.[72] Such homes had to provide a haven from the brutal and sinful outside world and this division between the public and private is described by the term 'separate spheres'.[73] The home was meant to nurture the appropriate emotional and, above all, religious attitudes in the husband and wife, and their children. These non-physical attributes were to be expressed through the choice of furnishings within the home. Many advice books were published that extolled the importance of homemaking. The most extreme were the religious texts such as those written by Mrs Ellis[74] however, these texts were also the least practical, and it was left to individual homemakers to interpret the instructions into actual choices of tables, curtains and chairs. Like all prescriptive literature the books on domestic ideology would have met with a mixed response in their readers. Even readers who wished to follow the tenets wholeheartedly would have first needed to produce an individual interpretation of the advice, and then to have maintained the home in the face of the demands of family life, and the economic restraints of most middle-class incomes. Advice literature perhaps had a general influence on homemaking, and similar ideas were expressed in many novels written at the time and therefore reflecting general attitudes without necessarily reflecting common practice.

Novels, like all forms of representation, used ideas that their readers would recognize and be in sympathy with. Novels also perhaps described domestic ideology in its most exaggerated form, since they tended to have ideas taken to extremes for dramatic effect. Many examples can be found of domestic ideology being used in novels as part of the story and characterization, where characters that are unable to create a real home are shown to be flawed and immoral. One of the most explicit examples of this is by Charles Dickens in the characters he created in *Our Mutual Friend*. He gives the nouveau riche family the name of Veneering. In the eighteenth century cutting veneers was highly skilled work and used exotic rare timbers. It was therefore associated with expensive and smart goods and was highly desirable. But by the 1830s veneers on wood had become an inexpensive method of making cheap furniture look more expensive and therefore associated with superficiality and sham.[75] The Veneerings had a smart house but not a home, and through them Dickens demonstrated how new and fashionable things were sometimes at odds with the ideals of homemaking.

> Mr and Mrs Veneering were bran-new people in a bran-new house in a
> bran-new quarter of London. Everything about the Veneerings was spick
> and span new. All their furniture was new, all their friends were new, all
> their servants were new, their plate was new, their carriage was new,

their harness was new, their horse was new, their pictures were new,
they themselves were new, they were as newly married as was lawfully
compatible with them having a bran-new baby, and if they had set a
great-grandfather, he would have come home in matting from the
pantechnicon, with out a scratch upon home, French-polished to the
crown of his head.[76]

The influence of domestic ideology on homemaking practice impacted on the value placed on older objects within domestic interiors. Such attitudes are discernible in the letter that the writer and critic John Ruskin wrote to *The Times* about the painting by Holman Hunt, *The Awakening Conscience*.[77] The painting depicted a man with his mistress in the house that he maintained for her. Ruskin suggested that the painter's comment on their immoral situation had not simply been expressed through the composition, which was littered with symbolic allusions, but also through the choice of furniture and furnishings. The immorality of the home was betrayed in the 'fatal newness' of all the bright and shiny new contents. His comments suggest that if the couple had been married then they would have inherited furniture from their families, resulting in an interior with items of different dates, some objects showing their age in their design and patina. Ruskin is suggesting that the result would have been a home rather than a shallow, fashionable and immoral interior.

Both Ruskin and Dickens were making a connection between furniture that was fashionable, new, shiny, and bought all at the same time, from a shop, with people who were shallow and who had dubious morals. Penny Sparke has commented on how the domestic ideology of the early-nineteenth century affected people's attitudes to objects within the home. One aspect was the desire for the home to look as well as be comfortable, and this was 'linked with the idea of the sanctuary and haven, suggesting safety and security. In material terms, this was more likely to have been represented by old, old-looking, or traditional goods'.[78]

However, for many middle-class homemakers in the early to mid-nineteenth century, there was no alternative to purchasing all the goods for their home since they did not have family items to inherit. Therefore purchasing some goods second-hand perhaps provided the suggestion of family history and background, and may have provided instant pedigree. Patina on furniture, darkened wood and faded textiles, even scratches and pulled threads, could carry emotional meanings. All goods acquired a new set of meanings when purchased second-hand and lost the meaning they possessed for their original owner. It is possible that good-quality, if slightly old goods were seen as desirable since they carried status with their patina.[79] Such goods carried associations of quality with them which homemakers could incorporate into their own furnishing schemes and personal home circumstances, making a home rather than just a fashionable interior.

Furniture in common with other objects can communicate meaning through a display of fashion or a particular taste. This could be described as 'fixed meaning' since such cultural values must be shared by society for their meaning to be understood. Objects can also be invested with meaning on an individual level through associations with events in the life of the owner or with the lives of past owners; as the personification of memories.[80] Inherited objects operated on this level but second-hand furniture was perhaps a good substitute.

By the early-nineteenth century particular attitudes to the home had developed that meant that these physical signs of age were desirable in at least some home furnishings. Purchasing a few pieces second-hand was not dissimilar to acquiring items from within the family, either when the home was first established on marriage or inherited later. Both of these sources of goods proclaimed their age in their patina.

Conclusion

The middle classes needed to pay attention to practical considerations in their homemaking. While wanting to have fashionable interiors that would impress their guests, they were also under economic pressure. Therefore, furnishing on marriage with a mixture of new and inherited things was a practical necessity. Some furnishings were retained for many years and every so often items were replaced to update interiors. Or some recycling could be practised by replacing the covers on a chair or making new curtains. Within such homes a few second-hand pieces would not look amiss.

The middle classes were also aware of their nouveau status. The gentility and fashionableness of their homes was important for reflecting their present position in society, rather than where they had come from. Many middle-class people did not have a previous generation that had been sufficiently wealthy to leave them good-quality furniture. Thus, the six Windsor chairs referred to above, inherited by Mary Wright in 1849 may have been special to her mother but would not have been considered fashionable or particularly desirable items of furniture by the mid-nineteenth century.

If inherited pieces were not available or if they were of too poor quality to retain then purchasing a few pieces of second-hand furniture could accomplish both practical and cultural needs. Domestic ideology was created primarily by and for the middle classes suiting their thrifty nature and their desire for the right moral and emotional ambience in the home. The acquisition of used goods and the continued use of older goods was as much a part of middle-class consumption practices as purchasing items in the latest fashion. These practices were a way of personalizing homes, marking out individual families and their histories.

Notes

[1]   Christina Hardyment (Introduction) (1987), *The Housekeeping Book of Susanna Whatman 1776-1800*, London: Century in association with The National Trust, p. 41.

[2]   *Cassell's Household Guide* (c. 1870-1), London: Cassell, Petter, and Galpin, volume 4, p. 46.

[3]   East Sussex Record Office, AMS 5569/66, p. 163.

[4]   Hardyment (1987), pp. 37-42.

[5] See Roszika Parker (1984), *The Subversive Stitch: Embroidery and the Making of the Feminine*, London: The Women's Press. For a contemporary source see A Lady (1838), *The Workwoman's Guide*, London: Simpkin, Marshall and Co.

[6] Catherine Hutton Beale (ed.) (1891), *Reminiscences of a Gentlewoman of the Last Century: Letters of Catherine Hutton*, Birmingham: Cornish Brothers, p. 213.

[7] J.C. Loudon (1838), *The Suburban Gardener and Villa Companion*, published by the author.

[8] Marcia Pointon has also commented on the practice of repairing furnishings. See Marcia Pointon (1997), *Strategies for Showing: Women, Possession, and Representation in English Visual Culture 1665-1800*, London: Oxford University Press, pp. 32 and 35.

[9] Birmingham City Archives, Matthew Boulton Papers (MBP). The household papers include many receipts for loaves of bread and other mundane articles as well as the furnishings receipts for Matthew Boulton's home, Soho House, his daughter Anne's home of Thornhill, plus some for his son Matthew Robinson Boulton.

[10] Birmingham City Archives, MBP 474.

[11] Henry Peat Day Book, begun in 1806 and kept for about seven years, although dates were entered spasmodically. West Sussex Record Office, Add Mss 2235.

[12] West Sussex Record Office, Samuel Peat Day Book Add Mss 2239.

[13] The main sources of information about the Newlands are the censuses for 1841 and 1851, and the inventory of Mrs Newland's home, made by the Peat firm in 1852. West Sussex Record Office, Add Mss 2245. The Newlands were an important family in Chichester; the men held various civic posts and the local newspaper carried stories of their involvement in public affairs. The houses occupied by the family still exist in North Street, Chichester.

[14] Fernleigh, a flint and brick house, is described in detail in Alec Clifton Taylor (1978), *Six English Towns*, London: BBC, pp. 36-37.

[15] The fabric was recorded in the 1852 inventory of Mrs G. Newland's home. West Sussex Record Office, Add Mss 2245.

[16] Staffordshire Record Office, Account book of John Foden 1822-1866, reference 3161.

[17] Birmingham City Archives, MBP 438. Letter dated 22 May 1838.

[18] The practise of purchasing textiles in London and then having the upholstery work done by a local firm was commented on in Chapter 1.

[19] Birmingham City Archives, MBP 479.

[20] Birmingham City Archives, MBP 438.

[21] See also Pat Kirkham (1995), '"If you have no sons": Furniture-making in Britain', in Judith Attfield and Pat Kirkham (eds), *A View from the Interior: Women and Design*, London: The Women's Press.

[22] Stana Nenadic (1994), 'Middle-rank Consumers and Domestic Culture in Edinburgh and Glasgow 1720-1840', *Past and Present*, number 145, pp. 122-156, pp. 132-133.

[23] Beverly Lemire (1997), *Dress, Culture and Commerce: the English Clothing Trade Before the Factory, 1660-1800*, London: Macmillan.

[24] Hetherington comments on the contemporary status of these 'conduits' for second-hand goods. See Kevin Hetherington (2004), 'Secondhandness: Consumption, Disposal and Absent Presence', *Environment and Planning D: Society and Space*, volume 22, pp. 157-173, p. 165.

[25] See Illustration 1:3 on page 37.

[26] Miles Lambert has demonstrated that dealers in second-hand clothing waited on genteel customers at their homes. Miles Lambert (2004), '"Cast-off Wearing Apparell?": The

Consumption and Distribution of Second-hand Clothing in Northern England during the Long Eighteenth Century', *Textile History*, volume 38, number 1, pp. 1-26, p. 8.

27   Jocelyne Baty Goodman (ed.) (1968), *Victorian Cabinet Maker: the Memoirs of James Hopkinson 1819-1894*, London: Routledge and Kegan Paul.

28   A Lady (1829), *The Home Book: or Young Housekeeper's Assistant*, London: Smith, Elder and Co., p. 107.

29   *Salopian Journal*, 30 July 1794.

30   *Salopian Journal*, 20 April 1835.

31   West Sussex Record Office, William and Henry Peat notebook, Add Mss 2245.

32   Cynthia Wall (1997), 'The English Auction: Narratives of Dismantlings', *Eighteenth-Century Studies*, volume 31, number 1, pp. 1-25.

33   Col. Egerton's property was given as 'Severn Hills, near Shrewsbury'. *Salopian Journal*, 11 May 1814.

34   Aris's *Birmingham Gazette*, 15 February 1796

35   Wall (1997), 'The English Auction', p. 10.

36   Grier comments on the importance of this for the middle classes. See Katherine C. Grier (1988), *Culture and Comfort: People, Parlors and Upholstery 1850-1930*, Rochester NY: The Strong Museum and University of Massachusetts Press, Chapter 1, 'Imagining the Parlor'.

37   Jon Stobart (forthcoming).

38   Birmingham City Archives, MBP 431.

39   Nenadic (1994), 'Middle-rank Consumers', p. 132.

40   Birmingham City Archives, MS 897, volume II, numbers 109 and 151. The images, probably bill heads, are not dated but the time of the move can be estimated from Rodderick's entries in trade directories.

41   Birmingham City Archives, MBP 438, letters dated September 1837. Perhaps this was the same sofa, noted already in this chapter, that was recovered in May 1838, see page 83.

42   Birmingham Archives, Auction details Norton Collection (2182) 820.

43   Carl Chinn (1998) Introduction to *The Life of William Hutton*, Studley, Warwickshire: Brewin Books, p. xxii.

44   Birmingham City Archives, MS 897, volume II, number 76, n.d. c. 1840s.

45   Birmingham City Archives, MBP 468. Matthew Robinson Boulton also purchased an oak chest from Samuel Pearson, a cabinetmaker in Worcester Street, in 1824. Birmingham City Archives, MBP 479.

46   See Elizabeth Stillinger (1980), *The Antiquers*, New York: Alfred Knopf; Clive Wainwright (1989), *The Romantic Interior*, New Haven and London: Yale University Press. For a contemporary source giving advice to collectors see *Practical Economy* (1822), pp. 115-123, 141-144.

47   Wainwright (1989) *The Romantic Interior*.

48   Catalogue Shropshire Record Office, D87.7 and 6001/153. House sale advertisement, *Salopian Journal* 8/1/1834. Wainwright (1989) suggests that many antiquarians in the 18th century were clergymen and other professionals, so Parkes was not atypical.

49   Adam Bowett (1994), 'The Commercial Introduction of Mahogany and the Naval Stores Act of 1721', *Furniture History*, volume 30, pp. 43-56.

50   David Parkes had a good reputation in Shrewsbury and nationally. An obituary notice appeared in the *Gentleman's Magazine* and numerous memorials to him are recorded. Shropshire Record Office, MS153, MS4073 and for biographical information see H.R.

Wilson (1978), *David Parkes*, published by the author (Shropshire Record Office, BP24).

[51] David Parkes drew mostly architectural subjects including picturesque ruins that were published in various books such as *Antiquities of Shropshire* (1807), London and *Beauties of England Wales* (1811), London. See Stanley Fisher (1972), *A Dictionary of Watercolour Painters 1750-1900*, Slough: W. Foulsham; H.L. Mallalieu (1986), *The Dictionary of British Watercolour Artists up to 1920*, Woodbridge: Antique Collectors Club.

[52] Nicky Gregson and Louise Crew (2003), *Second-hand Cultures*, London: Berg, p. 83.

[53] Amanda Vickery (1998), *The Gentleman's Daughter: Women's Lives in Georgian England*, New Haven and London: Yale University Press, p. 192.

[54] Vickery (1998), *The Gentleman's Daughter*, p. 190.

[55] Maxine Berg (1996), 'Women's Consumption and the Industrial Classes of Eighteenth-Century England', *Journal of Social History*, volume 30, number 2, pp. 415-434, p. 418.

[56] It was noted in Chapter 2 that the items most often singled out in wills were jewellery and portraits. Much of the research exploring the meaning of objects bequeathed or inherited has related to such objects. Berg (1996), 'Women's Consumption'; Pointon (1997), *Strategies for Showing*; Vickery (1998), *The Gentleman's Daughter*.

[57] Coventry Archives, Will of Thomas Robinson, 1853, 101/8/762. The contents of bequests in wills at Coventry Archives have been extracted and indexed allowing a search to be made for specific items. While this is unusual the wills themselves offer a representation of bequests generally for the period.

[58] A husband's business assets often went to a son rather than his wife. Susan Wright (1989), '"Holding Up Half the Sky": Women and their Occupations in Eighteenth-Century Ludlow', *Midland History*, volume 14, pp. 53-74, p. 61.

[59] Margot Finn (1996), 'Women, Consumption and Coverture in England, c. 1760-1860', *Historical Journal*, 39, pp. 703-722. Finn quotes the work of Amy Louise Erickson who found that 10 per cent of non-elite women protected their property rights in this manner, p. 706.

[60] Coventry Archives, Will of William Pickard, 1856, 101/9/57.

[61] Coventry Archives, Will of John Alcott, 5 January 1827, 101/1/485.

[62] Coventry Archives, Will of Anne Cave, 1 January, 1755, 487/1. See also Chapter 2, page 67.

[63] Coventry Archives, Will of John Derwas Haines, 1821, 101/9/72.

[64] Research on the contents of wills has emphasized that women were most likely to personalize objects in bequests. Berg (1996), 'Women's Consumption'; Vickery (1998), *The Gentleman's Daughter*.

[65] Coventry Archives, Will of Mary Bucknill, 1838, 101/4/150.

[66] Coventry Archives, Will of Elizabeth Parsons, 1849, 101/9/308.

[67] Coventry Archives, Will Catherine Wright, 1843, 101/7/314.

[68] Coventry Archives, Will of Fanny Downes, 1858, 1010/8/426.

[69] See Marcia Pointon (1999), 'Materializing Mourning: Hair, Jewellery and the Body', in Marius Kwint, Christopher Breward and Jeremy Aynsley (eds), *Material Memories*, London: Berg.

[70] John Burnett (1978), *A Social History of Housing 1815-1970*, Newton Abbot: David and Charles, p. 95.

[71] *The Family Economist: a Penny Monthly Magazine for the Industrious Classes* (1851), volume 5, London: Groombridge and Sons, p. 182.

72 For more elaboration on the notion of domestic ideology see Catherine Hall (1979), 'The Early Formation of Victorian Domestic Ideology', in Sandra Burman, *Fit Work for Women*, London: Croom Helm; Leonore Davidoff and Catherine Hall (1992), *Family Fortunes: Men and Women of the English Middle Class 1780-1850*, London: Routledge, pp. 149-192.

73 Amanda Vickery (1993), 'Golden Age to Separate Spheres? A Review of the Categories and Chronology of English Women's History', *The Historical Journal*, volume 36, number 2, pp. 383-414.

74 Mrs Ellis (1844), *Family Monitor and Domestic Guide: The Women of England, their Social Duties and Domestic Habits*, New York: Henry G. Lanley; Mrs Ellis (1845), *Daughters of England*, London and Paris: Fisher, Son and Co.

75 See Adrian Forty (1987), *Objects of Desire: Design and Society 1750-1980*, London: Thames and Hudson.

76 Charles Dickens (1960 first published 1865), *Our Mutual Friend*, Oxford: Oxford University Press, p. 6.

77 Ruskin's letter is reproduced in Caroline Arscott (1988), 'Employer, husband, spectator: Thomas Fairburn's commission of The Awakening Conscience', in J. Wolff and J. Seed (eds), *The Culture of Capital: Art, Power and the Nineteenth-Century Middle Class*, Manchester: Manchester University Press, pp. 172-173. This chapter also analyses the symbolic nature of the interior depicted.

78 Penny Sparke (1995), *As Long As It's Pink*, London: Harper Collins, p. 27.

79 McCracken says the use of patina in this way died out in the eighteenth century due to the adoption of the fashion system but this does not seem to be the case. Rather, patina continued to be associated with status albeit in a slightly different way, and hence the use of antiques as status markers into the twentieth century. Grant McCracken (1990), *Culture and Consumption*, Bloomington and Indianapolis: Indiana University Press. See Bourdieu on the subject of antiques and status. Pierre Bourdieu (1984), *Distinction: A Social Critique of the Judgement of Taste*, London: Routledge and Kegan Paul.

80 For a discussion of this idea see Marius Kwint (1999), Introduction, in Marius Kwint et al., *Material Memories.*

Chapter 4

Extended Households

In c. 1729 John Wood the Elder drew up plans for houses in Queen Square, Bath. The interior arrangements for the rooms are curious by the standards of today. Wood placed two bedrooms on the ground floor, one each behind a dining room and parlour and beyond them, at the back of the house, was the kitchen. On the first floor were two drawing rooms, both at the front of the house and divided by a dressing room that was meant to be used by one or other of the two bedrooms towards the back of the house.[1] While Wood was concerned with the positioning of public rooms at the front of the building the mixing up of bedrooms and dressing rooms with kitchen, dining room and drawing rooms must have led to curious usage; cooking smells in the downstairs bedrooms and people in a state of undress going between bedroom and dressing room.

Such arrangements in smart houses were less in evidence later in the century. Drawing rooms situated on the first floor continued in town houses but bedrooms were all moved to upper floors. These changes in wealthy homes were mirrored to some extent in middling-sort homes. Similarly, by the later-eighteenth and early-nineteenth centuries, multifunctional rooms were becoming less common in such homes. Instead rooms had clearer uses, often with single functions. Rooms specifically for dining emerged instead of meals being taken in any room. Parlours became solely for relaxation rather than doubling as a room for work and/or a bedchamber. These moves coincided with rooms taking on a gendered slant in their decoration and furnishing that was supposed to suggest use. The dining room was designated a masculine room and had more robust furniture and darker colours than the drawing room, a feminine room.[2] However, despite these developments many homes could not conform even if their inhabitants wanted to either because older properties resulted in odd arrangements, or because the extended family had to be accommodated.

At the same time domestic ideology was placing pressures on homemakers to produce homes that could fulfil the moral role assigned to the home. Thus it was becoming increasingly important to make a clearer distinction between the public sphere of work and the private sphere of the home. Therefore it was desirable for work to be divorced from the domestic sphere, but again many homes continued to accommodate workrooms and the storage of materials and stock. The idea of the extended household can also be interpreted as the furthest corners of the house: the attics, cellars and built-in cupboards used for storage. These areas of the house had a practical function to store items not in immediate use and keeping the house tidy of clutter. But sometimes the storage was halfway towards disposal without accomplishing it completely. This was because the emotional associations of these objects made homemakers reluctant to part with them.

People as well as objects needed to be accommodated in the extended home. Servants were present in most middling-sort and later, middle-class, homes. Their presence had to be accommodated without compromising the privacy of the family. Servants' access to the service areas and their sleeping arrangements were the subject of much architectural planning in the mid- to later-nineteenth century,[3] but in older and humbler properties homemakers had to fit in servants and their work where best they could.

A further complication in defining the space of domestic interiors was the need to accommodate a public role within the home. While primarily a domestic and private space, still, entertaining at home was necessary and even desirable as the home was a safer place for women than the public arenas of leisure that had been popular in the eighteenth century, such as pleasure gardens. Therefore, ways were devised for the household space and its furnishings to provide visitors with access to certain areas of the home so that they could be entertained at an appropriate level.

This chapter is concerned with how older arrangements persisted despite fashionable developments, and how the newer trends were superimposed over imperfect situations. For example, there were tensions between multiple use and single use of rooms. The public and private areas of the home and how they functioned for its various inmates whether family, servants, lodgers and temporary guests are all at least hinted at in the inventories of homes. While many of the examples in the chapter will be of homes that display less than perfect arrangements according to the ideas of their day, the chapter will end with an example of a home that was able to accommodate all aspects of the domestic environment and probably displayed them expertly to visitors. This home belonged to Mrs Newland, who lived in Chichester in the first half of the nineteenth century. Her home will be used to reconstruct the circumstances of a dinner party to show how her home, and others on a similar level, would have been able to provide genteel surroundings for guests in the public areas of the home. Elaborate food could be prepared in the kitchen and the requisite number of servants was available to perform tasks that linked both the public and service areas.

Old Arrangements

Old arrangements in the form of rooms with mixed uses are evident in the probate inventory, made in 1786, of Thomas Lovatt's Shropshire farmhouse.[4] The kitchen contents were listed first, and while it was clearly a working kitchen with cooking implements, it also contained decorative items: a dresser with numerous pewter plates and dishes displayed on it, a clock and a tea kettle and earthenware. Despite decorative possibilities and the newer commodities for tea drinking, and newer ways of serving food implied by these goods in the kitchen, Thomas Lovatt's parlour did not conform to what was expected in the 1780s. By this time it was usual to have a sitting room, described as a parlour, that was free of work and that therefore could be decorated and furnished in a more elaborate, fashionable and expensive manner than the practical areas of the house. Lovatt's parlour contained the usual table and chairs but also accommodated a saddle and bridle and two wagon ropes and some hemp, showing that farm goods had strayed into this room. Next door was a room designated the 'little parlour'. Despite its smaller dimensions it contained far more than the parlour, which might suggest that this was the room that performed that function. To this purpose it contained a couch and table and chairs, but there was also a night stool and pan with a pewter cover and a bedstead with hangings and blankets, and in addition, a servant's bedstead. The furnishing of the little parlour may have come about because Thomas Lovatt was too ill towards the end of his life to go upstairs to bed and the servant was there to take care of him (he was not married). But it was not uncommon for rural houses to have a bed in the parlour although the expectation was, by this period, that a parlour was meant to be free of sleeping and work-related functions.

Another farmhouse displaying odd arrangements was that belonging to James Mullock, in Whitchurch, Shropshire. The inventory, dated 1804, began with all the kitchen goods except that the inventory called the room the houseplace.[5] This was the old name for the general living room where cooking was also done, but by the later-eighteenth century this name had largely died out and cooking was relegated to the kitchen, although some households continued to eat their meals there. The sitting room element of the houseplace was replaced by a separate room, the parlour. In his houseplace, James Mullock had numerous tables and chairs as well as cooking and serving equipment. Farmhouse kitchens needed to perform additional roles beyond cooking food. The farm workers, together with the family, all ate their meals in the same room and this continuation of an old arrangement (dating back to the medieval, extended household) encouraged the continued use of the name houseplace even though it had largely died out, in polite circles, by the later-eighteenth century.

Even later references to the houseplace in homes, in the small town of Stone in Staffordshire, are found in a tradesman's account book.[6] John Foden, a joiner and wheelwright by trade, was employed to do a wide range of activities: repairing wooden and upholstered furniture, painting and decorating, taking down bedsteads and other spring-cleaning work (including delousing furnishings), making coffins and other funeral work, and furniture removals. The extensive range of his work was due to the lack of cabinetmakers and upholsterers in Stone, from the 1820s to the 1860s, when Foden was working there. The quiet rural nature of Stone perhaps also led some of its residents to continue with old-fashioned ways of organizing their homes. On several occasions in his account book Foden noted that he had white-washed or painted a 'houseplace'. In 1831 Foden recorded work for Mr Thomas Stevens, a gentleman living in the hamlet of Stonefield: 'Paint for window and Gates & Colers left for Slapdashing houseplace 4s 6d.' Slapdashing is a rather archaic term for applying paint to resemble paper.[7] The description of Thomas Stevens as a gentleman reinforces the impression that old-fashioned ways prevailed in Stone.[8] Foden was thought to be adequate, even by gentlemen, to carry out all manner of cabinetry and upholstery work, as well as painting and decorating, despite his lack of training, and his old-fashioned terminology that indicates a lack of fashionable knowledge. In a small town like Stone that was towards the bottom of the urban hierarchy, and receding rather than rising, it was still possible for regional methods that were far behind fashionable practice to continue well into the nineteenth century.

The Intrusion of Work in the Home

Birmingham and, to a lesser extent, Wolverhampton were more dynamic towns in comparison to Stone. They were moving up the hierarchy in terms of what they could provide in retail, commercial and leisure facilities, but at the same time industrialization provided a messy backdrop for homemaking, not just for the lower-status workers. Combined living and working conditions prevailed from the outset of the period and continued to its close.

One such example is provided in the home of Ann and Thomas Heeley, a brother and sister, who shared a house in Birmingham until Thomas died in 1764.[9] Ann kept a grocery shop selling tea, spices, dried fruit and tobacco. Thomas was a button and toy maker.[10] They were not particularly wealthy; their household goods only amounted to £78, but with the stock, materials, good and bad debts, Heeley's inventory totalled £639. Both shop and workshop were attached to their home and encroached on their living conditions. In the garrets were stored their clothes, two brown wigs and nine pairs of shoes along with 13 pounds of brass wire, 25 pounds of file dust, 27 pounds of waste metal and quantities of other materials for Thomas's business. Thomas needed several places to store his materials and stock as well as extensive workshops for all his tools and equipment. This left no room for a parlour. Next to the grocery shop was their kitchen, which also had to serve as a sitting room and dining room with just a small dining table and '6 wooden bottom chairs', offering little comfort. The only other domestic rooms listed were two bedchambers. Both rooms contained substantial feather beds, bedsteads, hangings, window curtains and blankets. In addition, they both had chairs and tables; the front bedroom's was described as a dining table. The old habit of eating meals in any rooms did continue at this date although it was falling from favour. In this instance it was a compromise to gain additional comfort and a pleasant alternative place, to the kitchen, to sit after the day's work.

The altogether smarter business carried out by James Eykyn in Wolverhampton nonetheless made full use of his family home as an extension of his shop, workshop and showroom. From the evidence of his inventory it is difficult to determine where these various aspects of his life began and ended.[11] Eykyn was a cabinetmaker and upholsterer with an extensive business. The value of his stock, equipment and household goods was £902 when he died in 1780. Of the long list of debts, £823 had been received but many debts were still outstanding.[12] Eykyn had clearly been in business for many years and had accumulated a huge stock of materials that were listed in a densely written list of the front shop contents; some individual entries were for large quantities; dozens of yards of furnishing textiles, lace and fringes, 10,000 tin tacks, 57 dozen Dutch tiles, 159 pieces of wallpaper in different colours and patterns. The inventory continued with the 'Dineing Room', but it would have been difficult for the Eykyn family to eat any meals there as it was so full of furniture. Listed were eight round mahogany pillar tables, several chests of drawers, a large mahogany two-leaf dining table and three breakfast tables, 14 mahogany tea chests, 16 mahogany tea boards, 11 dozen bottle boards and waiters, plus yet more overspill from the front shop: 40 yards of Manchester stripe, 'counterpaines', 300 pieces of wallpaper, and numerous items of glass and china ware. It seems that James Eykyn had extended into the room behind the shop and made it into a showroom for his furnishing stock.

The Eykyn family were surrounded by the business. At the back of the premises were the workshops, perhaps arranged in a similar manner to, the later, J. Mills in Bromsgrove Street, Birmingham[13] (Illustration 4:1).

Eykyn's premises included a cabinet workshop, a 'matt room', a stable, a feather room, a timber yard and an 'accompting' house. The front shop and workshops are to be expected in this line of business, even the use of an extra room in the house as a showroom merely indicates that the business was extensive. But Eykyn's work did not stop there and encroached on more intimate areas of the family home. This hints at a business strategy rather than simply overspill through lack of space. In between the list of contents for several bedchambers, the inventory maker inserted the 'Silvering Room', indicating that a bedchamber had been given over to making mirrors. Here were listed frames and finished looking glasses, some not completed and materials for making more. In the garrets at the top of the house more stocks of textiles and unfinished furniture were stored. Even four of the six bedchambers contained large quantities of furniture, some of it unfinished, particularly chairs minus their upholstery. Thus Eykyn was using his entire home not only for storage but also as a showcase for his work. Customers could see materials, semi-finished goods and finished items and choose from amongst them. The unupholstered chairs could be made up with the customer's choice of fabric from the stock in the front shop. This was probably quite a common way for cabinetmakers and other trades to organize their homes; using the domestic environment as a suitable backdrop to show off their wares.

An example of a customer viewing stock, in the private areas of a tradesman's home, is provided by Matthew Boulton when he purchased furniture from the prestigious cabinetmaker James Newton in London, between 1797 and 1805. In a letter to Boulton Newton referred to a chair that he was sending him, he described it as 'the one that you saw at my house'.[14] Using the home in this way demonstrates how the middling sort used the domestic environment, and the consumer goods that they acquired for it, as an advertisement for their businesses, their fashionable taste and their expertise. Consumption for the home can therefore be seen sometimes as a shrewd investment rather than emulation of the wealthy and fashionable.[15] By the early-nineteenth century a discernable middle class existed that made distinctions between people who bought and sold goods and others who 'got their hands dirty' however successful their business. It was at this period that living at a distance from the workplace became desirable and suburbs were increasingly situated around the perimeters of towns to accommodate the wealthier members of society. Some people were caught between the artisan class and the middle class while others, mainly elderly people, who were merchants and

4:1 The premises of Mills, cabinetmaker in Birmingham, gives an idea of the arrangement of James Eykyn's home and business in Wolverhampton in 1780, with front shop, workshops and living accommodation.

therefore belonged to the middle class, chose not to change their ways and move out of town away from their business premises. One of the latter was Jonah Bissell who had a substantial business as a merchant in brass cabinet wares, and fancy and hardware goods, as the catalogue of his effects announced, after his death in 1842[16] The list of his stock was substantial and in his will he left £600 in cash. The sale of his goods took place over three days with a gig, phaeton and various harnesses and so on sold on the first day, along with all his warehouse stock of guns, buttons, clock movements and every kind of decorative article. Further lots of jewellery and clocks were to be sold the following week at the auctioneer's offices. These were too numerous to be listed and a separate catalogue was announced. The warehouse consisted of a large room with an inner room, used as an office, and a lower warehouse and yard where boxes, hampers and a bench with a vice were situated. The last day's sale was of his furniture and household goods, the house being adjacent to the warehouse. The auctioneer listed each room, beginning at the top of the building with the attic rooms and ending with the cellar and yard. The movement through the house followed a clear pattern: on each floor the auctioneer listed the front room first followed by the room behind, at the back of the dwelling. Below the attic rooms were two chambers both with mahogany bedsteads and chintz hangings. Listed next was the ground floor beginning with the parlour at the front of the house.

Bissell owned furniture and ornaments to be proud of and that the auctioneer thought deserved to be described in detail. In the centre of the parlour was a mahogany pillar table with four matching dining chairs with hair seats.[17] A small mahogany sideboard and butler's tray completed the furniture needed for dining. To one side of the room was a 'well-made modern mahogany sofa, with hair squab seat, and two square pillows'. A green Kidderminster carpet was on the floor with a hearth rug before the wire-work fender, and steel fire irons in the fireplace. A fancy wire window blind in a mahogany frame was fitted to the window. On the walls was a pair of medallions of George III, two paintings of 'the Woodman', and a 'capital wheel barometer, by Pedretti'. On display were a clock in a spar frame, and two glass cases, one containing a stuffed pheasant and the other a pigeon and bantam cock. There were also several fancy japanned trays and a 'neat bronze coffee percolator'. Bissell had a fine parlour with comfortable and prestigious furniture and decorative goods. However, he probably kept this room for best and instead generally used the sitting room. This room is listed following a large store room and placed next to the kitchen. The methodical listing used by the auctioneer locates the sitting room at the rear of the building, next to and probably overlooking the yard. In comparison with the front parlour, then, this room was in a less attractive position and yet it contained almost as many decorative items as the parlour and was almost certainly used on a daily basis by Bissell, including for eating all his meals at the 'strong mahogany two-leaf dining table' and for writing letters at the oak bureau. It was not unusual for lower middle-class people to keep a front parlour 'for best',[18] but in Bissell's case, with a successful business and extensive stock, this rear sitting room was an unattractive setting for his 'genteel household furniture', as the auctioneer described it.

Bissell was surrounded by his work and the densely packed human activities of Bradford Street, in Birmingham. He was well situated for customers to his business and for keeping an eye on his affairs, but the property did not offer a genteel existence. The dirt and mess of work were all around. By 1842 the better off were moving to the west of Birmingham where Edgbaston was growing as a prosperous suburb and houses were being built to suit middle-class tastes.[19] The houses provided the necessary requirements for their domestic arrangements along the lines of rooms with separate uses and a clear demarcation between public and private, work and domesticity.

Accommodating Clutter

Observing the disposition of objects in a house can provide an indication of how a house was run, how objects were used and by whom. In the day-to-day existence of a family home many objects were in constant use. In a well-regulated house these items all had a resting place where they could be found easily. In other households untidy clutter would have been part of a dirty and chaotic lifestyle.[20] Many objects remained on show, placed on shelves and mantlepiece, not for display purposes but for convenience of use. Although the Shakers turned this procedure into a fine art they were merely refining a common homemaking practice.

Other items ceased to have an obvious usefulness and were stored in cupboards, in the attic or cellar more or less permanently. Such items were still retained by homemakers in case they proved useful in the future or because the materials they were made from could be utilized in some way, as suggested in Chapter 3. Thriftiness went alongside good housewifery and husbandry. Many eighteenth-century inventories record cheese, bacon and wool being stored in attics. Alongside them the inventory maker recorded 'lumber': timber or broken furniture stored for future use. In Thomas Thomas's farmhouse in Bobbington, Shropshire, for example, one of the upper rooms was described as the 'Cheese Chamber' in the inventory made in 1796.[21] This room seems to have been above the 'Best Parlour' and contained:

> 48 Cheeses
> 3 quart of Clover seed
> 12lb of Turnip seed
> Part of a [illegible] of Hops
> 2 Pieces of Blanketing
> Sundry Lumber

Beyond such practical disposing of goods around the house it was also common to store objects that were probably never to have a further use. Such temporary storage could last many years before finally the objects were sold, given or thrown away. Kevin Hetherington has referred to this kind of storage as 'liminal, betwixt and between', since the goods existed in an uncertain position within the house.[22] Hetherington suggests that such objects provided an 'absent presence'. Sometimes people were not able to fully dispose of things, because they retained an emotional bond with the objects. In this way the miscellaneous contents of a cupboard, cellar, attic or unused bedchamber still formed an important part of the household even though the contents were out of sight, since they could contain objects that exerted a strong 'effect upon social relations'.[23]

Although inventories do not provide obvious comments on the importance of objects to their owner, still the disposition of goods within the home can provide a clue as to their status. An instance of absent presence is suggested by the 1811 inventory of John Staunton's Kenilworth home. In this gentleman's house a store room was situated between the study and the dining room on the ground floor.[24] A host of useful things were stored here. Some were connected with serving food and were conveniently placed for the servants of the household. These items included a bronze tea urn, a coffee mill, three lamps, a pewter wine strainer funnel, two mahogany, and two papier mâché tea trays. The presence of such useful objects next to the dining room suggests that this was a store room in constant use. Other objects were for occasional use, such as two mouse traps, a set of weights and a marble mortar. However, other items would have obstructed access to the contents of the room. These items included 13 deal packing boxes, an oak bureau, a chest of drawers, three nests of drawers and shelves, seven baskets and a mahogany stand. The presence of pieces of furniture along with service items suggests that this was a store for unused furnishings. These seem to be items that the Stauntons had no particular use for but were not ready to discard from their home.

The most surprising item in the store room was a set of needlework hangings for a bed. Textile bed hangings were amongst the most costly items in many eighteenth-century homes. Although the date of the inventory, made on John Staunton's death, was 1811, he was 76 years old by this time and would have acquired most of his furnishings many years earlier. Much of his homemaking would have been done with his first wife, the mother of his children, four of whom were still living at the time of his death. John had married his second wife, Anne, in about 1800. As we saw in Chapter 1 they made one visit to London during their marriage and chose new textiles for the bed hangings and window curtains for their bedchamber. Might these needlework hangings, discarded in a store room, have been replaced by the new ones, of yellow chintz? Perhaps the needlework had been carried out by John's first wife, Maria? The origin of these needlework hangings and the reason for their being stored so unceremoniously in a store room with a tea urn, packing boxes and mouse traps, will never be known. But there is the possibility that they were an example of what Hetherington has described: an item removed from sight, and not encountered on a daily basis, but still able to exert an emotional presence, for John of his dead wife, and for his children of their mother. Perhaps the presence was most keenly felt by Anne, the new wife, who lost her home when John Staunton died and had to return to live with her father in Coventry.[25]

The Accommodation of Additional People

Beyond the nuclear family other people inhabited the house whether on a temporary or permanent basis. The middling-sort household commonly consisted of four to seven people.[26] Elderly mothers and fathers lived with a son or daughter, lodgers brought in extra money, and some tradespeople had apprentices living with the family, although the practice was dying out by this period. The homes of the gentry had tutors or governesses to instruct the children and most middling-sort, and later middle-class, homes had live-in servants, ranging from just one young maid to three or four servants, or more, including a cook and butler.

Providing a room or two for a lodger meant losing either a sitting room or a bedroom, as well as giving up some of the family's privacy. There was the extra work, too, of providing meals and perhaps doing their washing. But for many families, it was an economic necessity.[27] While some households furnished the lodging room completely, leaving little for the lodger to personalize[28] other people, like Elizabeth Jeffries, in Bridgnorth, just provided the basics of a bed, bedsteads and hangings, a chair and a box for clothes.[29] John Anderson was her lodger and presumably he had further possessions that were not included in the inventory made when Elizabeth died in 1768. Her house was a modest one, comprising a kitchen and parlour and the 'lower lodging room' with two bedchambers upstairs. Thus an extra room was squeezed in on the ground floor and indeed, in her will, Elizabeth Jeffries left John Anderson the bed, bedsteads and hangings that he had used in the 'Little Room'.

Accommodating a lodger and being a lodger in someone else's house was a compromise born out of economic necessity, but, as in the case of Elizabeth Jeffries and John Anderson, friendly relationships could also develop. Perhaps, too, this was the case in the Wilson household in Chichester. In 1841 Joseph Wilson was a surgeon living in North Pallant, a road just off East Street, which contained some substantial houses.[30] In the house, as well as Joseph, his wife Sarah and their young family of four boys and two girls, lived Henry Pickriss, also a surgeon, and Edward Romney, an architect, both about 20 years old.[31] These two young men seem to have shared the attic room, which contained two tent bedsteads with dimity hangings and a commode each. The Wilson household met the requirements of these three professional men by having an extra 'masculine' sitting room in the house. Joseph Wilson had his surgery at his home in one of the front rooms, his parlour being in the other. Behind the surgery was a library and across the hall the dining room. Both the dining room and the library at this period were considered masculine rooms and would have been decorated accordingly. The library had woollen, moreen window curtains and a piece of Brussels carpeting, the dining room had a painted floor cloth beneath the mahogany dining table. By contrast the front parlour was 'feminine' with a greater use of textiles and more decorative items. It contained a sofa upholstered in striped cotton and a large rosewood loo table in the centre of the room, a pier glass in a gold frame, a Brussels carpet fitted to the room and cotton window curtains hung from a cornice. The furnishing of the living rooms provided the men in the household with their own space in which to spend their evenings with books and papers and conversation, away from the children and the domestic tasks of the household. Joseph Wilson mixed with the professional class of Chichester that included John Lush a portrait painter, who spent evenings at his house, and who also painted a portrait of Mrs Wilson in 1833.[32] The Wilson household, despite its professional status and good connections, was probably struggling financially and this made the extra income from lodgers attractive as well as providing Joseph with male company and in Henry Pickriss, a junior colleague.

Accommodating Servants

Servants were another matter. In Susannah Whatman's instructions to her servants she was largely concerned with detailing what work she expected from each person and how they were to carry out their duties in order that her house was well maintained and ran smoothly.[33] Some published books gave instructions to servants that provided more personal advice. Thomas Cosnett cautioned against spitting and nose blowing and gave other advice that employers would have wanted to be observed, especially when the servants in question were waiting at table.[34] Perhaps Susannah Whatman and most employers, or their head servants, would have passed on instructions on personal hygiene and etiquette.

Accommodating extra people, in the form of servants, who were wanted on hand to perform their duties but who were also intruders in the family home became a more pressing problem as the nineteenth century progressed, since the number of servants increased as well as people's expectations of privacy in the home. Bell pulls were introduced to summon servants so that they could respond from distant quarters rather than being on hand all the time. The same desire for privacy resulted in the elaborate floor plans, segregating family and servants, that Jill Franklin has evaluated.[35] But older and smaller properties were again at a disadvantage. This problem is hinted at in Anne Boulton's hand-written instructions to her servants.[36] Anne Boulton's instructions went beyond the care and maintenance of her house; she was also concerned with security. She gave details to each servant about what time the doors and windows were to be fastened. She was also concerned with the behaviour of her servants. Her instructions to the female 'Upper Servant' included the comments that 'when there is company the men servants dine in the kitchen and sit before and after dinner in the laundry, no men servants except those belonging to the house to be admitted into the Footman's Pantry or the Housekeeper's Room'. During the day, she stated, 'no one allowed to work upstairs'. Amongst the many instructions to the footman was the comment that he was to see that his soiled linen was given to the housekeeper every Saturday when she gave out the clean. But no clothes were to be kept in the pantry (part of his province); he must always dress upstairs. To the coachman she said, 'no servants to sit in the Saddle House.' The footman gave out the ale to the servants. He was instructed to give a pint a day for the male servants and half a pint for each of the female servants.

Anne Boulton was trying to control the behaviour of servants, both her own and those of visitors to the house. It would clearly have caused embarrassment if the footman took to changing his linen in the pantry and servants congregating in the saddle room might have been up to mischief, while too many male servants in the butler's pantry or housekeeper's room could become raucous and be overheard by the company in the dining room or drawing room.[37] It was important for employers to dictate what was required of servants with regard to their work but also to control their movements, the times that they were in certain parts of the house, and ensure their absence from areas where it was inappropriate for them to be.

If the family was often inconvenienced then servants were doubly so. Many houses had 'odd' arrangements for fitting live-in servants where they could. Farmhouses were often rambling premises with stairs and passages leading to rooms added on at different times. The work of the farm intruded in the private areas of the house, particularly the rooms used by servants. In Catherine Hutton's fictitious account of the family home, a farmhouse in Derbyshire, the servants slept in dark rooms with small windows and no ceilings, being open to the 'beams and thatch' which the 'men servants and the maid servants, [shared with] pigeons and cheese, wheat, malt and apples.'[38]

The picturesque arrangements, described by Catherine Hutton, were perhaps not entirely realistic but they give a flavour of rural methods of organizing the home. William Field's family had farmed at Rumboldswhyke in Sussex for generations and after his death in 1841 his son Alfred continued the farm.[39] When the 1841 census was made two other children were still living at the farmhouse, Ellen aged 25 and Charlotte, who was 15. The Fields needed their servants to help them with the multitude of indoor tasks associated with living on a farm; the kitchen and wash house contained an extensive array of implements for food preparation including '8 tin milk pails and a churn' for making butter. The Field men were keen sportsmen; both father and son shot game birds, and William Field prided himself on his skills at pigeon shooting.[40] So meat and game preparation were additional tasks along with cleaning the silver, washing and ironing the clothes and linen for the household, and keeping the house clean and tidy. The Fields had made the farmhouse smart despite its rambling architecture with a nicely furnished parlour and dining room. These rooms had fitted Brussels carpets, an upholstered sofa and polished mahogany and rosewood furniture. In the less important areas of the house, the service areas, regional items were still in evidence. Windsor chairs and oak and deal furniture were relegated to an upstairs passage or to the kitchen.

The distinction between the furnishing of the smart living rooms and service areas was repeated in the family and servant bedrooms. The room designated by the inventory for the servants was a sparsely furnished bedchamber with only a French bedstead, whereas the other bedrooms had four-poster or tent bedsteads, all with hangings. The servants' beds had only a flock mattress while the other beds were filled with feathers. The furniture was basic, poor quality and sometimes described as old: a deal chest for clothes and linen, an old oak table and two old chairs. If the servants listed in the 1841 census all lived in, then Emily Shepherd and Harriet Dyer, both aged 20, and Harriet Horner, just 13 years old, would have had the additional hardship of sharing a room and a bed, and had little privacy after their working day.

In wealthy homes better provision was made for servants; ideally the butler had a room next to his pantry and the cook and housekeeper also had rooms downstairs near to the kitchen. The lady's maid was more likely to be on the same floor as the family and near to her mistress, to help her dress and do her hair. Other female servants probably shared rooms at the top of the house and were segregated from the male servants who were in a separate area of the house. The truly segregated and hierarchical arrangements in larger houses were created in the mid- to later-nineteenth century. In smaller country houses or the town residences of the lesser gentry, rather more makeshift arrangements might be needed.

At the Stauntons' house in Kenilworth for example the bedrooms for servants, family and visitors were spread over the first and second floors. Leading from a vestibule, on the second floor there were three rooms designated 'servant room' along with two bedrooms called by the predominant colour in their furnishing, the Green Room and the Red Room, plus a small study.

Unlike the later-nineteenth century, when furniture was produced specifically for servants, there were no obvious indications, from the inventory, that the furniture was intrinsically different in the servants' rooms.[41] It was not made specifically for servants, nor was it predominantly regional in construction. However, the differences would have been immediately visible. All the bedrooms had bed hangings and window curtains, pieces of carpet on the floor, items of furniture made in fashionable woods, mahogany and walnut; all had a looking glass, a wardrobe or chest of drawers for storing clothes, a table or dressing table and chairs.[42] The clues are there, however, that indicate that some rooms were less comfortable, attractive and fashionable. The three rooms on the second floor that were intended for family or guests all had much longer lists of items in them, they had more substantial furniture and were more consistent in the materials. They had mahogany chest on chest, a dressing table, a dressing glass and a pillar and claw table and chair, rather than simply a chest of drawers with a small looking glass. So although one of the servant's rooms contained damask bed hangings and a mahogany chest of drawers, the rest of the furniture was oak. The walnut and mahogany furniture in the servants' rooms was probably older and had been moved there from another part of the house. Whereas the family rooms had cane seated chairs that were appropriate for a bedroom, the servants' rooms had rush seated chairs that were probably regional items.

The Red Room contained a sofa and had a small study next door. These two rooms could have been used for guests making a long stay, the study serving as a sitting room. The Green Room contained a child's chair and an easy chair also indicating extended family use or for guests. Since no bedrooms were listed on the ground floor, near to the service areas, most of the servants slept on the top floor. The exceptions were the coachman and the lady's maid. On the first floor there was just one servant's room, next to the bedchamber described as the White Room. Sally, Mrs Staunton's lady's maid, would have occupied this room.

In the early-nineteenth century, the Stauntons had three female and two male servants. Mary Welton was the housekeeper and was paid 11 guineas a year. Another member of the same family, Sarah Welton, or Sally, was paid seven guineas a year. Mary Hopper was the cook and she also received seven guineas.

Thomas Welton the butler was no doubt related to Mary and Sally. Mary was usually referred to as 'Welton' suggesting seniority, though of course Thomas earned the higher sum of 18 guineas and received extra payments for helping in the garden. The last servant was the unnamed coachman, who slept in one of the outbuildings near to the horses. The Stauntons took care of their servants but still they dominated their lives. In his account book, for example, John Staunton listed payment to a doctor for seeing Mary Welton. After he died in 1811 generous sums of money were given to Mary (£180), Sarah (£50) and Mary Hopper (£30), so that they could buy annuities; however, the wages they paid them were rather low for the period.[43] Rather casual arrangements existed for paying their wages that were due on Lady Day (25 March) but were invariably paid later in the summer and sometimes two years in arrears. John Staunton was very regular paying his bills to tradesmen: once a year, every December. When Edmund took over paying the wages, when his father became ill, he paid Mary Welton 10 guineas and then entered a further guinea in the account book with the comment that he had discovered that 'her wages are 11gns instead of 10 which she herself had forgotten'. A hint of the master/servant relationship is perhaps revealed in the provision of mourning clothes for all the servants, ensuring that they reflected credit on the family at the funeral. Margot Finn suggests that by the nineteenth century the gift of mourning clothes was seen as manipulative since it put an obligation on people to attend the funeral.[44]

The disposition of paintings in the Staunton's home offers a further insight into master/servant relationships in this household. The best public rooms on the ground floor all had prestigious paintings, which were omitted from the house sale following the death of John Staunton. The large study on the first floor and all of the bedrooms contained family portraits; again these were omitted from the sale. However, there was also a family portrait listed in each of the servant bedrooms.

Each evening Mary Welton, or Mary Hopper, would go to the second floor, proceeding from the small vestibule with its ticking eight-day clock and enter her own bedroom that was largely taken up by a four-poster bed with check hangings and an oak wardrobe. There was a fire grate and fender, and perhaps sometimes a fire was lit. Sitting on the stool at the oak pillar and claw table, she would see above her, by the low light from a candle, an oil painting, four feet eight inches by three feet ten inches, of a member of the Staunton family. A comfortable room, but surveillance continued into their private space. Although the Stauntons might have been close to their servants and took care of them, still the master/servant relationship was reinforced by the presence of the family portraits in each of the servants' bedrooms.[45]

Accommodating Visitors

Social visiting was important to all levels of middling-sort and middle-class households. The domestic environment was growing in importance, as, too, was the consumption of commodities to make the home more attractive, decorative and comfortable. So, visiting and entertaining visitors gave people the opportunity to variously display possessions and to observe other people's homes. This was not simply to show off but to demonstrate that you were part of polite society. Providing for guests was an extension of making a home for a family. The prevailing notions of domestic ideology suggested that a house should be able to accommodate both family and guests, providing them with comfort and ease. While the furnishings, food and entertainment might provide an impressive show, they should also contribute to the comfort of the home.

In the article that Catherine Hutton wrote for *La Belle Assemblé* on the tendency, in the early-nineteenth century, for some people to put fashion before home comforts, she was particularly outspoken about the poor hospitality that was provided. Writing in the first person, although describing a fictitious family, she was disgusted with her 'sister-in-law' for the changes she had made to the home of her grandparents. Matters were brought to a head when she found her bed damp.[46] Hutton implied that her sister-in-law was wholly concerned with appearances and not with the comfort of guests, any more than she had shown proper feelings concerning her husband's ancestral home.

Throughout the period, people paid extended visits. At Matthew Boulton's home, Soho House in Birmingham, he entertained the men of the Lunar Society to dinner, but in addition their families met frequently and wives and children paid each other visits lasting a few days. The dining room at Soho witnessed erudite conversation and the laboratory next door was used for their scientific experiments, but the whole house was affected when the Darwin or Wedgwood family came to stay.[47]

Family and friends expected a reasonable level of comfort and privacy. The bedchambers at the top of the Stauntons' house, referred to above, furnished in red and green damask, both provided sleeping requirements together with comfortable chairs for sitting by the fire with a book, and a table or desk for writing letters. It is this kind of room that is depicted in a pencil drawing entitled 'My Room, Normanby'. This drawing, dated 1819 but not signed, had been folded so was probably sent along with a letter to a friend by a visitor to Normanby Park. This house was built in the sixteenth century and designed by Robert Smythson although the room depicted was a fashionable, if modestly furnished sitting room for the early-nineteenth century.[48] This guest had a sitting room, as well as a bedroom, with a small desk for writing letters, comfortable seating beside a fire lit in the grate and a bell pull to summon a servant[49] (Illustration 4:2).

Serving food and drink was an essential part of entertaining guests: appropriate food and drink, served using the right kind of equipment and in a way that showed an understanding of etiquette. In the later-eighteenth century dinner was eaten in the middle of the afternoon; supper, a simpler meal, was eaten in the evening. Rosemary Sweet suggests that it was supper that was the meal for inviting guests to share.[50] The hard-working middling sort preferred to keep socializing until the evening, after their working day. But also, for women the practice of taking tea with friends was becoming a social habit. These practices continued into the nineteenth century, although by then the main meal of the day was eaten at six o'clock or later. By this time more emphasis was placed on evening dinner parties as the polite way to entertain guests.

4:2 'My Room, Normanby'. This pencil drawing of a sitting room was probably produced by a visitor to the house and sent to a friend with a letter, in 1819.

Advice books warned middle-class families, especially the lower middle classes, not to go to extremes when they entertained guests. *Cassell's Household Guide* stated that 'a great many persons aim at giving set dinners, without particularly caring for the comfort of their guests'. According to this *Guide* 'English society has been termed a pre-eminently *"dinner-giving society"'*. The main reason for discomfort, it suggested, was due when:

> a person of more slender means is liable to fall into the error of supposing that his friends do not care to dine at his table, unless he imitates the surroundings of the wealthier classes. It occurs to comparatively few persons that the chief charm of a dinner party lies in ease of manner on the part of the host and hostess, together with the arrangements of the entertainment being in accordance with the income and the natural mode of living of the entertainer.[51]

Throughout the first half of the nineteenth century, cookery books and etiquette books gave advice on giving dinner parties: how to lay out the table, what dishes to serve and instructions for servants.[52] While wealthy and fashionable society placed increasing emphasis on the evening dinner party, the less affluent middle class were unable to participate fully. (How this difficulty affected some sections of society will be explored in the next chapter.) Leaving aside the richest families who could provide for guests on a lavish scale and the lower middle class who were advised, by the Cassell *Guide*, to avoid dinner parties, what could the moderately wealthy middle class provide for their guests, to impress them but also to provide comfort and ease?

Dinner with Mrs Newland

The remainder of this chapter will consist of a reconstruction of how the Newland home in Chichester was able to entertain guests to a dinner party. The size of their house and its number of rooms, the contents of their home, their number of servants, and their position in society enabled them to participate in this way.[53]

The size and status of Mrs Newland's home and her complement of servants placed her in a similar category to the Boultons and even to the Stauntons, although all three families had different backgrounds, sources of wealth and social circles. The Newlands were professional people, who held important positions in the society of Chichester, whereas the Boultons were industrialists in Birmingham and the Stauntons were gentry in rural Warwickshire. Each family had a substantial house that was capable of entertaining on a large scale and each had three female servants and at least one male servant, at a time when male servants were an additional expense to which only the wealthier members of the middle strata of society could aspire.

Sufficient information exists about Mrs Newland's home and the members of her household from which to reconstruct the kind of dinner party that in all likelihood she gave on many occasions. An inventory of her house, Fernleigh, was made in 1851 when Mrs Newland died.[54] The house still survives in Chichester with its original layout discernable. From these sources it is possible to see how the rooms were used, where the servant areas were and what furnishings and domestic articles were available for a dinner party. Where objects were stored was recorded and how access by servants was achieved can be surmised. Mrs Newland's house had three female and one male servant. This was a similar number to that of Anne Boulton; therefore her instructions to her servants[55] provide an insight into how Mrs Newland's home would have been organized. In addition to these details some published sources will be utilized, but they will be interpreted to fit the particular circumstances of Mrs Newland's home.

Mrs Newland and her household contained all the ingredients for an elegant dinner party; she possessed plentiful china and cooking equipment, she had sufficient servants to wait at table and cook the meal. Apart from a morning room for family use she had a smart dining room and a drawing room. Both rooms could accommodate a dozen people comfortably.

The production of ceramic goods in the first half of the nineteenth century suggests the great importance placed on table layout and ritualized methods of serving food by middle-class consumers.[56] Different ceramic materials provided goods for a range of uses: blue and white under glaze ware for every day and porcelain china, or, by the early-nineteenth century, bone china, for special occasions. Tea services could be in earthenware but china, particularly with gilding, was more desirable. Dessert ware was also produced in both materials and so again allowed for different degrees of outlay. Since serving dessert was a luxury in itself the possession of any kind of dessert ware was prestigious.

In Mrs Newland's case, the quantity of china and tableware enumerated in her inventory was prodigious. The common ware, described as 'blue and white', was for everyday use by the family, and was kept in the kitchen.[57] In the passage leading from the service area to the main house was the china closet, and here the dinner ware was stored. Although the ceramic material is not specified, the dinner service allowed for a large number of people and numerous courses; it included two dozen soup plates and five dozen dinner plates.[58]

A cupboard in the breakfast room contained all the paraphernalia for breakfast, including a white and gold china tea set. The storage of these wares in the breakfast room, which would have doubled as a daytime sitting room for the ladies of the house, gave easy access by the family. But when visitors were being entertained in the drawing room the servants could access these tea wares for serving tea and coffee in the best room. Anne Boulton instructed her male servant to see that the tea tray was laid correctly, to carry it into the drawing room, and to wait on the company.

Details for conducting an elegant dinner party were fully described in books of recipes and prescriptive literature, including that ostensibly aimed at servants such as James Williams' *The Footman's Guide*, which included diagrams for table settings.[59] Such books tended to describe ideal conditions to which most people could not aspire. Anne Boulton seems to have written her instructions to servants by copying the advice given in a published source. For example she began with stock comments that did not apply to her own home, but then she warmed to her subject. The instructions became more personal and better suited her house and requirements. Her instructions to a 'Butler' and to a 'Footman' became condensed into instructions for one male indoor servant. Similarly, she gave instructions for an 'Upper Servant' who appears to fulfil the role of a housekeeper. Anne's home had a housekeeper's room, and as her instructions continue, she addresses them to a housekeeper. She also gave advice for a cook and housemaid.

In the 1841 census Mrs Newland was listed with three female servants, all in their twenties. Their rooms in the house were up in the front and back attics. In the same census Mrs Newland did not have a male servant listed; although in the inventory of her home, taken after she died in 1851, a bedroom was listed as 'Manservant's Room'. Even if there were periods when Mrs Newland was without a male servant, her nephew and brother-in-law, living on either side of her, both had a male servant, recorded in the census, one of whom she might have borrowed for parties. In London servants and extra china and plate could be hired for special occasions, but this was not so easy in a small town. According to James Ayres the hierarchy that existed amongst servants meant that housekeepers would set a table differently to a butler[60] and therefore guests may well have been able to tell at a glance the level of servicing that existed in the house.

Further evidence that Mrs Newland had a male servant was the listing of a butler's pantry to the left of the front door. This small room had a window so that the servant working there could be on hand to answer the door to guests. Here was kept the glasses, cruets, decanters and water jugs, as well as items for servants to use at table: a table brush, knife tray, tea tray and plate basket. It was the male servant's job to clean the silver plate. Anne Boulton instructed her footman to clean the plate, but he should first make sure that the window was locked and he was never to leave anything standing within its reach.[61]

Cosnett and Williams both gave very precise details for bringing food to the table and the removal of used plate and china, to ensure minimal disruption to the company, the safety of breakables and the safekeeping of expensive plate.[62] Directing the operations of the dinner party and keeping the plate safe under lock and key was ideally the province of the footman or butler. Anne Boulton covered this in less detail than the published manuals, simply saying that her man should wait at dinner and deal with the wine and port. Her 'Upper Servant' or housekeeper along with the maidservant should wait at table when there were visitors; when numbers were large, the coachman was also expected to help. The presence of a male servant to deal with the wine at the table, and male members of the household to order it and take an interest in its quality were important requisites for an elegant dinner party. Although Mrs Newland was head of her household, her son was present to undertake these 'masculine' duties.

Anne Boulton gave only instructions on cleaning the kitchen to her cook. She seems to have taken for granted the specialist knowledge that was also necessary to cope with early-nineteenth century conditions and the demands of a dinner party. The variety of dishes, the complicated preparations, and the difficulty of cooking on a range for a large number of people, all needed skill and careful planning. The number of cookery books published increased in the nineteenth century and gave recipes for plain and fancy dishes, although until Mrs Beeton's *Book of Household Management* in 1861, the instructions were not always precise.

Giving a large and elaborate dinner party required expensive ingredients, a variety of cooking implements and, in some instances, specialist equipment. The kitchen of Fernleigh was equipped with a range at a time when many people still relied on an open fire. There was a separate spit with dripping pan and ladle. So food could be boiled on hobs, roasted in front of the fire and also dry baked in the ovens. Although ranges were becoming more common in the early- to mid-nineteenth century, they were still expensive pieces of equipment and many did not have dry-baking facilities. That Mrs Newland's did is demonstrated by the presence in her kitchen of a number of utensils connected with baking: a bread pan, flour dredge, flour bin, two cake tins, two cake moulds, a paste board and rolling pin.

Apart from the versatility of her kitchen equipment, Mrs Newland's kitchen could also cope with large quantities and a variety of dishes being cooked at the same time. Using James Williams's suggested menu for a dinner party for 14 and Eliza Acton's *Modern Cookery for Private Families*, first published in 1845,[63] the number of pans for cooking and serving a meal is summarized in Table 4:1.

Table 4:1 Cooking and serving a dinner party menu

1. Menu	2. Preparation	3. In Mrs Newland's kitchen	4. Serving	5. In Mrs Newland's china closet
Soup	Large soup pan	Large iron pot	Tureen	Soup tureen
Fish	Fish kettle & drainer	Fish kettle & strainer	Large plate & cover	Large dish with cover (total of 4)
Entrées e.g. rissoles, pastries	Frying pans, saucepans, paste board, rolling pin	6 frying pans, 5 saucepans, pastry board & rolling pin	Entrée dishes	7 corner dishes for entrées
Roast joint, poultry	Spit or roasting jack	Spit with dripping pan	Large covered dishes	Large dish with cover
Tongue	Tongue pan	Tongue pan	Covered dish	Large dish with cover
Boiled joint	Stew pan & skimmer	2 stew pans, 6 iron skimmers	Covered dish	Large dish with cover
Vegetables, sauces	c. 4 saucepans	5 saucepans	Vegetable & sauce tureens	6 vegetable dishes & 4 sauce tureens
Dessert	Cake mould	2 Cake moulds	Cake basket or epergne	2 cake dishes

In Table 4:1 columns 1, 2 and 4 give a menu together with the utensils to prepare and serve the meal. The items listed in Mrs Newland's kitchen and china closet, in columns 3 and 5, show that she was able to offer such a meal to guests.

How Mrs Newland's dinner party was served would depend on which method was favoured by Chichester society at this date. The old method required several courses to be placed on the table at the beginning of the meal and the joints of meat and poultry being carved at the table. Then everything was removed, including the cloth, for the dessert to be placed on the table with some ceremony.[64] By the early-nineteenth century the new method, called à la Russe, had been gaining ground in fashionable circles, but it did not oust the old method until after the middle of the century. Cosnett and Williams both employed the old method in their table arrangements, and even in 1861 Mrs Beeton assumed that most of her readers were still following it. The new method required each course to be served separately, most of the carving was done at the sideboard and servants handed round the dishes to each guest. This method, then, required more servants, and they needed to be well trained. The lower middle-class household with just one housemaid would not have been able to cope with such elaborate arrangements. The dessert course was placed down the middle of the table, now less cluttered with savoury dishes, and remained on the table as an attractive display throughout the meal. It seems likely that in Chichester, which was a traditional although cultured society, the old style of serving persisted into the 1840s.[65]

Mrs Newland's dining room was furnished with the necessary equipment for a dinner party: a cellaret, a sideboard, and a dining table made up of a middle section and two round ends to provide a larger table when there was company. The cellaret for wine and the sideboard for plate, glasses and cutlery were both items specific to dining rooms. There were only '8 single and 2 arm chairs with cushions' but in the breakfast room were the same number, and there were 12 chairs in the drawing room, so there would have been no shortage of seating.

The dining room at Fernleigh was a rather small room, 16 feet by 10 feet, at the back of the house with French windows overlooking the extensive garden, complete with fern house. The size of the room probably dictated that furnishings were kept to a minimum: moreen curtains, which were appropriate for a dining room, and carpet, roller blinds, fender and fire irons with just two cups and saucers and a vase on the mantelpiece for decoration. This room had been wallpapered, by Samuel Peat, in 1841.[66] The simple furnishings show that this room was used exclusively for dining and that it had been deliberately furnished in a style to contrast with the richer and more ornate style of the drawing room.

Following the meal, the ladies could adjourn to the drawing room and leave the men to their wine. This room was situated at the front of the house, with two windows, and measured 17 feet 6 inches by 21 feet. The drawing room was meant to be the best sitting room, and it was designated a feminine space. Mrs Newland's conformed to this arrangement. On the floor was a carpet and hearth rug with curtains and blinds at the two windows. Rather than an open fire Mrs Newland had a stove with brass fender and fire irons, two candlesticks stood on the mantelpiece, and two screens were provided to shield the ladies' complexions. A chiffonier was placed against one wall and 12 chairs with cushions were around the room ready to be moved to where they were needed. In the centre of the room was a loo table. Comfortable seating was provided by a sofa with squab and bolsters, two ottomans and two easy chairs. Three small tables could be set beside them for the tea cups and saucers. The feminine character of the room is hinted at in the list of additional ornaments: 44 unspecified ornaments and three scent jars for containing *pot pourri* or for burning incense. When tea and coffee were served in the drawing room by the butler, the gentlemen would have joined the ladies for conversation, music or cards. Mrs Newland's drawing room contained a music stool and stand although no piano was listed.

No evidence survives that indicates that Mrs Newland gave dinner parties but there are good reasons for thinking that she did. Apart from the provisions that her home could offer for such entertainment there were personal circumstances as well as general trends that support this idea. The most likely occasion for a dinner party at Mrs Newland's home would be to entertain her extended family. The four households lived next door to each other and consisted of 11 adults in the 1840s. The professional connections of her male relatives would have given Mrs Newland ample opportunity to provide hospitality to aid business. Her son, John, who still lived at home, was aged 30 in 1851 but no occupation was given in the census. However, her brother-in-law, William Charles Newland, had been mayor of Chichester several times and was a councillor or alderman throughout the 1830s. One of his sons, Henry, who still lived at home, was a solicitor, and another, William, lived next door to Mrs Newland with his family, and was a junior partner in the Chichester Old Bank.[67] The Newland men had political as well as professional connections in Chichester and were often mentioned in the local press when public affairs were reported. Entertaining professional and political associates and their families would have required dinner parties to be held.

The Newlands were a sociable family and participated in many social and cultural events that took place in Chichester.[68] Visiting military and the nearby Goodwood Races were typical of the town's social life.[69] Some events were held in the public realm and attended exclusively by men. But private functions often paralleled the public ones. Mark Girouard quotes an example happening much earlier in 1771 when Mrs Lybbe Powys visited Ludlow for the races and recorded that 'all the gentlemen in town' dined together at an inn and 'every lady of any consideration is invited to a Mr Davis's, a gentleman of large fortune in Ludlow, and having been formerly an eminent attorney, of course acquainted with the surrounding families. She is a very clever, agreeable woman and we had everything in the highest elegance.'[70] By the early- to mid-nineteenth century, ladies had become increasingly excluded from public events, and this made private parties even more important, and more common, than in Mrs Powys's time. Mrs Newland's connections, through her late husband, her son and brother-in-law, gave her an elevated position in Chichester society and meant that she could function at the same level as that of Mrs Davis in Ludlow.[71] While the men enjoyed a grand public event Mrs Newland could have entertained a select gathering at Fernleigh with her silver displayed on her mahogany sideboard, her best china and glassware resplendent on the table, elaborate food and sufficient well-trained staff to serve her guests with aplomb.

The success of a dinner party required a smooth-running house with well-trained servants who could produce the elegant dishes and serve them graciously. But after the meal had been eaten the work of the servants was not over. While the guests enjoyed the remainder of their evening in the drawing room, the servants continued to work, clearing the table and washing up the dishes. Anne Boulton directed her housekeeper to see to the candles 'when the gentlemen leave the dining room' and the dishes were always to be washed the same evening. The female servants would have had plenty to do with the dishes and cooking utensils in the kitchen while the silver and glassware were the province of the footman in the pantry. At the end of the evening after the guests had left and the family had retired for the night the servants then had to extinguish all lamps and candles, lock away the valuables, and lock the windows and doors.

In the nineteenth century the dinner party was an important method of entertainment. While it was held in the private sphere of the home it still produced a public arena for entertaining guests who would be left in no doubt of the social standing of their hosts and their household. Every part of the house and all its occupants had their part to play in producing the image of elegance.

Conclusion

This chapter has used the idea of the extended home to explore how people who lived in the same house, whether family, lodger or servants, constituted a household and used different spaces within the home. New ideas about the use of the home evolved during the period but older houses and less wealthy households were not always able to accommodate them. Such ideas included specific functions being ascribed to certain rooms in the house. For example the parlour was expected to be a room for entertaining and relaxation. It was no longer fashionable to allow work or sleeping arrangements to take place in this public room in the house. By the early-nineteenth century the ideal was for the home to become completely divorced from the place of work. But many families did not achieve these distinct roles for either their parlour or their home more generally. So, despite changing attitudes to what was fashionable, people lived with older arrangements and made the best of them. Similarly, attitudes to privacy and propriety dictated that servants should live in separate quarters from the family but many homes had not been built with such ideas in mind. This became more problematic in the nineteenth century when middle-class families employed more servants than previously.

The home had a public role as well as a private one. Entertaining guests in the home meant that the public rooms, the dining and drawing room, needed to reflect the position of the household. Holding a dinner party was a means of communicating status still further by the choice of dishes, and their preparation, the table display and how the meal was served. All these elements required not only that the public areas were comfortably furnished but also that the service areas were correctly organized. Sufficient servants were necessary and they needed to be well trained. In Mrs Newland's home in Chichester in the 1840s all these requirements were in place. Family and guests, whether business associates, friends or local dignitaries, and servants all had their role to play. The house with its beautifully furnished public rooms and well-equipped service areas provided the perfect setting. But not all middle-class homes were this well provided for and were incomplete by comparison. This is the subject of the next chapter.

Notes

1 Reproduced in Nathaniel Lloyd (1975), *History of the English House*, London: Architectural Press, p. 248.

2 A survey of the contemporary literature on this idea can be found in Juliet Kinchin (1996), 'Interiors: Nineteenth-Century Essays on the "Masculine" and the "Feminine" Room', in Pat Kirkham (ed.), *The Gendered Object*, Manchester: Manchester University Press.

3 The organization of the internal arrangements of houses culminated in the complicated plans suggested by Robert Kerr (1864), *The Gentleman's House or How to Plan English Residences from the Parsonage to the Palace*, London: Murray. See also Jill Franklin (1981), *The Gentleman's Country House and its Plan, 1835–1914*, London: Routledge and Kegan Paul.

4 Lichfield Joint Record Office, Probate inventory.

5 Shropshire Record Office, Inventory and family papers, 6000/12161–12167.

6 Staffordshire Record Office, John Foden account book 1827–1866, MSS 3161.

7 The *OED* definition states that it was a northern, country colloquialism. Foden also used the expression 'flitting' to mean a house removal, and again this is a Scottish or northern term.

8 Even as late as 1863 Foden made a reference to papering a houseplace. This was in a rented house for which he did maintenance work. Another indication of lack of fashionable practice is that Foden mostly recorded whitening rooms and sometimes using stone or buff colours, but only on a few occasions did he use more expensive colours and oil. For a discussion of relative costs of paint see Ian C. Bristow (1996), *Architectural Colour in British Interiors 1615–1840*, New Haven and London: Yale University Press, p. xi.

9 Lichfield Joint Record Office, Inventory and will of Thomas Heeley.

10 A toy maker made small decorative objects in metal, such as buckles.

11 Public Record office, Kew, Probate inventory for James Eykyn, PROB 31/678/155.

12 For comments on Eykyn's large and diverse range of customers see Diane Collins (1993), 'Primitive or Not? Fixed-shop Retailing before the Industrial Revolution', *Journal of Regional and Local Studies*, volume 3, number 1, pp. 23–35, p. 29.

13 Birmingham City Archives, MS 897, volume II, number 143, n.d., c. 1840s.

14 Birmingham City Archives, MBP Correspondence Box 'N', number 70. See also Nancy Cox on this subject, Nancy Cox (2000), *The Complete Tradesman: a Study of Retailing 1550–1820*, Aldershot: Ashgate, pp. 135–139.

15 Emulation theory was suggested by Veblen, Thorstein (1994 first published 1899), *The Theory of the Leisure Class*, with an introduction by R. Lekachman, Harmondsworth: Penguin. The idea is continued in Harold Perkin (1968), *The Origins of Modern English Society*, London: Routledge and Kegan Paul; Ferdinand Braudel (1973), *Capitalism and Material Life 1400–1800*, London: Weidenfeld and Nicolson; Neil McKendrick, John Brewer and J.H.Plumb (1982), *The Birth of a Consumer Society*, London: Europa. But it is problematized by Grant McCracken (1990), *Culture and Consumption*, Bloomington and Indianapolis: Indiana University Press; Colin Campbell (1987), *The Romantic Ethic and the Spirit of Modern Consumerism*, Oxford: Blackwell; Lorna Weatherill (1988),

Consumer Behaviour and Material Culture in Britain, 1660–1760, London; Routledge; Lorna Weatherill (1993), 'The Meaning of Consumer Behaviour in Late-Seventeenth and Early-Eighteenth Century England', in J. Brewer and R. Porter (eds), *Consumption and the World of Goods*, London: Routledge; Daniel Miller (ed.) (1995), *Acknowledging Consumption*, London: Routledge. It is now generally thought that emulation is too simplistic a notion to explain people's motives for consumption.

[16] Birmingham City Archives, Catalogue of house sale and family papers, MS 319/1–31.

[17] Horsehair, usually dyed black, was woven to form geometric patterns and provided hard-wearing seats for chairs. It was a cheaper alternative to leather, the most desirable covering for the seats of dining chairs.

[18] This later became a feature of working-class homes; see John Burnett (1978), *A Social History of Housing 1815–1970*, Newton Abbot: David and Charles.

[19] For analysis of the separation of work and home in Birmingham see Leonore Davidoff and Catherine Hall (1992), *Family Fortunes: Men and Women of the English Middle Class 1780–1850*, London: Routledge, pp. 364–369.

[20] For analysis of present-day homemakers' relationship to storage and clutter see Jane Graves (1998), 'Clutter', *Art, Architecture and Design*, volume 5, number 2, pp. 63–68; Saulo B. Cwerne and Alan Metcalf (2003), 'Storage and Clutter: Discourses and Practices of Order in the Domestic World', *Journal of Design History*, volume 16, number 3, pp. 229–239. See also Judy Attfield (2000), *Wild Things: The Material Culture of Everyday Life*, London: Berg.

[21] Lichfield Joint Record Office, Probate inventory.

[22] Kevin Hetherington (2004), 'Secondhandness: Consumption, Disposal, and Absent Presence', *Environment and Planning D: Society and Space*, volume 22, pp. 157–173, p. 162.

[23] Hetherington (2004), 'Secondhandness', p. 159.

[24] Birmingham City Archives, Inventory 397968.

[25] This event was recorded in an account book. Birmingham City Archives, 397971.

[26] Rosemary Sweet (1999), *The English Town 1680–1840: Government, Society and Culture*, London: Longman, p. 182.

[27] It is not known how many people at any time lived as lodgers, although from the 1851 census onwards more detail was recorded of the make-up of households. Richard Lawton (ed.) (1978), *The Census and Social Structure*, London: Frank Cass.

[28] Davidoff and Hall (1992), *Family Fortunes*, p. 358.

[29] Lichfield Joint Record Office, Probate inventory and will of Elizabeth Jeffries.

[30] An inventory of Joseph Wilson's home is recorded in Henry Peat's notebook. West Sussex Record Office, Add Mss 2245. No reason was given for the inventory. Joseph Wilson was still living in Chichester in 1851, but at a different address.

[31] The 1841 census is not reliable for ages since it rounded them up. Pickriss had probably trained with Wilson for some time; the artist John Lush recorded going on a trip, in 1833, with Mr Wilson and his pupil. Diary of John Lush, West Sussex Record Office, Add Mss 19026.

[32] West Sussex Record Office, Diary of John Lush, Add Mss 19026.

[33] Christina Hardyment (Introduction) (1987), *The Housekeeping Book of Susanna Whatman 1776–1800*, London: Century in association with The National Trust, p. 41.

[34] Thomas Cosnett (1825), *The Footman's Directory and Butler's Remembrance*, London: Simpkin, Marshall and Henry Colburn.

[35] Franklin (1981), *The Gentleman's Country House*. See also Tim Meldrum (1999), 'Domestic Service, Privacy and the Eighteenth-Century Metropolitan Household', *Urban History*, volume 26, number 1, pp. 27–39.

[36] Birmingham City Archives, MS 3782/14/83/20–21.

37   See the floor plan in Illustration 1:1 on page 28.

38   Birmingham City Archives, Hutton, Beale Family Papers 106/12.

39   West Sussex Record Office, Inventory in William and Henry Peat's notebook, Add Mss 2245.

40   *Sussex Agricultural Express*, 23 December 1837, William Field took part in a pigeon shooting competition and was described as a crack shot; 23 September 1843, Alfred Field was recorded buying a game certificate.

41   See Adrian Forty on the furniture made specifically for servants in the later-19th century. Adrian Forty (1986), *Objects of Desire*, London: Thames and Hudson.

42   Christopher Gilbert suggests that the furniture in servants' bedrooms in country houses was made especially for their use, even in the 18th century. He quotes Chippendale supplying Nostell Priory with such furniture in the 1760s. This kind of furniture was larger than that made for the family and of elm, ash and painted pine; less important houses favoured oak. He also includes examples of grand furniture that was past its best and no longer fashionable finding its way into servants' rooms. Christopher Gilbert (1977), *Backstairs Furniture from Country Houses*, exhibition catalogue, Leeds: Temple Newsam.

43   See David N. Durant (1988), *Living in the Past*, London: Aurum Press.

44   Margot Finn (2000), 'Men's Things: Masculine Possessions in the Consumer Revolution', *Social History*, volume 25, number 2, pp. 133–155, p. 147.

45   Marcia Pointon suggests that portraits, especially older ones, often ended up in garrets when they were no longer valued and because of the fashion for having wallpaper by the late-18th century, although this does not seem to apply in the Stauntons' case. Marcia Pointon (1993), *Hanging the Head: Portraiture and Social Formation in Eighteenth-Century England*, Paul Mellon Centre for Studies in British Art and Yale University Press, p. 175.

46   Birmingham City Archives, Hutton Papers, 106/12.

47   See Jenny Uglow (2002), *The Lunar Men: the Friends Who Made the Future*, London: Faber and Faber.

48   The owners completely remodelled the house in the 1820s using the architect Robert Smirke. See Simon Jenkins (2003), *England's Thousand Best Houses*, Harmondsworth: Allen Lane. The indication, in this drawing, of the presence of a spinning wheel is a curious addition, perhaps with nostalgic connotations, to the furnishings of a bedroom in such a smart house.

49   In a private collection.

50   Rosemary Sweet (1999), *The English Town, 1680–1840*, London: Longman. p. 184.

51   *Cassell's Household Guide* (1870–1), volume 3, London: Cassell, Petter, and Galpin, p. 243.

52   Dinner parties are covered in detail in Mrs Isabella Beeton (1861), *The Book of Household Management*, London: Ward, Lock and Co.

53   See Illustration 3:1 on page 84.

54   West Sussex Record Office, Inventory in William and Henry Peat's notebook, Add Mss 2245.

55   Birmingham City Archives, MS 3782/14/83/20–21.

56   See Sarah Richards (1999), *Eighteenth-Century Ceramics: Products for a Civilised Society*, Manchester: Manchester University Press.

57   In the scullery were listed oddments of pottery and 'coarse ware' that would have been used for food preparation and for the servants' use.

58   Anne Boulton's pantry contained a china dinner service in blue and gold consisting of 120 soup, meat, pudding and cheese plates plus serving dishes to match; also, a blue and white ironstone dinner service, for everyday use, of almost the same quantity, a cut glass

dessert service, and a china tea and coffee service. Birmingham City Archives, MBP 286/23.

[59] James Williams (1847 4th edition), *The Footman's Guide*, London: Thomas Deane and Son. See also A Lady (1829), *The Home Book: or Young Housekeeper's Assistant*, London: Smith, Elder and Co. It gives sample menus, table arrangements and quantities for giving dinners and suppers for large numbers of guests.

[60] James Ayres (1993), 'Domestic Interiors in Britain: a Review of the Existing Literature', in David Flemming (ed.), *Social History in Museums: a Handbook for Professionals*, London: HMSO, p. 148.

[61] In the plan of Anne Boulton's home, made by Bridgen's, a Breakfast Room was placed to the right of the front door and next to the Dining Room. In the catalogue when her home was sold no Breakfast Room was listed. The Butler's Pantry followed the Dining Room items. So, perhaps this room beside the front door had a change of use at some point.

[62] Thomas Cosnett (1825), *The Footman's Directory and Butler's Remembrance*, London: Simpkin, Marshall and Henry Colburn.

[63] Eliza Acton (1860 first published in 1845), *Modern Cookery for Private Families*, London: Longman, Green, Longman and Roberts.

[64] See Mary Ellen Best's dining room with table set for the first course, reproduced in Caroline Davidson (1985), *The World of Mary Ellen Best*, London: Chatto and Windus.

[65] The Mace Club held a dinner at the Swan Inn when 50–60 gentlemen had an 'elegant dinner…after the removal of the cloth the most sumptuous dessert appeared that ever decorated a table in this city. It groaned under the wait of pines, grapes, peaches, filberts etc.' At least in public dinners then, the old method of removing the cloth for the dessert was still practised. *Sussex Agricultural Express*, 2 October 1841.

[66] West Sussex Record Office, Add Mss 2239.

[67] For background information on the Newland family see *Chronology of Chichester*, West Sussex Record Office, Add Mss 29,710.

[68] For example in 1843 a large party was held at the Anchor Hotel for a visiting dignitary and was hosted by William Charles Newland.

[69] In 1803, for example, a Race Ball and Supper were held during the Goodwood Races; tickets for which cost 15s for gentlemen and 7s 6d for ladies. *Sussex Chronicle and Chichester Advertiser*, 21 April 1803.

[70] Mark Girouard (1990), *The English Town*, New Haven and London: Yale University Press, p. 113.

[71] An indication of Mrs Newland's standing in Chichester society is revealed by a rare mention in the *Sussex Agricultural Express*, 7 October 1837. The Duchess of Richmond was reported as patroness of a Grand Bazaar to raise money for charity; the select few making up the committee included Mrs Newland.

Chapter 5

Incomplete Households

Margaret Higginson, a widow living in Bridgnorth, Shropshire, died in 1762. The probate inventory of her goods consisted of 32 items, almost every one of which was described as old, small or little.[1] A section of the inventory reads:

> a small butter tub
> an old warming pan and frying pan
> an old joyned stool
> an old chair
> an old cast mettle boiler
> an old cast mettle pot
> 8 trenchers
> an old candle box and an old tundish
> an old spinning wheel
> a very small fire grate and cheeks
> a little looking glass
> an old clock

Margaret Higginson's belongings were valued at just £9 8s 1d plus £6 for the lease on her house. The exact circumstances of her life are not known and other goods owned by her may have been dispersed before her death, either given away or sold. However, the designation of so many goods as old or small, and their low value, certainly suggests a reduced household. Her son, Richard Higginson, was set to inherit very little. Many homes were poorly furnished, but the nature of Margaret Higginson's home may have been strongly influenced by the death of her husband and a decrease in income and status.

What concerns us in this chapter are the influences of gender, on homemaking practices, produced by a household consisting of a single man or woman, or a household where the husband or wife has died. A widow or widower needed to exercise some retrenchment in household arrangements after the death of a husband or wife due to reduced income. Whether unmarried or widowed a household that consisted of a single man or woman was also more likely to show gendered preferences in household furnishings since the occupant was pleasing themselves rather than a spouse. Other households had limitations from the outset if they were headed by a single female occupant since the public role of the home could not be fully realized, certainly if their income was modest. This chapter, then, will examine the homemaking decisions that might have resulted from a woman being widowed, the gendered choices made by unmarried or widowed men, and the limitations on the public role of homes headed by a spinster or widow.

Chapter 5 deals with what I am terming 'incomplete' households since they did not contain a family and therefore, according to contemporary views, they did not constitute the ideal home. John Tosh suggests that the ideology of homemaking placed 'a high premium on the quality of relationship between family members'.[2] It was not simply the practical and economic aspects of homemaking that were affected by the makeup of the household, but according to the ideology, the moral welfare of the inhabitants of a house were affected likewise. Thus 'the bachelor returned to his lair of an evening; only the married man dwelt in a home.'[3] The examples of homemakers used in this chapter were creating homes against this backdrop of moral pressures. Financial considerations might have affected many homemaking decisions, but as the nineteenth century progressed the moral obligation to create a good home increased.

Widows and the Need to Retrench

The need to retrench was more of a concern for women since men were usually better paid, and therefore it was easier for a man to establish his own household, and widowers were slightly more likely to remarry.[4] Women who had been comfortable while a husband lived might find themselves without an income on his death; wives did not always inherit business assets when a husband died, instead they were left to a son, or to settle debts.[5] Employment opportunities for middle-rank women seem to have decreased in the later-eighteenth and nineteenth centuries. Surviving evidence, in wills and inventories, usually state what work a man did. This is less true for women. Although, as Susan Wright says of the eighteenth century, the 'lack of evidence, does not, by any means, imply lack of economic activity.'[6] But there were fewer opportunities for middle-class women in the nineteenth century since they were less inclined to accept manual work. To be comfortable, and to avoid manual work, a widow (or spinster) needed other forms of income. This might be from renting a room to a lodger, or from renting out properties, or income from an annuity. Few women were substantial landowners or had a large annuity, but even a small addition to the annual income would have made a big difference to their lives and it was a surer way of maintaining an income than depending on employment or producing and selling commodities. Although it is difficult to judge how common land ownership and annuities were, in towns like Ludlow (and Chichester and Shrewsbury) there were probably 'many women [who] must have had a substantial annual income which enabled them to survive independently.'[7]

In the example of Margaret Higginson it is not known whether the poor quality of her home furnishings was a result of her widowed status. In an early-nineteenth century example of a widow's home there are much clearer indications that this was the case. The household goods of Ann Chandler were rather meagre and she shared her home in Shrewsbury with a lodger, indicating straitened circumstances. And yet many of the items in her home would have been classed as luxuries at the time of her death in 1814. The upstairs part of the house was used by her lodger, and Ann had a kitchen and parlour downstairs, the latter doubling as a bedroom. This parlour, at the back of her house, contained many objects that the maker of the inventory ran together, rather than putting them in a neat list. This adds to the impression of a crowded room.

> Back parlour
> A tent Bedstead and Furniture, A Feather Bed Bolster and two Pillows, A Mattress, Five Blankets, A Counterpane, A pair of Sheets, One Window Curtain, One Chest of drawers (no lock), One Arm Chair and Cushion, One Night Chair and Pan, 2 Common Chairs, One Round Table, A Swing Looking Glass, One Large Looking Glass over Chimney, One Small ditto side of Bed, Two Family Pictures, One Poker Tong and Shovel, An Iron Hanger, A Pair of Bellow, One Flat Iron, One Iron Candlestick, One Tin ditto, Four China Bowls, One Tea Caddy, A Tin ditto, Three Small Basons and Six Cups and Saucers, A Pint Metal Mug, A Knife Tray, A Walking Stick with Ivory Handle, A Japan Tea Tray, A Large Chest containing Clothes and other Articles (locked), A Bible and two Prayer Books, Three Other Books[8]

Many of these items were decorative and would, under other circumstances, have been used to indicate status. They would have displayed gentility and refinement, as demonstrated by the presence of a window curtain as well as bed hangings,[9] three looking glasses, including a large one over the fireplace, and all the necessary prerequisites for the tea ceremony. Owning five books, besides a Bible, was an indication of education and culture – her own or her dead husband's.[10] The item listed that most clearly reveals that Ann Chandler had previously enjoyed a higher status was the inclusion of two family portraits. Although having portraits painted was more common than now it was still relatively unusual.[11]

Despite the fact that Ann Chandler owned goods that could have been used to indicate status, her home reveals instead her reduced circumstances. Her position may well have dated from the time of her husband's death. Owning objects that carried status was not sufficient for that status to be apparent to visitors to the house, since objects needed to be displayed to advantage, and the context was just as important as individual items. This point needs to be borne in mind when quantitative studies remove objects from their context and put them into tables of ownership.[12]

The influence of context is perhaps also a useful way of problematizing Veblenesque theories of conspicuous consumption.[13] Ownership of particular goods does not necessarily confer status on the owner. This was realized by contemporary consumers who would have been able to read an interior for status markers and interpret the context as well as individual objects within it. Ann Chandler had retained many goods that had previously indicated her status and which had given her pleasure. She had acquired her possessions over her lifetime, including inherited items. Although she could have sold some of her belongings in order to supplement her income, even if only slightly, the emotional and sentimental value of some objects outweighed their monetary value. In her little house in Shrewsbury Ann Chandler lived in just two rooms: a kitchen and a parlour that doubled as a bedchamber. The parlour was full of furniture and objects with decorative, practical and, above all perhaps, sentimental value, to make her present existence comfortable, and to remind her of her former life.

In rare cases it is possible to compare the ownership of goods before a male householder died, and later when his widow died. This is the case for John and Susannah Marrian. The Marrian family were farmers in Bobbington, Staffordshire. John died in 1761 and a probate inventory of the house was made. Nine years later Susannah died and the process was repeated.[14] While most of the household goods were the same there were a few changes that indicate Susannah's preferences, rather than a retrenchment of the household after her husband's death. Susannah had already enjoyed a parlour with table, chairs, a large map on the wall, a corner cupboard for storing glasses, a mahogany tea chest with silver tongs and tea dishes and saucers; all these items were in place in 1761 and were repeated in the inventory of 1770. It was in the kitchen that the changes occurred. From the 1761 list it is clear that this was a working farm kitchen, full of cooking implements and items for preparing and serving food to a large number of people. An open fire had various methods of roasting meat before it: an iron 'maid' with crane hooks, two spits, a dog wheel, a Dutch oven, frying pans, and chaffing dishes with basting spoons. A rack for bacon was suspended from the ceiling. A dresser with frame was against one wall and held a quantity of pewter; 12 dishes and 26 plates, plus some delftware. Food was eaten at a large table with two forms and four chairs; an oak screen protected the diners from draughts. But a few small changes had taken place between the two inventories. When John Marrian was alive 20 trenchers were present and were probably the habitual method of serving food. No trenchers were present in the kitchen when the later inventory was made. Instead the six delftware plates had increased to 12, and tea cups and saucers were present in the kitchen. These are small changes but are significant for suggesting changing methods of serving food; from a rural and rough method to a more genteel and fashionable one.[15]

Susannah made another change in the farmhouse kitchen that further indicates a feminine touch; she hung curtains from a rod at the window. Comparing the two inventories, then, suggests that rather than needing to retrench, Susannah had been able to make changes in the farmhouse to reflect her preferences. Susannah had been married previously to Richard Shepherd and her eldest son by him inherited the goods in the farmhouse that belonged to her. Margot Finn has demonstrated how many women were able to subvert and evade the law of coverture, by which a married woman's property became her husband's. One method of this was by coming to informal settlements by which a woman's property rights were protected.[16] As a widow with belongings from a previous marriage Susannah probably had a greater say in the disposition of the household goods and was therefore able to express her taste.

Masculine Decisions in Furnishing Homes

Much of the work on consumption practices in the eighteenth century has stressed the particular relationship of women to commodities.[17] In her reappraisal of men consuming, gifting and their general interest in goods, Margot Finn has suggested that men were enthusiastic consumers for the home.[18] John Tosh, however, asserts that by the mid-nineteenth century men were less involved in the commodity culture of the home due to the prevailing domestic ideology.[19] There were exceptions to this trend; Charles Dickens for example was obsessively involved in the furnishing of his homes.[20] Throughout the period people's relationships to goods and to the home were evolving. The part played by gender along with occupation, age, status and location cannot be discounted. But the further ingredient of marital status needs to be included as a probable factor governing male participation in homemaking, their interest in newer commodities, objects with expressive qualities as well as how they organized the house into the framework of a home. It is with these considerations in mind that two male homemakers are examined, with details of their possessions from the late-eighteenth and early-nineteenth centuries.

The inventory of James Wakeman Newport's home was made in 1785, although he did not die for another 40 years, by which time he was a good age.[21] James Wakeman adopted the name Newport in recognition of the source of the family's prosperity: his mother was the heiress of John Newport. Due to this inheritance the family home was an extensive one, in the tiny hamlet of Hanley William, in rural Worcestershire. James Wakeman Newport never married and devoted much of his life to his career, holding a number of commissions in the Worcestershire militia. His house had 21 rooms listed, 14 of which were bedrooms, although at least half were poorly furnished. Some bedrooms were probably intended for servants, although it seems likely that the majority of the bedrooms were unused most of the time.

Despite the obvious grandeur of this gentleman's house, its size and smart-sounding furniture, there seem to be omissions in the provision of ceramics and textiles. The china pantry contained a small quantity of imported porcelain, with enamelled decoration, including special dishes for pickles and fruit. But apart from six dessert plates no ceramic dinner plates were listed, here or in the kitchen. The only plates listed in the inventory were two dozen pewter plates plus a further 23 'old' pewter plates and five for soup. By 1785 the Staffordshire potteries were producing large quantities of earthenware, which was preferable to pewter in fashionable homes, even if porcelain were not affordable.[22]

The other aspect of Newport's house that was deficient was textile furnishings. None of the three living rooms had window curtains or carpets listed. The only window curtains were listed for the first bedroom, which generally had good-quality furnishings: carved mahogany bedsteads with 'superior yellow worsted damask hangings' and two festoon curtains to match and a 'superior Wilton carpet to fit round the bed'. These were indeed superior-quality furnishings.[23] But none of the other bedrooms had curtains. This might be explained by the bedrooms being unused, although this only emphasizes the constrained circumstances under which Newport lived.

Ceramics and textiles were the goods traditionally associated with female consumption.[24] So, it seems that James Wakeman Newport inherited a fine home, with goods that had been fashionable and of good quality in about the 1760s, but he had added little to the interiors. The omissions may have been caused by his unmarried status and his lifestyle as a military man.

A bachelor living in rather different circumstances to James Wakeman Newport was James Mullock. He was elderly when he died in 1804; he was certainly old-fashioned in his homemaking practices. The other influences were his occupation as a farmer and butcher, living in rural Shropshire, his masculine gender and bachelor marital status. All these aspects came together in his ownership of goods, their disposition in the house and the usage that is implied by the inventory of his home.[25]

The farmhouse, in Whitchurch, consisted of three main rooms on the ground floor and four bedrooms above, with cellars, a brewhouse, and stables and a 'slaughter house' arranged around a yard. An old-fashioned note is struck at the outset; the first room listed was described as a houseplace. This was an old name for a general-purpose kitchen and living room. The name had gone out of general use by this time. All the elements were present to conform with this designation: oak tables, dresser, a screen, a total of 11 chairs, most of which were described as oak and of turned construction, indicating local production, 16 pewter plates and 26 dishes, and numerous cooking implements. Rather more surprising was the presence of 43 books and a 'lot of unbound books and papers'. At this date books were still produced by a printer, with only a paper wrapper, so that they could be taken to a book binder for a more permanent cover of the owner's choice. Mr Mullock may have been a farmer and butcher living in rural Shropshire, but he was a keen reader. Unfortunately the titles were not listed.

His dining room was adequate for the purpose with an oak table and a cupboard for storage. Alcoholic consumption is indicated by the presence of one stone, two wooden and eleven glass bottles, and a silver-mounted jug with Mr Mullock's name on it. This last item was perhaps a ceramic piece with the inscription painted on. The only other ceramics in the house were also listed in this room: just five dishes and two plates. The nature of the dining room is duplicated in the parlour; masculine items were present and feminine objects are noticeably absent. The parlour had a small mahogany dining table but with only rush-bottomed chairs to go with it. Regional chairs often had woven rush seats, but not smart chairs. Mr Mullock's chairs therefore were not in keeping with the mahogany table. There were two barometers and a thermometer, which were useful objects for a farmer who needed to be mindful of the weather. The 11 plaster figures and seven prints could have provided decorative possibilities in this interior, although both were as likely to express masculine tastes as feminine; figurines and prints were often of political and sporting subjects. During his evenings, after his work on the farm was done, Mr Mullock was able to survey the furnishings of his parlour. He could sit in comfort in one of two 'smoking chairs'[26] that the room contained, with a pint of his home-brewed beer, amidst a cloud of smoke from a pipe, and with a book open beside him.

The masculine nature of Mr Mullock's home and his way of using it, continued in the rooms upstairs with numerous objects stored in inappropriate places. The first bedroom contained the usual items plus eight small cheeses, a 'butcher's pad' and some lead weights. Out on the lobby was another butcher's pad. In a closet was stored an old kitchen grate and fire guard. In Mr Mullock's own bedroom was the usual furniture, mostly in oak and which included three 'smoking chairs'. A further reference to his literary interests was also present with the item '39 no.s of the Life of Lord Clive'. The inventory maker's reference to numbers rather than volumes suggests that this book had been first published in parts. Owning this work might suggest that Mullock was a supporter of Lord Clive, who had been a big landowner in Shropshire and the Welsh border country, as well as Member of Parliament for Shrewsbury in the later-eighteenth century. However, the only biography to appear by this date was Charles Caraccioli's *The Life of Robert, Lord Clive, Baron Plassey.*[27] The first volume of this book was published in 1775, the year after Clive died, and a further three volumes appeared over a number of years. Caraccioli used the book to attack Lord Clive's controversial public and private life. Mr Mullock could well have held strong opinions about Clive's activities as a landowner in the same area that he farmed.

The fourth bedroom led off Mr Mullock's room and, apart from the bed, this room chiefly contained a large oak chest in which was stored 38 guineas, two gold rings, two mourning rings, a 'good' shilling, and six 'bad', a 'bad' sixpence, a silver stock buckle, a bad half crown, a silver tankard, a silver pint, and a silver half-pint tankard, three broken silver tablespoons, a pistol, two tablecloths, a small silver cup, a pair of money scales, and a pair of money scales 'from the kitchen'. Mullock was keeping these valuables safe, in a chest within a room that could only be accessed through his own bedroom. The impression of a careful, even perhaps miserly existence is suggested by the presence of the money scales and bad coins. Overall James Mullock had little of great value in his home. There were virtually no items that were associated with newer ideas of homemaking: ceramics, upholstered furniture, window curtains or carpets. Instead what was most in evidence were articles that had a political content, items connected with alcohol consumption and smoking, and objects connected with his butchering trade.

James Mullock was well established as a farmer and butcher in Whitchurch. He was following the family traditions in this respect[28] and owned land and rented some from neighbouring farms. He left all his estate to Thomas Hinton, a great nephew, who was a ward of John Knight of nearby Dodington until he came of age in 1812. James Mullock's home was therefore an expression of his family traditions, his occupation, his age, his bachelor status and his gender. If he had been married there would no doubt have been differences in his homemaking practices, and even if only slight these changes would have been in evidence throughout his farmhouse.

The Public Role of the Homes of Independent Women

A large number of households were headed by an independent woman, whether unmarried or widowed. Lawrence Stone has suggested that there was an increase in the number of unmarried people within the middling sort in the eighteenth century.[29] Throughout the period a significant number of women did not marry. In eighteenth-century Ludlow Wright found a quarter of all households were headed by women and about 3 per cent of all households were headed by a spinster.[30] By the mid-nineteenth century the numbers of spinsters had increased, although many of them were unable to live independently and were lodgers in other people's households.[31] The status of women limited their participation in society and, therefore, the public role of their homes. On the other hand independence often gave women the opportunity to emphasize certain aspects of homemaking that were in keeping with their lives.

The position of independent women in a provincial town is difficult to determine. Mark Girouard has suggested that they played an important role. He gives the example of Ludlow in the late-eighteenth century when ten independent women lived in the main street. Girouard claims that it was about this time that the practice for independent women to set up their own home, rather than live in the extended home, became usual in England, unlike on the continent.[32] Most of the examples to be used in this section are drawn from towns with similar conditions to Ludlow: Bridgnorth, Shrewsbury and Chichester. These towns attracted gentle- and middling-sort women to set up home due to the favourable conditions for a genteel existence.[33] One example comes from the smaller town of Cleobury Mortimer, a market town near to Ludlow that was described in 1844 as a town that had formerly been 'a place of good trade, having extensive iron works; these have disappeared'.[34] So, by the time that our example lived there in the early-nineteenth century, the town was once again largely rural with about 1500 inhabitants.

The households of independent women would have varied quite considerably, from very wealthy to the quite humble, on which level it would have been difficult to maintain gentility. *The Home Book* of 1829 gave tables for household expenses for families of different size and status.[35] Two tables dealt with independent ladies. The first included two female and one male servant, the second was for a household with just one female servant. Both households however consisted of two ladies living together. Whether this was suggested as an economic measure or because it was more respectable is unclear. The larger household had expenses of £216 18s 6d a year and the smaller came to £112 18s 6d; £150 a year was usually taken, at this time, as the minimum to sustain a middle-class household.[36]

However, in rural areas rents and servants' wages were lower; therefore genteel lifestyles could be accomplished on less money. Somewhere between the two sizes of household given in *The Home Book* was the home of the Croft sisters. Harriet and Margaret Croft lived in West Street, Chichester, a few doors away from the Peat firm of cabinetmakers. They had two female servants, Sarah Gee who was 70 years old in 1841 and Caroline James, aged 20, but no male servant. Harriet Croft was about 70 and her sister was 75 in the early 1840s.[37] Samuel Peat recorded doing a few repair jobs for them at this time.[38] In January1843 Margaret Croft died, and Samuel Peat made her coffin. Following her sister's death Harriet may have benefited from additional income, such as annuities inherited from her sister's estate. This would be one explanation for the flurry of homemaking activities that followed quickly on Margaret's death. On 7 March Peat recorded five days of papering and jobbing work for Harriet. This indicates a considerable amount of work since Peat usually only needed one or two days for papering a room. Later the same month he was back at the house in West Street, preparing the walls and repapering three bedrooms, the staircase and a living room. Each of the bedrooms was furnished with new mattresses in April. One of these rooms was the best front bedroom, so perhaps Harriet had taken possession of this room after her elder sister's demise. Harriet continued to enjoy her home for at least another eight years since she was still living in West Street in 1851.[39]

Two spinster sisters who shared a home and whose financial circumstances were closely connected were Catherine and Hannah Poyner, who lived together in Bridgnorth, Shropshire until their deaths, in quick succession, in 1765. The sisters enjoyed a comfortable income derived from the rents on properties that they owned. They had a high status within Bridgnorth. Their father had been a successful timber merchant who had been a burgess and churchwarden in the town in the early-eighteenth century, and the family had enjoyed a respectable position. But their brother John ran up debts and their goods were to be sold for the benefit of his creditors.[40] Their home consisted of a hall, parlour, kitchen, brew house, two bedchambers, a servant's room and garrets used for storage. The contents of their house in many ways reflected the opposite style of homemaking to that of James Wakeman Newport, although their lower status inevitably meant that the sisters had a smaller house with less grand furnishing schemes. The gendered slant to their home and its contents is revealed by the comparatively large quantities of ceramics and linen, including 24 pair of sheets, ten tablecloths, four dozen napkins and six dozen towels. While Newport had substantial furniture but very few ceramic items the Poyners had a long list of tea and dinner wares, but meagre furniture in their one living room.[41] They also had an extensive list of linen, although like Newport, their home had few items of textile furnishings present, but this is understandable in a middling-sort home as early as 1765.[42]

An emphasis on textile furnishings and ceramics is then to be expected when the home of the comfortably off spinster Ann Fox, of Cleobury Mortimer, is considered. She died in 1813 and left various sums of money in legacies, and £50 to buy land to fund a charity for the poor of the parish.[43] Her house had extensive gardens for vegetables and cows and pigs, with fields for pasture and hay. The outbuildings included a brew house, dairy and cheese room. Both of the last rooms were well equipped, and a large quantity of 'family' cheese was included in the sale of her household goods after her death.[44] Ann Fox had at least three servants, since the accounts kept by her nephew after her death included settling their wages for the previous year. Nancy received ten guineas, Sally six guineas and John Dallance ten guineas. Whether John Dallance was a house or outdoor servant is not clear. Miss Fox's residence, The Lea, was substantial with five bedrooms and attic rooms with two stump bedsteads for the female servants. How did Ann Fox organize her home? What was her life like, as a spinster, living in her own house, in Cleobury Mortimer, in the early-nineteenth century? The catalogue of her house contents made for a sale by auction gives a few clues.

The kitchen at The Lea was well equipped with implements for preparing and cooking food. Tea and coffee preparation was also provided for. The comfort of her servants was considered with armchairs, a small looking glass and a 'Handsome Screen' to protect them from draughts. These conveniences were however in contrast with other elements present in the kitchen. The emphasis on spits, a wind-up Jack with pulleys and weights, and toasting forks, and the lack of items for baking all suggest that there was no cooking range installed.[45] A large number of pewter plates, dishes and salvers were arranged on built-in shelves, since no dresser was mentioned. Although many households retained pewter at this date it had lost its prestige value and had been replaced by earthenware and china in more fashionable households. The final country touch in the kitchen was provided by the 'Good fowling Piece' that was listed, perhaps for the use of John Dallance to shoot birds and rabbits for the table.

After the working nature of the kitchen the living rooms at The Lea struck a more genteel note. They were described as a breakfast parlour and a dining parlour. The names alone suggest that the breakfast parlour was the daytime sitting room, or everyday room, and the dining parlour was for evening or best use. In many ways the rooms duplicate each other with table, chairs, a pier glass and Turkey carpet in each. However, the breakfast room had only a round oak tea table, whereas the dining parlour had a large round oak dining table with two additional square tables, each with two leaves, suggesting a large number of diners could have been seated. The breakfast parlour had just six mahogany chairs, while the dining parlour had 12. The dimensions of the Turkey carpets confirm that the dining parlour was the larger room.

Ceramics were stored in the house according to their quality and frequency of use. Some tea china was stored in the breakfast parlour, while the dining parlour had a further tea set of 'rich foreign China', some dessert plates and a large quantity of glassware. The earthen dinner ware was kept in a separate pantry, and included two and half dozen dinner plates.

Both the breakfast parlour and the dining parlour appear to have been furnished in an elegant manner. They were probably decorated in different ways that would have signalled different uses, especially in the textiles and wallpaper. It would have been usual for the breakfast room to be lighter in colour and less formal than the dining parlour.[46] Wallpaper was not listed of course since this was a sale of moveable goods. But neither was there any textiles listed to help determine the nature of the rooms. No window curtains were listed and no furniture appears to have been upholstered, beyond the hair seats on the chairs. No sofa was recorded for either room. Items were omitted from sales for a variety of reasons, but the lack of this fashionable item was in keeping with the other characteristics of the house, as already suggested by the kitchen. The Lea was smart but not entirely fashionable and there were clear indications of its rural location, not far from the Welsh border. Apart from household linen that she left to a cousin there was a lack of textile furnishings. Key items of furniture were made of oak rather than a more fashionable imported timber.[47] All of these traits point to a house that had not kept up with fashion, despite a comfortable income.

It is difficult to determine how the home of Ann Fox functioned in the wider context of entertaining visitors since not enough is known about the social lives of spinsters. In the case of Ann Fox her extended family were certainly safe options. She had a brother and sister; another brother had died in 1779. She was also close to her nephew since she left him most of her 'real and personal estate'. In his summary of her accounts, after her death, this nephew, John Fox, referred to her as 'My Dear Aunt Fox'. She seems to have had close friends too, leaving £50 to each of Obadiah Whitchurch's children, and £300 to Mary Stevens. Unfortunately the accounts do not indicate how these people were related to Ann Fox. She was also closely involved with the church in Cleobury Mortimer; she left £50 to buy land, and the proceeds from rent were to purchase bread to be distributed to the poor twice a year.[48] So, to some extent a sociable life can be assumed even if the possibilities of entertaining were not extensive and the household could not aspire to a fashionable gathering in the dining parlour.

A similar position in society was occupied by Miss Mayor of Meole Brace, a village on the outskirts of Shrewsbury, Shropshire. She died in 1831 and the sale of her household goods was advertised in the *Salopian Journal* where they were described as 'Genteel and nearly new'.[49] The list included some substantial pieces of mahogany furniture. The list did not mention the rooms from which the furniture came, but the auctioneer clearly began with bedroom furniture, before moving on to living room items; although where any possible division came, between a parlour, drawing room and dining room, is not obvious. This part of the list consisted of:

> handsome solid Spanish mahogany Bureau and Bookcase, Spanish Mahogany Stand Table, 4 Mahogany Chairs (hair seats), 4 imitation Rosewood Chairs (cane seats), excellent Spanish Mahogany Pembroke Table on Pillar and Claw, neat Couch stuffed with Hair and Hair Squab and Bolsters, mahogany Lady's Work Tables, Portable Writing Desk, Handsome small Spanish Mahogany Bookcase (glazed doors)

While this list contained good-quality items there were some omissions. Although the newspaper advertisement would not have listed the entire household, auctioneers always listed the best goods that a house had to offer potential buyers. Therefore the lack of certain items might indicate a reduced household. Only eight chairs were listed: just four mahogany and four imitation rosewood. The different timber indicates that they were used in two rooms. Advice books at this period dictated that mahogany was the ideal wood for dining rooms and rosewood should be used in drawing rooms.[50] But having only four chairs in each room suggests a small household that did not attempt entertaining many guests. This point is reinforced by the omission of any table that was described as a dining table; neither the stand table nor pembroke table would have been adequate for seating a large number of people to dinner. The list made no mention of the other essential items for a smart dining room, a cellaret and sideboard. So, although Miss Mayor may

have had a comfortable home, with numerous items of smart furniture, she probably did not have a separate dining room, and did not have the necessary equipment to give a dinner party.

As we have seen in the previous chapter, by 1831 giving dinner parties was a growing form of social function and part of the public role of the home. The homes of Hannah and Catherine Poyner, Miss Fox and Miss Mayor almost span the period. In the earlier years many homes of independent women seem to have placed an emphasis on ceramics and linen textiles, as in the case of the Poyner sisters and Ann Fox, and no doubt these objects played an important role in the lives of their owners. However, the homes that have been examined were not especially fashionable and certainly seem to have lacked the all-important textile furnishings and upholstered items that became an increasingly significant part of interiors by the later-eighteenth century. The limitations of how these homes might have sustained a public role are also hinted at in the lack of certain items, all connected with the furnishings of dining rooms.

The Homes of Six Independent Women in Chichester

While the sources for the three homes examined above only allow speculation on the point of how independent women could participate in giving dinner parties, more can be achieved for a group of women living in Chichester. Whilst still using inventoried lists of household contents the uniform method employed by the Peat family allow detailed reconstructions to be made of a few homes in Chichester in the 1840s.[51]

Inventories were not written by the individuals themselves, but were made often after their death, usually for legal reasons. Therefore the individual was not involved in describing their home's contents. The representation of the home was made by another person.[52] When Lorna Weatherill compared male and female ownership of goods for the earlier period of the late-seventeenth century and early-eighteenth century, she discovered no significant difference in most geographical areas, and for most of the goods that she looked for, leading her to conclude that there was no evidence of a 'separate female material culture'.[53] However, the instance of individual items in someone's home does not tell us how the items contributed to the overall organization of the home, or the meaning they had for their owners. Maxine Berg's study of wills made by women in the later-eighteenth century suggests that although ownership of goods may have been similar, women invested goods with rather different symbolic values to men.[54] Together with other supporting evidence, the few inventories of independent women to be considered here have been closely scrutinized to ascertain how these homes were viewed by the maker of the inventory, and how the individual goods may have contributed to the material culture of these women's lives.

Among the 20 inventories that Henry and Richard Peat made during a 20-year period were seven for independent women, all living in this small cathedral town at the same time and who were probably acquainted with one another. The six to be studied here are Marie Ann Drinkwater, Elizabeth Stamper, Mary Fisher,

Mary Ann Livingston, Celia Parker and Caroline Smelt. The seventh was Mrs Newland whose home was examined extensively in Chapter 4. Her home is used here to contextualize the other six women's homes.

Trade directory entries for the period reveal that all these six women were listed in the 'Nobility, Gentry and Clergy' list; a clear indication of their relatively high social status, since the list always consisted of less than a hundred names at a time when Chichester's population was around 9000. The trade directory entries also show that all these women lived in the better streets in Chichester, and of course their presence in the list indicates that they were heads of households. What is known of these women's circumstances can be summarized before speculating on how these homes might have sustained a public role.

Marie Ann Drinkwater lived at 45 East Street (Illustration 5:1) and would therefore have been very familiar with the street scene painted by Joseph Francis Gilbert, described in the opening section of Chapter 1. She was 85 years old when she died in 1841. The Drinkwaters had been a prominent family in Chichester in the eighteenth century; her father had been a merchant and they had owned large amounts of land. Miss Drinkwater was one of four daughters. Her sister Mary had married John Drew and they lived in his house close to the cathedral. John Drew was a wealthy and prominent figure in Chichester, an alderman and a partner in one of the banks.[55] Miss Drinkwater's will stipulated that she was to be buried in her family's vault in the cathedral. She therefore enjoyed an elevated position in Chichester society and her will gave details of her investments, from which it can be estimated that she had a comfortable annual income of about £200. Miss Drinkwater had three servants: a housekeeper, Grace Tuffin, aged 65, Barbara Cobby and Caroline Stanley, both aged 20. In her will she left Grace Tuffin all her clothes and £100.[56]

Elizabeth Stamper either came from, or had married into, a family with a wealthy and illustrious background in Chichester. The Stampers had been successful merchants and aldermen in the eighteenth century. She lived in West Street until her death in 1844.

Little is known about Miss Mary Fisher, who died before the 1841 census, and her exact address was not given. Apart from her inclusion in the trade directory list she was also recorded owning land in Bognor, West Sussex, which she sold in 1824.[57] Both of these points give her a modest but securely middle-class status.

When Mary Ann Livingston died in 1843, aged 47, she lived in a street named Little London. This consisted mostly of small houses although some, including hers, was three storeyed. Although the trade directories refer to her as Mrs Livingston this was almost certainly a courtesy title.[58] She had only one servant listed in the 1841 census, Martha Deadman, aged 15, but the other visitor or occupant was Ann West, aged 20 and described as 'Independent'. So perhaps she lived as a companion or lodger in Miss Livingston's home.

Trade directories in 1839 and 1845 gave Miss Caroline Smelt's address as North Street, another of Chichester's main streets and the same one lived in by the Peat cabinetmakers and the Newland family. John Smelt, Caroline's brother, may have lived with her, for a few years at least. Caroline was not at home when the census was made in 1841, but John was recorded in the house, between Mrs

5:1 The home of Miss Drinkwater in Chichester. Her drawing room was on the first floor.

Newland and her sister-in-law, Miss Sarah Newland. John Smelt's age was given as 60, and Caroline was a few years younger.[59] She died in 1847. The servants for the house were Anna Palmer, aged 45 and Caroline King, aged 15.

Not much is known of the remaining woman; Celia Parker died between 1848 and 1850. She lived in Priory Street, which consisted mostly of small houses. She was 60 in 1841, as was her one servant, Elizabeth Knight.

All these six women had substantial houses with extensive home furnishings. They probably all had live-in servants. But how did their gender and marital status affect their social position, and to what extent could their homes have a public role for entertaining? This question will be addressed by considering the use of space within the house: the furnishing of public rooms, the quantity and storage of objects involved in providing food and serving it to guests.

Of the six only Miss Drinkwater's home had a room described as a dining room. The rooms used by the other women for dining were listed as front parlours, or in one case, a back parlour.[60] It seems unlikely that they could not afford dining tables, or that their homes were too small to justify setting a room aside for this purpose, since all the women had numerous items of fashionable furniture, including dining tables in two homes, and all of them had at least two living rooms.

The nature of these rooms was sufficiently unlike a dining room for the Peats to use another name. This must have been due to the style of decoration and the type of furnishings being different in some way to what was usually expected of dining rooms at this period. In only one case is there sufficient evidence to test this; Mary Anne Livingston had rather different furnishing schemes in her two public rooms. The drawing room had printed cotton curtains and Venetian carpeting.[61] These would be in keeping with the ornamentation expected of a drawing room. Whereas her front parlour had woollen curtains and Brussels carpeting,[62] this seems to indicate a room with the 'masculine' style of a dining room. Although these two schemes suggest that the front parlour was a dining room Richard Peat did not describe it as such. Similarly, all the women had one room furnished with mahogany furniture. This was the same room that they appear to have dined in, and this furniture would have given the room the formal nature of a dining room. If these rooms had been a breakfast or morning room then it would have been more usual to furnish them with light furniture in unpolished wood.[63] This kind of room would have been used primarily during the daytime and was not considered a public room.

The real difference seems to be the inclusion of items that do not belong in a dining room. This tendency is demonstrated, in Table 5:1, by comparing the list of items in Elizabeth Stamper's front parlour, which was her living room that most closely suggested a dining room, with the appropriately furnished dining room in Mrs Newland's house. Whereas Mrs Newland had the specialist items of furniture and nothing else, Elizabeth Stamper also had comfortable seating and tables that suggest other uses of the room, besides eating. This was also true of all the women who did not have a dining room listed.

As we have seen, Mrs Newland had everything that was required for a formal dinner party. It is, therefore, useful to compare her furnishings and equipment with the other six women. Miss Drinkwater had an extending mahogany dining table, seven chairs, several side tables and a sideboard. Elizabeth Stamper and Mary Fisher both had dining tables and eight chairs. Mary Anne Livingston and Celia Parker had loo tables and eight chairs. Only Caroline Smelt was deficient with only a pembroke table and four chairs.

All the women, except Mary Fisher and Caroline Smelt, had cooking ranges listed in their kitchens, which would have greatly increased the variety and sophistication of dishes that could be cooked. All of them had numerous cooking pots and pans listed, including specialist items such as fish kettles. The one exception was Caroline Smelt.

Table 5:1 The contents of Elizabeth Stamper's front parlour and Mrs Newland's dining room as recorded by the Peat firm

Elizabeth Stamper's Front Parlour	Mrs Newland's Dining Room
Dining table & two round ends	8 single & 2 arm chairs with cushions
Pair of card tables	Cellaret
8 mahogany chairs	Sideboard
Easy chair & cushion	Set of dining tables with 2 round ends & middle table
Chaise longue	Fender, poker & tongs
Stove, fender & fire irons	Carpet & hearth rug
Work table	Moreen window curtains
Pier glass	Copper coal scuttle
Chimney glass	Roller blinds
2 chimney ornaments	Bell pulls
Carpet to plan of room	2 cups & saucers & vase
Druggett and rug	
Pole fire screen	
Footstool	
Curtain & roller blind	

All the women had extensive lists of dinner and tea ware that far exceeded what was required for such small households. Dinner ware was usually described as 'blue and white' and therefore would have been earthenware. Tea ware was sometimes described as china, which at this period usually denoted porcelain or bone china. Once again Caroline Smelt is the exception; however she did have a silver tea pot, coffee pot, cream jugs and cutlery listed.

It is clear from this summary of the cooking and serving items in the inventories that five and possibly all six of these women had the necessary equipment for entertaining. But would they have given dinner parties or provided another kind of repast for guests? The way that these rooms were used when visitors were present is hinted at in the inventories. In particular the storage of objects provides a clue. Miss Drinkwater, along with Mrs Newland, did not store objects in her dining room, the principal room for serving food to guests. Miss Drinkwater and Mrs Newland gave their servants easier access to these objects and therefore they could rely more on their servants to deal with serving food. They also had more servants than the other women. This also indicates that the objects kept by the other women, in their front parlours and drawing rooms, were considered 'best' china and cutlery and therefore not used very often. In each case a small quantity of these items were kept in the kitchen, for everyday use.

To summarize the points arising from the six inventories, only Miss Drinkwater had a dining room. The other five women had a living room that provided most of the necessary ingredients for a dining room, but these rooms were sufficiently different for Henry and Richard Peat to describe them as parlours. These five women had fewer servants for serving an elaborate meal, when compared to Miss Drinkwater and Mrs Newland. They all had quantities of dining objects, including specialist items, that indicate participation in entertaining but their storage in five of the homes suggests less formal use and/or less frequent use.

It seems therefore that these women were unlikely to have entertained guests to a formal dinner. It is far more likely that their homes welcomed visitors to tea and biscuits or cake, or perhaps supper. There are a number of reasons for supposing this. Serving tea and supper was easier because they were less formal and required fewer servants, since the hostess and guests participated in handing round tea cups and plates. Baking cakes was considered a genteel activity that the hostess could engage in. Catherine Hutton recorded many of her favourite recipes including one for tea cakes. The recipe required 'twelve ounces of flour, dry and warm; a little nutmeg and lemon peel, half a pound of sugar. Twelve eggs well beaten; six ounces of butter melted with one or two spoonfuls of cream. Make it into a paste; work it well, roll it thin; cut into small cakes.'[64]

Hosting a dinner party was far more complicated than a tea party, and required trained servants to wait at table. Female hosts and female servants were less knowledgeable about serving wine, which was considered a male province. Tea and supper would also be served in the drawing room not the dining room. James Williams, in *The Footman's Guide*, observed that supper parties usually followed tea parties, rather than dinner parties, since dinner was served late. The food he suggested consisted generally of cold dishes, and therefore would have been less trouble to serve.[65] He directed that the 'noise of moving tables, rattling knives and forks and the jingling of glasses' should be kept to a minimum. This problem occurred because a servant would bring in the refreshments on a tray, and place it on a table, where the company were gathered. Training a servant to be able to do this quietly and efficiently was clearly an important requirement for the evening to go smoothly. Anne Boulton, in her directions to her servants, stipulated that it was her footman's job to set out the tray things and to bring in the tea or supper tray, thereby ensuring that it was done satisfactorily.[66] But none of the independent women looked at in this section, who were of more modest means than Anne Boulton, had a male servant.

It was possible for some independent women to use their homes for formal entertaining, as was the case for Anne Boulton. A higher level of income and more numerous servants, including at least one male servant, were required, but also the appropriate social sphere and an extended family. The widow Mrs Newland had all the practical and economic necessities for giving a dinner party, but she also had a grown-up son living at home, and she had influential male relatives living nearby. Therefore perhaps, to some extent, it was not so much her higher status as a widow (rather than a spinster) as her position in this extended family that allowed her to participate in society in a fuller way to many other independent women. If this were the case it would explain the presence of a dining room in the home created by the spinster Miss Drinkwater, who had important male relatives in Chichester. So perhaps she had led a socially active life, and entertained at home, particularly when she was younger.

A rather negative image of the lives of spinsters and widows was often portrayed in novels from the period. The expectation that they would lead a quiet life, out of the social and public realm, was implied in Jane Austen's *Sense and Sensibility.* When the widowed Mrs Dashwood and her three daughters were discussed by her son, John Dashwood and his wife, the latter exclaimed: 'Altogether they will have five hundred a-year amongst them, and what on earth can four women want for more than that? They will live so cheap! Their housekeeping will be nothing at all. They will have no carriage, no horses, and hardly any servants; they will keep no company, and can have no expenses of any kind!'[67]

'No company' clearly indicates that she expected them to lead a quiet life. The link between a widow's lifestyle and her material goods was then reinforced, when the elder Mrs Dashwood's china was referred to: 'the set of breakfast china is twice as handsome as what belongs to this house. A great deal too handsome, in my opinion, for any place *they* can ever afford to live in.'

About 50 years later, in *Cranford*, Elizabeth Gaskell deliberately portrayed an almost exclusively female society and in doing so presented a very positive view of the socializing that took place between independent women. Her more positive reading of the lives of independent women in the early- to mid-nineteenth century is complemented by recent recognition of the radical line taken by Elizabeth Gaskell in this novel, although she softens it with humour.[68] Although Gaskell is looking back with nostalgia for the quiet life of a country town, she is also presenting a relatively modern point of view. Gaskell held positive views on the single state for women that were expressed in her correspondence.[69] Her views were part of a wider campaign affecting the position of women in society. In the 1830s a campaign to reform the marriage contract resulted in numerous articles being published in the Unitarian journal, *The Repository.*[70] As Elizabeth Gaskell was a Unitarian she would have been familiar with these views, and they found their way into her fiction. Gaskell celebrated the independent state of the ladies of Cranford in subtle ways. She suggests that they avoided giving dinner parties; the one occasion when Miss Matty had to entertain a male relative in this way illustrated the problems involved, mainly due to the lack of trained servants. But still Elizabeth Gaskell suggested that a strong network of socializing existed nonetheless. The ladies met frequently at each other's houses for tea and supper parties, often with card games being played.

The Chichester ladies were quite probably also sociable and met for tea and supper parties. Cards and music could have been provided as entertainment. All six women had card tables, described variously as square mahogany card tables, or as mahogany loo tables. The latter were circular and often placed in the centre of a room for playing this popular card game, as well as for other purposes. It was in Celia Parker's home that music was most likely to have been heard; she had a square piano with a music stool in her drawing room. All the women also had work tables listed. These were small tables that had a drawer or fabric bag suspended, for storing sewing requisites. So, sewing parties could also have taken place.

When considering the social possibilities of the homes of independent women the context of time and place must also be considered. As dinner parties became increasingly important in the nineteenth century and the ritual increased with the adoption, around the 1860s, of the à la Russe method, which required more servants, so people in less illustrious positions were disadvantaged. No doubt the growth of urbanization and suburbanization in the nineteenth century would also have greatly affected social groupings. For such women to have a social life depended on being part of a network of women in a similar position. The circumstances prevailing in a genteel town like Chichester were dying out, although many country towns, particularly in the south, did not change dramatically. It is possible, therefore, that the social position of independent women became more marginalized as the century progressed, and that they could not enjoy to the same extent the socializing that was possible and that these independent women of Chichester were able to enjoy in the 1830s and 1840s.

Conclusion

From the examples of homemakers and their homes looked at in this chapter it seems clear that marital status and gender did affect homemaking practices. For women especially the death of a spouse could mean retrenchment. But with the single state could also come independence that allowed women to match consumption for the home and its organization to their own individual taste. The expression of taste could take subtle forms but the clues provided by inventory evidence point to the different ways that people lived in and used their homes. A positive slant on the lives of six women in Chichester has been prompted by Elizabeth Gaskell's portrayal of women in a similar position in the village of Cranford. Gaskell was aware of the difficulties faced by women but also of the advantages to being independent, providing sufficient income was available.

In all the examples of homes drawn on in Chapters 1–5 the evidence of homemaking practice was fragmentary. Other unknown factors would also have played a part. But this is always the case with historical enquiry. The purpose of these chapters has been to interpret the evidence that does exist by placing it into context of time and place, and to take into account the influences of status and gender, in order to reconstruct narratives about the homemaking strategies of individuals. Whilst they mostly followed trends of the period they can also be seen to have inhabited unique homes that reflected the particular circumstances of their lives.

Notes

1   Lichfield Joint Record Office, Probate inventory.
2   John Tosh (1999), *A Man's Place: Masculinity and the Middle-Class Home in Victorian Britain*, New Haven and London: Yale University Press, p. 27.
3   Tosh (1999), *A Man's Place*, p. 29.
4   S.J. Wright's research on Ludlow found that more women than men became lodgers and concluded this was because men were better placed to found or retain a household. S.J. Wright (1990), 'Sojourners and Lodgers in a Provincial Town: the Evidence from Eighteenth-Century Ludlow', *Urban History*, volume 17, pp. 14–35; Barbara J. Todd (1996), 'The Remarrying Widow: a Stereotype Reconsidered', in Mary Prior (ed.), *Women in English Society 1500–1800*, London: Routledge.
5   Susan Wright (1989), '"Holding up Half the Sky": Women and Their Occupations in Eighteenth-Century Ludlow', *Midland History*, volume XIV, pp. 53–74, p. 54, p. 62.
6   Wright (1989), 'Holding up Half the Sky', p. 54. She shows evidence of women engaged in all manner of work throughout the eighteenth century in Ludlow.
7   Wright, (1989), 'Holding up Half the Sky', p. 63.
8   Lichfield Joint Record Office, Probate inventory.
9   Susan Prendergast Schoelwer (1979), 'Form, Function and Meaning in the Use of Fabric Furnishings: a Philadelphia Case Study, 1700–1775', *Winterthur Portfolio*, volume 4, number 1, pp. 25–40.
10 Ann Chandler had been unable to sign her name on her will; perhaps she had been too ill, although Lorna Weatherill suggests that it was not uncommon for uneducated women to learn to read but not to write. Lorna Weatherill (1986), 'A Possession of One's Own: Women and Consumer Behaviour in England, 1660–1740', *Journal of British Studies*, volume 25, pp. 131–156, p. 142.
11 Marcia Pointon has suggested that family portraits were the item 'least often disposed of' when families needed to retrench. Marcia Pointon (1993), *Hanging the Head: Portraiture and Social Formation in Eighteenth-Century England*, New York: Paul Mellon Centre for Studies in British Art and Yale University Press, p. 14.
12 Margaret Ponsonby (2003), 'Ideals, Reality and Meaning: Homemaking in England in the First Half of the Nineteenth Century', *Journal of Design History*, volume 16, number 3, pp. 201–214.
13 Thorstein Veblen (1994 first published 1899), *The Theory of the Leisure Class*, with an introduction by R. Lekachman, Harmondsworth: Penguin.
14 Lichfield Joint Record Office, Probate inventories.
15 When Catherine Hutton wrote a nostalgic account of life in a farmhouse she described how the farmer resisted the use of ceramics for eating his meals and instead continued to use a trencher. Birmingham Archives, Hutton Beale Papers 106/12.
16 The inheritance of goods owned by a woman in an earlier marriage was commented on in Chapter 3. Finn quotes the work of Amy Louise Erickson who found that 10 per cent of non-elite women protected their property rights in this manner. Margot Finn (1996), 'Women, Consumption and Coverture in England, c. 1760–1860', *Historical Journal*, 39, pp. 703–722, p. 706.
17 Neil McKendrick (1974), 'Home Demand and Economic Growth: a New View of the Role of Women and Children in the Industrial Revolution', in Neil McKendrick (ed.), *Historical Perspectives: Studies in English Thought and Society in Honour of J.H. Plumb*, Cambridge: Cambridge University Press; Beverly Lemire (1991), *Fashion's Favourite: The Cotton Trade and the Consumer in Britain, 1660–1800*, Oxford: Oxford

University Press; Maxine Berg (1996), 'Women's Consumption and the Industrial Classes of Eighteenth-Century England', *Journal of Social History*, volume 30, number 2, pp. 415–434; Marcia Pointon (1997), *Strategies for Showing: Women, Possession, and Representation in English Visual Culture 1665–1800*, London: Oxford University Press; Elizabeth Kowaleski-Wallace (1997), *Consuming Subjects: Women, Shopping and Business in the Eighteenth Century*, New York: Columbia University Press.

[18] Margot Finn (2000), 'Men's Things: Masculine Possession in the Consumer Revolution', *Social History*, volume 25, number 2, pp. 133–155.

[19] Tosh (1999), *A Man's Place*.

[20] Madeline House and Graham Storey (eds) (1965), *The Letters of Charles Dickens*, Oxford: Clarendon Press.

[21] Birmingham Archives, MSS 394886 for a transcription and notes see Malcolm Wanklyn (ed.) (1998), *Inventories of Worcestershire Landed Gentry 1537–1786*, Worcestershire Historical Society New Series, volume 16, Worcester: Worcestershire Historical Society.

[22] Adrian Forty (1987), *Objects of Desire: Design and Society 1750–1980*, London: Thames and Hudson.

[23] Mary Schoeser and Celia Rufey (1989), *English and American Textiles: 1790 to the Present*, New York: Thames and Hudson.

[24] Kowaleski-Wallace (1997), *Consuming Subjects*.

[25] Shropshire Record Office, Inventory and family papers, 6000/12161–12167.

[26] Smoking chairs were the name given to certain regional chairs, of the Windsor type, with a back rail that was curved to fit the back of the sitter snugly.

[27] Charles Caraccioli (1775), *The Life of Robert, Lord Clive, Baron Plassey*, London: T. Bell.

[28] Shropshire Record Office, 12165 contains a 1720 reference to Thomas Mullock of Whitchurch, a butcher.

[29] Lawrence Stone (1979), *The Family, Sex and Marriage in England 1500–1800*, Harmondsworth: Penguin, p. 243.

[30] Wright (1989), 'Holding Up Half the Sky', pp. 71–72. Population in Ludlow was 3000 in the 1750s and 4150 in 1811. Wright (1989), p. 53.

[31] The 1851 census statistics show that out of every 100 women over 20 years of age, 12 were widows and 30 were spinsters. Quoted in Martha Vicinus (ed.) (1972), *Suffer and Be Still: Women in the Victorian Age*, London: Methuen, p. 57.

[32] Mark Girouard (1990), *The English Town*, New Haven and London: Yale University Press, p. 103.

[33] Girouard (1990), *The English Town*, p. 113.

[34] *Directory of Shropshire* (1844), Manchester: Pigot and Slater.

[35] A Lady (1829), *The Home Book: or Young Housekeeper's Assistant*, London: Smith, Elder and Co., pp. 169–170.

[36] See John Burnett (1978), *A Social History of Housing 1815–1980*, Newton Abbot: David and Charles, p. 96.

[37] 1841 census.

[38] West Sussex Record Office, Samuel Peat account book, Add Mss 2239.

[39] Although the census again recorded her age as 70.

[40] Lichfield Joint Record Office, Probate inventory. Family details for the Poyners can be found at Shropshire Record Office, St Leonard, Bridgnorth, parish records.

41 Lorna Weatherill's analysis of the contents of inventories, between 1660 and 1740, suggested that fewer tables were found in the homes of independent women compared with the homes with a male head. Further research on the reasons for this is needed. Weatherill (1986), 'A Possession', p. 142.

42 For a discussion on the order of acquisition of textiles in the home see Schoelwer (1979), 'Form, Function'. For comments on women and the ownership of linen see Berg (1996), 'Women's Consumption'.

43 Shropshire Record Office, Extracts from Miss Fox's will, 6000/15317.

44 Shropshire Record Office, Auctioneer's catalogue, 6000/15309.

45 This situation continued well into the 19ᵗʰ century for many middle-rank homes. For example, the Carlyles in fashionable Cheyne Walk in London had only an open fire for cooking. Burnett (1978), *A Social History*, p. 96.

46 Juliet Kinchin (1996), 'Interiors: Nineteenth-Century Essays on the "Masculine" and the "Feminine" Room', in Pat Kirkham (ed.), *The Gendered Object*, Manchester: Manchester University Press.

47 The latter may be explained by oak being readily available for local production of furniture.

48 Family papers record that her brother had also left a legacy on his death, in 1779, to provide £50 to teach the poor children of the parish to read. Shropshire Record Office, 6000/15298.

49 *Salopian Journal*, 20 December 1831.

50 For example see J.C. Loudon (1833), *Encyclopaedia of Cottage, Farm and Villa Architecture*, London: Longman, Orme, Brown, Green and Longman.

51 West Sussex Record Office, Henry and William Peat notebook, Add Mss 2245.

52 Marcia Pointon has made the point that 'history often works on the basis of an assumption that description is access, whereas description is, of course, representation.' Marcia Pointon (1997), *Strategies for Showing*, p. 9.

53 Weatherill (1986), 'A Possession', p. 132.

54 Berg (1996), 'Women's Consumption', p. 421.

55 West Sussex Record Office, Family papers, Add Mss 8454, and 'Chichester Papers', volume 5, p. 15.

56 West Sussex Record Office, Miss Drinkwater's will, Add Mss 11,128.

57 West Sussex Record Office, Family papers, Add Mss 16,607.

58 Mary Ann Livingston had work done by Samuel Peat who always referred to her as Miss in his account book. West Sussex Record Office, Add Mss 2239.

59 The International Genealogical Index (IGI) records Carline Smelt christened in 1781 and John Smelt, her brother, christened in 1775.

60 Setting a room aside specifically for dining had become normal by the later-eighteenth century, at least in wealthier homes. Such a room was often referred to as a dining parlour. However by the 1840s the expectations of homemakers had grown to encompass a room with a particular style of furnishings through which the function could be expressed. See Kinchin (1996), 'Interiors'.

61 This was a smooth woven fabric, probably in bright colours and either striped or in a zigzag pattern.

62 This was a tufted carpet in traditional patterns and sombre colours.

63 See Mary Ellen Best's painting room which had all the characteristics of a breakfast room, reproduced in Caroline Davidson (1985), *The World of Mary Ellen Best*, London: Chatto and Windus.

64   Quoted in Audrey Duggan (2000), *A Lady of Letters: Catherine Hutton 1757–1846*, Studley: Brewin Books, p. 151. The recipe was first published in Catherine Hutton Beale (ed.) (1891), *Reminiscences of a Gentlewoman of the Last Century: Letters of Catherine Hutton*, Birmingham: Cornish Brothers.

65   James Williams (1847 4th edition), *The Footman's Guide*, London: Thomas Dean & Son, p. 78.

66   Birmingham City Archives, MS 3782/14/83/20–21.

67   Jane Austen (1994 originally published in 1811), *Sense and Sensibility*, Harmondsworth: Penguin, pp. 10–11.

68   Compare, for example, the introduction to a 1976 edition of the novel which describes the women's lives as 'sterile' with the 1992 reappraisal of Elizabeth Gaskell's novels that sees the single state of the Cranford women as 'empowering'. P. Keating (1976) Introduction to Elizabeth Gaskell, *Cranford*, Harmondsworth: Penguin; H.M. Schor (1992), *Scheherezade in the Marketplace: Elizabeth Gaskell and the Victorian Novel*, New York and Oxford: Oxford University Press.

69   J.A.V. Chapple (1980), *Elizabeth Gaskell: A Portrait in Letters*, Manchester: Manchester University Press.

70   J. Perkin (1989), *Women and Marriage in Nineteenth Century England*, London: Routledge.

PART II

The previous chapters aimed to establish what the experience of homemaking was like for individual homemakers: the particular influences that determined their consumption practices for the home, how the space within the home was used, and the public role that different homes were able to sustain. Various influences were considered. One was living in a provincial town or rural location where the desire for a fashionable home was tempered by the constraints of provincial living. Another was the desire for the home to be a permanent and secure place and how this led to various strategies to maintain the general fabric of material goods, and to safeguard objects of particular significance to the family and to individuals. The home was viewed as a whole with public and private areas but also cupboards and attics with the objects that had been stored for later use or simply for sentimental reasons. Tensions existed due to an increasing desire for a private space for family life, away from the intrusion of work and servants, contrasting with economic necessities and older houses not designed for such segregation. Finally, the influence of gender on homemaking was considered and whether accommodating a public role within the home was affected during the period if the householder was a single woman. All of these influences combined to produce unique homes that reflected the particular circumstances of individual homemakers. While they might overall follow general trends, homes in the past were a product of individual lived experience.

In Part II Chapter 6 leads on from the issues raised in Part I. It explores whether the individuality of homes and how they functioned is conveyed to visitors of historic houses. Do such houses reflect the lived experience of their occupants? Do they represent individual homes and the idiosyncratic choices made by real homemakers or are they generic room settings of a particular period? Or in other cases do they merely present a collection of antiques? Do they show how people inhabited those interiors or have they been tidied up physically, socially and aesthetically? To answer these questions the history of houses being open to the public is briefly outlined and the different methods that have been employed are considered, since this background has shaped the physical elements of historic houses and how they are presented to visitors. While the buildings and objects survive from the past into the present the stories that they tell are a product of the method of interpretation adopted. Finally, the stories that emanate from historic houses are explored through a number of examples that display a variety of interpretation techniques.

Chapter 6

Representations of Home

> Every disposition of the ground was good; and she looked on the whole scene, the river, the trees scattered on its banks, and the winding of the valley, as far as she could trace it, with delight. As they passed into other rooms, these objects were taking different positions; but from every window there were beauties to be seen. The rooms were lofty and handsome, and their furniture suitable to the fortune of their proprietor; but Elizabeth saw, with admiration of his taste, that it was neither gaudy nor uselessly fine; with less splendour, and more real elegance, than the furniture of Rosings.
>
> 'And of this place,' thought she, 'I might have been mistress!'[1]

Elizabeth Bennett's description of Pemberley conveys to the reader of Jane Austen's *Pride and Prejudice* that not only would this be a desirable home for the heroine but also that Darcy, its creator, would make her a suitable husband. The interior is meant to convey his character. In fiction this matching of place and person might take exaggerated form but in practice too the homes of people in the past were a reflection of their character, gender, status and circumstance. This chapter seeks to determine how much of that character survives in historic houses that are open to the public gaze.

The survival of homes from the past, either intact or as recreated interiors, provides us with an insight into the internal arrangements of houses, their furnishings and style of decoration, and some notion of how they might have functioned as homes for their inhabitants. Visiting such houses is a popular pastime for many people; not only to see the bed that Queen Victoria/George Washington slept in but also because it gives them the chance to 'inhabit' the three-dimensional space of previous generations, whether they were well known or not.[2] Domestic interiors offer perhaps the most accessible form of history since it is something we have in common with people in the past, even if the reality of homes was very different to our own. Objects are seen in the settings for which they were intended – the domestic. But there are a host of difficulties concerned with opening a house to the public. Leaving aside all the financial considerations there are fundamental philosophical decisions to be made concerning how the interiors will look and be furnished, and how the 'story' of the interiors will be conveyed to visitors.

This chapter will examine how different approaches result in different 'products for consumption'. Each approach produces a particular version of the past. The methods employed to present interiors has varied over time just as written histories also reflect the period when they were written. All representations of history tell us something about the past. They also tell us about the present by highlighting the particular concerns of our own period.

When a historic house opens to the public it takes on at least some of the characteristics of a museum, whether or not this is explicitly acknowledged. A museum is a collection preserved for the future, and these collections are presented to the public using some kind of interpretation. As Diane Barthel declares 'History is not God-given, it is humanly made. And what was once socially constructed can be socially reconstructed, through interpretation.'[3] At historic houses open to the public the interiors we see have been interpreted by curators and historians who produce a subjective view of the past influenced by class and ethnicity. They bring assumptions to the interpretation.[4] In addition, different styles of interpretation have prevailed at various times and the houses that are presently open for visiting offer a variety of interpretation techniques. The methods are often not made explicit or even referred to in brochures and guidebooks or by guides at the sites. The visitor to a historic house must take in their stride the method of interpretation presented to them and mentally accommodate the choices that have been made.

To highlight the subjectivity of the interpretation of historic houses the rather different approaches adopted in England and the United States will be compared.[5] These differences have come about due to the preservation movement in each country evolving independently. The background to historic houses being opened to the public will be outlined along with an exploration of how the interpretation process is put into practice. Finally, the chapter will look at some examples in more detail to see how a variety of methods can produce quite individual representations of domestic life through historic interiors.

Representation

The care of historic domestic buildings and their contents is just one part of the preservation movement. The presentation of these homes, and the process of interpretation and all that that involves has always been done in such a way that the visiting public will gain an insight into their significance to history. However, the representation of historic interiors is far from straightforward. Stuart Hall has argued that exhibits in museums are a 'practice of representation'.[6] Inevitably the methods chosen have changed over time as our understanding of how homes looked and functioned has evolved. But on a deeper level the interpretation has changed according to current thinking about what it is a historic house should provide its visitors. Thus the window on the past becomes a reflection of the present.

There are various methods that can be chosen to present historic interiors. The reasons behind the decision making will reflect the circumstances of the particular site and the aims of the owners. While each method that is adopted might offer particular insights, so too, each method produces difficulties and requires compromises. The chief ways of interpreting, or presenting, a historic house to the public can be reduced to three distinctly different methods, although recognizing that there are overlaps. These methods are restoration, preservation of layers of occupation, and preserved as found.

The first method is restoration to a chosen date, either when the house was first built, or to a later date or a broader period of perhaps 30 years, that was significant in its history. In this method the interior is presented as it would have looked and how it would have been used at the date chosen.

The second method is to preserve the layers of occupation. This method accepts that changes to the structure and interiors have occurred over time. The most recent layer/s of occupation might be peeled back and sometimes missing furniture is replaced by repurchasing items that once belonged to the house, or else objects of the same period.

The third, and most recently evolved method, is to conserve and preserve 'as found', that is how it looked when it passed into the ownership of a public body such as English Heritage or the National Trust. Every detail is deemed worthy of preservation and the interiors and arrangements of furniture are preserved as the last occupant used them.

In theory any of these methods could be adopted in each instance of a house being presented for public consumption. In practice the precise circumstances of the house and its interiors prompt certain methods to be adopted. If the house is in the United States it is more likely to be restored than if it is in England. Whether the layers of occupation are preserved or if the interiors are preserved 'as found' will often depend on the status of the interiors and their condition. Each house elicits a different response. Whether restored or preserved, the variety of method does not correspond with the presentation of interiors as an individual home. No particular method encourages this more than another method. Capturing the individuality of a home and the lived experience of its occupants is a product of present-day interpretation or, more correctly, representation.

A Comparison between England and the United States

The preservation movements in England and the US developed along different lines in the nineteenth century and these differences still influence present-day attitudes and decision making when a historic house is interpreted for public viewing. The history of the preservation movement in both countries is summarized in Table 6:1.

Preserving and Opening Houses to the Public: England

Visiting country houses in England has a long history and one not entirely related to the preservation movement.[7] As Peter Mandler has demonstrated the habit of visiting country houses has changed from wealthy people visiting new houses, furnished in fashionable style and still fully lived in, if only for part of the year, to the post World War II era when old houses were opened to the general public.[8] By

6:1 Preservation Trends in England and the United States

England	Trend	US	Trend
18th–early 19th centuries	Wealthy people visit new country houses	Mid-19th century	Patriotic sites are saved for the nation
Late-19th century	Preservation movement – SPAB and National Trust	Later-19th century	Colonial Revival Movement
Early-20th century	Interior decorators influence 'country house' look	Early-20th century	SPNEA founded influenced by SPAB and NT
Interwar period– 1960s	Country House Scheme founded by NT preserves layers of occupation	Interwar period– 1960s	Colonial Williamsburg, Sturbridge Village etc – restorations influenced by Colonial Revival
1970s–1980s	Academic Restoration projects	1970s–1980s	Academic Restoration projects
1990s–present	Layers continue with less aesthetic influence + some restoration + some preserved 'as found'	1990s–present	Less extreme restoration + some preserved 'as found'

the 1950s the emphasis was on large country houses. The families who owned them opened some, and the National Trust owned others. The Trust had begun as a preservation pressure group and only seriously became involved in saving country houses after World War II.[9]

The British preservation movement began in earnest in the mid-nineteenth century under the influence of John Ruskin. He spoke out against the over-restoration of ancient buildings, and encapsulated the attitude to preservation to be taken in England. Restoration was, Ruskin claimed:

> the most total destruction which a building can suffer: a destruction out of which no remnants can be gathered: a destruction accompanied with false descriptions of the thing destroyed. Do not let us deceive ourselves in this important matter; it is impossible, as impossible as to raise the dead, to restore anything that has ever been great or beautiful in architecture.[10]

The Victorians were keen on restoring buildings especially churches and cathedrals but also country houses. One example was Charlecote, a Tudor structure but during the early nineteenth century it was doubled in size and heavily restored inside and out. Mark Girouard says that here the work was carried out 'with considerable panache'. However, the restoration of many 'houses as well as churches, scraped off the accumulated texture of several centuries and replaced it with detailing whose mechanically worked stonework and slight differences in proportion remorselessly marked it down as Victorian and brought no compensating gains.'[11] The architect George Gilbert Scott is most often mentioned in connection with this tendency, since he was responsible for many restoration schemes, but he was part of a much wider attitude.

Ruskin's vociferous condemnation influenced William Morris, who called for an association to be founded that would campaign against the restoration of buildings. The Society for the Protection of Ancient Buildings (SPAB) was formed with Morris as secretary, in 1877. According to Girouard the SPAB:

> radically altered the way people looked at buildings. It made them cease to think of them in the abstract as pieces of design, and look at them as living pieces of history, on which each succeeding generation had left its mark. Once this point of view was adopted, any attempt to 'restore' back to an earlier period was just a piece of forgery, which in addition unforgivably erased the historical value of the building.[12]

This meant that country houses that displayed various ages and periods of growth were increasingly valued, and rather than modernize them the owners took pride in 'owning a splendid example of rambling old English charm.'[13]

The same spirit that had created the SPAB led in turn to the founding of the National Trust in 1895 to preserve countryside from the encroachment of urbanization and industrialization.[14] The first building that they saved was the Clergy House at Alfriston. This was a fairly humble half-timbered building. Its importance was as an example of a traditional regional (vernacular) building. The Trust's involvement in country houses truly got under way with the setting up of the Country House Scheme.[15] The necessary legislation, passed in 1937, allowed owners who could not afford the upkeep, especially in the face of rising taxation, to make the house over to the Trust. Christopher Rowell and John Martin Robinson have said that at this time 'the Trust regarded itself as an institutional embodiment of the enlightened private owner'.[16] Although the donor family was allowed to remain in part of the house, the decision making rested with the Trust. Each house presented a unique situation, with some families more in evidence than others, and the completeness of the contents that came with the house varied considerably.

The Trust has often needed to replace furniture that had been previously sold or was not included when the house came to them and they have a store of appropriate period furnishings for this purpose. One example of this process is Hanbury Hall in Worcestershire, an early-eighteenth-century house with a notable painted staircase by Thornhill. Since very little of the household furniture belonging to the family came with the house a grant from the Merrill Trust was used to acquire suitable furnishings along with loans from various institutions and bequests of paintings and furniture from private individuals.[17] This situation does not arise with privately owned houses where the family continues to live in the house and make changes to the decoration and furnishings. More than 200 houses are members of the Historic Houses Association. The HHA was formed in 1973 to help members maintain their houses and by issuing advisory material. Unlike the National Trust and English Heritage properties – owned by corporate bodies – the HHA is 'an association of individuals trying to run our own properties.'[18]

Speaking of HHA houses Sproule and Pollard state that 'It is a rare house that expresses the tastes of only one owner, and it is partly this crowded quality – this feeling that one is in the presence of several generations at once – that gives Britain's historic homes and their contents part of their special appeal.'[19] The distinction they are making is that the family are changing the interiors rather than a curator or historian. This situation has resulted in some criticism of the Trust. In 2004 *Country Life* commented on the death of the Duke of Devonshire. It praised his achievement in opening his family home, Chatsworth, to the public without making it into 'another "cultural institution", a northern offshoot of the Victoria and Albert Museum or a National Trust property where the visitor would search in vain for signs of the true spirit of place.'[20]

The National Trust is, conversely, criticized for allowing the donor family to continue to live on the premises, since this is seen by some as preserving an elitist way of life as well as the buildings. Robert Hewison is particularly critical on this point. He states that the 'National Trust's commitment to the continued occupation of houses for whom it accepts responsibility by the families that formerly owned them has preserved a set of social values as well as dining chairs and family portraits.'[21] Hewison believes that the policy of permitting the donor family to remain in residence allows the Trust to claim that the houses in their care are not museums, but this simply adds to the confusion of how to define these houses. Hewison claims that it is not enough to show objects 'in their natural setting and in the ambience of the past', but that this evidence of the past also needs interpreting for the present day.

In England historic houses, whether owned by individual families or by the National Trust, are rarely referred to as museums, whereas in the US historic house museums is the standard term. The reasons for the varying nomenclature are central to the differences inherent in historic house treatment in the two countries. However, the rooms in English houses that are opened to the public are museum exhibits, whether this interpretation process is made clear or not. Generally, the donor family does not continue to use the staterooms at Trust properties. Interiors, especially staterooms, in privately owned houses, have a somewhat ambiguous status. Are they domestic spaces, museum exhibits or even commercial spaces? Many privately owned houses hire out rooms for functions. Weston Park, in Staffordshire, for example, holds wedding receptions and conferences in the main house and a number of bedrooms have been made into bathrooms for the guests to use.[22] Whoever owns the house, even if the family still live there, the public is viewing an illusion. In most houses open to the public, the viewer is no longer looking at someone's home in the strict sense. In addition, these houses present interiors that preserve a style of decoration that is not historically correct. They are frozen in time. But what time is not clear.

The Influence of Aesthetic Taste on the Preservation of Layers

The National Trust has tended, in the past, to preserve the layers of occupation and this is the only method used by the many houses that continue to be privately owned, such as those that come under the Historic Houses Association. As the HHA suggests, many houses have remained in the same family 'for several centuries and who now open them to visitors. Each, in its own way, exhibits that sense of continuity, individual taste and eccentricity that successive owners inevitably impose upon their homes and which is difficult to create artificially. It is this human element so clearly evident in a private house, which brings the building to life.'[23] There are various reasons for the National Trust also preserving layers of occupation. Most National Trust houses have tended to be large and grand houses where the decorative schemes and furniture are 'important' from the point of view of the history of decorative art, and the history of collecting, both what was first assembled but also the later additions and changes. For this reason it has been common to place furniture in these interiors turned towards the visitor route, so that these precious objects can be seen and appreciated, rather than placed as they might have been used. To remove or erase anything from the collection would be to lose something of artistic and historical interest. But the preservation of a collection does not completely explain either the Trust's attitude to presenting country house interiors or their popularity with the public.

Anthony Mitchell has summed up the National Trust approach to country house interiors as 'presenting a palimpsest of decorative history'. Rather than restoring to a particular period they preserve interiors using conservation that uses minimal intervention to change them as little as possible. He concludes that '*Authenticity* is a current, not uncomplicated, concept but enhancement of a *sense of place* is surely an impeccable aim.'[24] The phrase 'sense of place' echoes the *Country Life* comment about Chatsworth, quoted above. So, both private owners and the National Trust aim to preserve similar things, but for the National Trust this has been problematic, as evidenced by Hewison's comments.

Mandler's explanation of the appeal of country houses to the visiting public suggests that it is their display of 'taste', through the creation of a particular style of furnishing that can be described as the country house style. This is 'an adaptation of the John Fowler style (itself an adaptation of eighteenth-century styles for the modern aristocrat), which has dominated interior-decoration magazines and middle-market tabloid features since the 1980s',[25] as well as the popularity of antique collecting and the programmes on television that promote it. This theme is more fully explored by Louise Ward who has traced the history of the Fowler style and its influence on English country houses.[26]

There seems to be an assumption in England that historic house interiors should look old, that they should display patina. Generally, the visiting public holds this assumption, and it seems to influence how conservators and curators preserve and present the interiors for public consumption. Mitchell has made some telling comments on the aesthetic decisions made by the National Trust at a number of its properties. On the subject of conservation methodology he suggests that the Trust try to practise a 'conservative' approach, that will stabilize but do as little as possible to change the look of both individual objects and the interiors which form the setting for them.

> We should…aim to arrive at an essential harmony, which depends on the considered balance of the tonality of oil on canvas, of the textures of woodwork and furniture with textiles, the controlled brilliance of metalwork and … the qualities of gilding. Moreover, whatever their individual history and character, a series of rooms should also be in harmony as we pass through them. Even the pace of a picture hang through the rooms should be balanced…[27]

This seems to be a subjective approach that seeks to produce an aesthetically pleasing result. Mitchell says that the personal preferences of Trust employees are not encouraged when redecoration is needed, but he concedes that conservation is an art as well as a science. He gives the example of Kingston Lacy where the saloon had been painted a dark grey before coming into Trust hands. The owners had intended to hang tapestries on the walls but this had never been carried out. The Trust tested various shades of grey for use in the redecoration but all were rejected. The walls were finally painted in 'an unhistoric but agreeable rich yellow' because it seemed 'solid and fresh enough to enhance the paintings, yet discreet enough to support the [painted] ceiling.'[28] A similar decision was made to tone a scheme in order to make it harmonize, in the Trust's work, at Stourhead. The original carpet was in poor condition so a replacement was made: 'the colour shades arrived at being a compromise between the brightest found on the underside of the carpet and the dullest on the damaged side. Thus the harmony of this most calm and elegant of English antiquary's libraries is still preserved.'[29]

The country house style is still in evidence in recently carried out decorative and furnishing schemes in many privately owned houses. At Eastnor Castle, in Worcestershire, for example, the great hall had been sparsely furnished since the 1840s, and hung with suits of armour in true Gothick style. However, in the 1980s it was turned into a drawing room complete with new comfortable seating that had been upholstered in old fabric to make a pleasing arrangement. Sarah Hervey-Bathurst has explained her approach to the restoration of the castle: 'we add things to "dress" the rooms, old fabrics, which sadly have a limited life, are replaced with new ones on cushions or chair covers … [when] one thing which has long been away at the restorers is returned to the rightful place starting a cascade of alterations in the room as everything has to be adjusted to accommodate it.'[30]

Barthel draws the conclusion that the UK preservation movement has been elitist whereas that of the US has been more democratic.[31] It is true that more middling-sort homes have been preserved in the United States than in England, where country houses have dominated. The introduction of the National Trust's Country House Scheme meant, according to Paula Weideger that 'the National Trust changed from being a charity focused on "the people" to one that was focused on its properties instead.'[32] There have been recent moves to change the Trust's elitist image and make it 'more relevant to ordinary people ... and to create a wider interpretation of heritage and social history.'[33] This has been attempted through the acquisition of properties such as a Victorian workhouse at Southwell, Nottinghamshire, and a Chartist cottage in Worcestershire. Clearly though, for most of its members, the grand houses with their fine architecture, collections and gardens are the main draw. Still, Barthel's definitions of 'elitist' and 'democratic' are not particularly useful for understanding the nature of representing historic interiors, in the present discussion. The historic background to the US preservation movement has influenced not only what was preserved but also the nature of the preservation process, which has, like the English examples, manipulated the arrangement, and the physical evidence of history.

Preserving and Opening Houses to the Public: The United States

The first historic house museum in the US was the Hasbrouck house in Newburgh, New York. This had been George Washington's headquarters on the Hudson River during the Revolution. It was opened to the public in 1850.[34] At this time there was a campaign to save George Washington's home at Mount Vernon. This process was not straightforward and it was not until 1858 that the house was secured for the nation, thanks largely to the Mount Vernon Ladies' Association of the Union.[35] Various female organizations were directly involved in the preservation movement in its early days.

Homes of American presidents and houses that were the site of important historical events, especially with connections with the Revolution and Civil War, were preserved and restored to the moment of their significance to history. They are used as three-dimensional history lessons to evoke a particular moment in the past. With this purpose in mind it was felt important to return the buildings and their interiors to how they looked at the time of their 'significant' moment in history. Restoration has therefore been the favoured method of preserving historic buildings in the US.[36]

The history of preservation in the US is well documented and has been far more thoroughly analysed than that of the UK.[37] Although the preponderance of restored interiors and the lack of preserving layers has yet to be scrutinized. Jan Cohn has suggested that there are two reasons for turning buildings into historic house museums. These are nostalgia and defining national history. She claims that these reasons produced an impetus to save more homes and create 'more house-shrines in America than in any other country in the world.'[38]

In the US as in England, the nineteenth century produced unparalleled urbanization and industrialization, and old values have often been celebrated at times of threat. In the US at this time there was the perception of the additional threat of immigration. Therefore the purpose behind preservation was largely due to a nationalistic impetus to preserve the homes of famous people important to American history, and the promotion of particularly patriotic attitudes. The preservation of the village of Deerfield, Massachusetts and the preservation/creation of Greenfield Village, Michigan and Colonial Williamsburg, Virginia[39] all stemmed from a desire to preserve sites of national significance and to celebrate the lifestyles that were thought to have existed before the onset of industrialization.

The states that had formed the early colonies that made up New England were particularly keen to preserve the past. They had led the country politically and culturally but they feared that this was likely to change with the expansion west and the influx of new people. Numerous attempts were made to preserve individual buildings and even whole villages that were felt to encapsulate the charm and values of old New England. The attitudes expressed through these sites also influenced the style of restoration practised.

William Sumner Appleton founded the Society for the Preservation of New England Antiquities (SPNEA), in 1910.[40] He had been influenced by the ideas of John Ruskin, William Morris and the SPAB and was keen to preserve historical evidence in the houses acquired by the Society. However, Appleton, declared: 'As a rule it is quite difficult for us to raise money for the purchase and preservation of the old houses unless it is understood that the building is to be put back as nearly as possible into the condition it originally presented.'[41] Some of the early buildings 'preserved' by the SPNEA had later additions and changes removed so that they could be returned to their supposed original appearance.[42] Already by the early twentieth century the desire to restore was firmly in place. However, the SPNEA was less in favour of restoration to the original appearance than were many other owners of historic houses in the US. The National Trust for Historic Preservation was founded in 1949 and it now owns 26 houses.[43] Although based on the UK organization and with a remit to preserve it has restored a number of its properties to a date of significance. In the US, apart from the state, individual historical societies and local history groups, rather than large organizations, own most historic houses. Personal interests are important and consequently methods vary but there has still been a general impetus to restore houses rather than to preserve layers of occupation.

The Influence of Aesthetic Taste on Restoration

Restoration to a particular date suggests that historical accuracy and objectivity rather than prevailing taste should have dominated the decoration and furnishing of American historic houses. But this was not the case. The Colonial Revival was as much an influence as the country house style was in Britain. The Colonial Revival promoted certain ways of seeing the past, the kinds of furnishings that were thought 'appropriate'.[44] An early example of the nostalgic view of the past that the Colonial Revival promoted was in 1858 at a fair in Boston. The bedchamber and parlour of the 1706 birthplace of Benjamin Franklin was recreated, together with costumed guides. 'In this exhibition, the cradle, tall case clock, blazing hearth and spinning wheels were firmly established as essential components of New England period rooms, and living history may have been born.'[45]

Typical elements in Colonial Revival interiors were Turkey carpets, spinning wheels, patchwork quilts, polished brass cooking pots, pewter plates in abundance and generally more objects, and of better quality, than was appropriate for moderately wealthy homes. Colonial Revival taste influenced how rooms in historic house museums were displayed. While many utilitarian objects were included they were arranged as art exhibits, rather than as they might have been distributed about a room when in use. This was particularly noticeable in service areas. Cooking pots and pans were displayed attractively around the hearth and food containers became decorative objects on the shelves of pantries.

Colonial Revival taste together with the method of paint analysis used at the time influenced the colour palette for interiors. The painted decoration was decided by paint scrapes. This method literally scraped away the layers of paint to decide what colour had been used first. However, it is difficult to be accurate using this method and in addition it is impossible to judge the colour with the naked eye since different types of paint and the pigments used would have aged in particular ways. Scientific paint analysis has comparatively recently evolved as a more accurate means of establishing old paint colours and the order of application.[46] But paint that had darkened with age gave a subdued palette of colours that suited the Colonial Revival taste in interiors. As a style for furnishing historic houses it was also tremendously popular with the public.

Apart from the influence of a particular stylistic taste on interiors, the restoration of many houses in the US suffered from overzealous restoration/preservation work. Some interiors were removed from houses and put into a museum, leaving the original house with poor imitations of its decorative schemes. One example of this is the Powell House in Philadelphia where several rooms were removed and installed in the Philadelphia Museum and the Metropolitan Museum of Art, in New York. The house had inaccurate and plainer versions of mouldings and plasterwork ceilings recreated. Originally displayed in Colonial Revival style and now reinterpreted as accurate eighteenth-century interiors it has lost much of its authenticity.[47]

Old houses have often undergone far too many structural changes to be able to 'go back in time', partly because it would mean sacrificing the later historical material, but also because if the history of the building had not been carefully recorded it would be pure conjecture to recreate what was there before. Attitudes have changed as to how to treat structures. A well-known example of an early restoration that was drastic but probably inaccurate was the House of Seven Gables. This house in Salem, Massachusetts was the prototype for the novel of the same name by Nathaniel Hawthorn. But over the years the house had lost four of its gables. The evidence for them, on which to base the restoration, was flimsy. The house almost had an extra window added, since it was described in the story, although no evidence for it existed.[48]

Reappraisal of Historic Preservation in England and the United States

Academic research and new scientific approaches to conservation and restoration resulted in a reappraisal of historic house interpretation, on both sides of the Atlantic. In the US the move away from the cosy image of the Colonial Revival in favour of more accurate, authentic recreations of interiors happened in the 1980s. This development was spearheaded by the redecoration of Mount Vernon, in historically correct schemes.[49] A similar programme of reinterpretation at Colonial Williamsburg took place.[50]

In England too there was a similar desire to restore some historic interiors, especially amongst museum professionals and academics. Rowell and Robinson suggest that in the early days of the National Trust's Country House Scheme 'There was no concept of curatorial responsibility like that of a museum.'[51] However, over time they suggest employees of the Trust became more professional and modelled themselves on museum practice. Research was undertaken on the Trust's houses and collections. A professional adviser on paintings was appointed in 1956 and Gervaise Jackson-Stops, the Trust's architectural adviser from 1975 to 1995, was instrumental in encouraging a more thorough academic approach. Academic research is plainly visible in the restorations carried out by the National Trust at such properties as Kedleston Hall in Derbyshire.

At the same time research was promoted by the Victoria and Albert Museum and their curator of furniture Peter Thornton, who had been influenced by the work being done in institutions such as Colonial Williamsburg.[52] The staff of the museum produced numerous books on historic decoration, and put their ideas on restoration into practice at Ham House, in Surrey, Osterley Park, in Middlesex and Apsley House, in Piccadilly.[53] All of these were well-documented houses and the treatment they received was based on archival research. This was backed up by paint analysis. In this way their original appearance and use was recreated in the decorative schemes and in the arrangement of furnishings.

Barthel says that it came as something of a shock when it was discovered that in the past interiors were painted in bright colours and that seemed, to our eyes, to clash. These colour schemes she suggests upset 'up-market heritage tourists when the past does not mirror their expectations of faded gentility'.[54] At Williamsburg, for example, the new palette of colours was completely different to the faded colours that had been promoted by paint companies as 'colonial shades'. But it was not only 'upmarket' tourists who were dismayed by the new-style restorations. Tourists generally found the cosy, nostalgic Colonial Revival interiors more acceptable than the starker and gaudier reality of the past.[55]

It was not only the colours of paintwork that changed as a result of more scientific analysis but also those of textiles. It has become increasingly common in the US for fragile historic textiles to be 'retired'. At Winterthur Museum for example, when the museum was first established the original textiles were kept on display. These original textiles, in their faded colours, suited the Colonial Revival aesthetic that was followed at the time. There is now a programme to replace all the textiles with reproductions that capture period colours. This practice also protects the artefacts from further deterioration and establishes a study collection for scholars, and for further investigation of manufacture and structure.[56]

The desire for more authentic historic interiors has proved difficult to achieve. Since many interiors of historic houses have lost their original furniture and ornaments, then replacements need to be used. At Apsley House for example, even though most of the interior furnishings had survived in situ, some guesswork was still needed. One carpet was missing, and there was no record of its appearance; therefore, as David Phillips recounts, 'a fragment of carpet found in the attic of the duke's country house [was used as] the model for the replica carpet…The point at which even this sort of thing becomes a kind of forgery is hard to define.'[57] The use of reproductions in restored interiors can often detract from an authentic look since they often appear too perfect, like a stage set.[58] As George L. Wrenn puts it 'The beautiful furniture, in excellent repair, looks as if it had never been used. It is difficult to imagine the owner coming in, tired and sweating, to flop down with an ale or a pipe and newspaper.'[59] Even the perfectly matched paint and textile colours do not entirely ring true since pigments in the past were more fugitive than in the present and so would have faded in a few years.

By the 1990s new methods had gained ascendance in historic house interpretation. In the US it had been usual to restore houses to the date when they were built or one particular and precise 'date of significance'. But this rule has been relaxed. Instead a date of significance is established within its history that often encompasses a longer period of perhaps 30 years, so that additions to the building can often be retained. Gradually too houses have had one or more rooms interpreted to different periods. This is done because decorations and furnishings have survived or where good documentation exists to support the interpretation.

Some historic houses continue in their Colonial Revival style. In a few instances houses that were restored to a more authentic interpretation have even had their Colonial Revival schemes re-established.[60] In most cases the earlier schemes were the work of noted interior decorators and their part in creating the interiors is fully acknowledged as an example of the taste of when it was done. This idea has also been practised in England where some examples of the country house style are now preserved and interpreted as a particular taste in historic interiors. The National Trust, for example, now owns the Treasurer's House in York, but Frank Green who died in 1930 arranged the interiors when he owned the property. The Trust recognizes that they are twentieth-century creations and these interiors are preserved as such.[61] The work of John Fowler, for both private clients and for the National Trust, has presented a few difficult decisions; whether to restore to more authentic colour schemes or to preserve the work of this well-known interior decorator.[62]

Differences still exist between the approach favoured in the United States and England and this continues somewhat to reflect the earlier tendencies described above. So, for example, even when restoration to a particular period is practised in England, some layers of occupation tend to be preserved. At Petworth, for example, the picture gallery had its early nineteenth-century picture hang recreated by the National Trust in the 1990s, but they did not reinstate the white walls of the decorative scheme of that time. Instead a surviving fragment of dark red paint was matched, although this colour had been used in the late-nineteenth century. This decision was taken because the paintings had darkened and deteriorated and this would have been more obvious against white-painted walls.[63]

Conversely, when the layers of occupation are preserved in the United States it is typical for some restoration to take place too. At Lyndhurst, New York, for example, owned by the National Trust for Historic Preservation, the three owners of the house are represented in the accumulation of furnishings. However, it was felt that the earliest inhabitants were not sufficiently in evidence so the decision was taken to fully restore one room to its appearance at their time of occupation.[64]

Historic Houses as 'Tangible Evidence of the Past'

Recent writing on the preservation of interiors has focused on the notion of the structure and contents of houses as physical evidence of the past. As Barthel has put it: 'Their very tangibility separates them from historic texts and media representations.'[65] Similarly William J. Murtagh has stressed that historic houses are three-dimensional and their structure, interior decoration and contents are tangible evidence of the past that can never be replaced.[66] How this evidence is treated; whether it is preserved or not and the methods used all affect the survival of the evidence and what it can tell us about the past, and in turn this affects how we view the past.

Louise Ward has commented on the ephemeral quality of interiors. They frequently undergo changes when they are in use by occupants but curators and historians of historic houses tend to treat them as permanent. Rooms are she says shaped 'by social and cultural conventions and the desire to create an environment, which has, or reflects, an identity. Rooms can act as a projection of personality and/or lifestyle, and even stand for aspects of character; a room is always greater than the sum total of its material parts.' [67] The interpreted interior thus offers a 'highly selected, edited version of the subject.'

Discussions around how to treat historic interiors are reflected in the current methods used by conservators. Increasingly they take into account entire interiors rather than individual objects in isolation. Methods have been developed that do not overly intervene with the nature of the object but at the same time arrest decay.[68] Everything that is an essential part of an object is retained and methods that are reversible are used whenever possible.[69] However, such attitudes do not always prevail and Phillips gives the example of the treatment of the 1890s wallpaper, designed by Walter Crane, at Wythenshawe Hall. The paper was removed and conserved but not put back. Instead the room was restored to how it may have looked in the early nineteenth century. So, although the wallpaper had been an authentic element of the history of the house it was replaced by a conjectured earlier scheme of decoration. He concludes that the restoration in this house could not 'retrieve internal creative unity ... either an interior environment was constructed in the past by and for a particular household, and to a substantial extent preserved, or it was not.' [70]

Preserving as Found

Ideas such as those expressed by Phillips have led to the most recent method of historic house interpretation, that of preserving the interiors as found. The premise of this method is that the interiors will be 'frozen in time' even if that means preserving intact the disorder and decay that the last occupant allowed to accumulate. Such houses have been termed 'time capsules'. Every detail is deemed worthy of preservation and the interiors and arrangements of furniture are preserved as the last occupant used them. While in theory this method should preserve authentic historical evidence, in practice, it is as open to interpretation as all others. It is even open to the influence of aesthetic judgements. The preserve as found method has been realized in various ways at different sites.

The National Trust for Historic Preservation now owns the eighteenth-century plantation house, Drayton Hall, just outside Charleston, South Carolina. The house is unfurnished and has not been restored but the original paint schemes retained and consolidated. The visitor leaflet refers to it as a time capsule, stating that 'the house remains in nearly original condition and has never been modernized'.[71] The house is used as a backdrop for guided tours when the history of the house is told: its architecture and use over time, including the lives of the slaves working in the house and on the plantation. If the interpretation at Drayton Hall had been carried out 30 or more years ago, it would have been restored to its eighteenth-century splendour and all trace of its original paint schemes would probably have been lost. However, due to the total lack of furniture the house in its present state preserves its abandoned state but does not show the arrested conditions of recent habitation, as in true 'preserved as found' sites.

Similarly the Aiken-Rhett House in Charleston, owned by Historic Charleston Foundation, is claimed, in the leaflet, to have 'survived virtually unaltered since 1858. Gilded looking glasses, a French chandelier and a portrait of Mrs William Aiken, Jr. are among the early furnishings in the drawing room'. However, the leaflet does not point out that these are among the small number of furnishings that are exhibited in the house.[72] With few exceptions this seems to be the method used in the US. In England, most houses that are preserved as found also preserve them fully furnished. Perhaps with its record of preserving layers of occupation, the UK is more practised at this approach. The National Trust tried out this process at Erddig in the early-1970s. The idea was taken further at Calke Abbey in the mid-1980s and English Heritage was even more scrupulous in their treatment of Brodsworth.[73] This last house had been built in the 1860s but had undergone some changes and additions such as bathrooms with modern sanitary wares. English Heritage preserved these additions along with the surviving original and fine decorative schemes.

Ightham Mote in Kent is a curious example of the preserved as found method. The manor house dates back to the fifteenth century with new wings added over time. Internally too additions were made, for example, early panelling and wall paintings were covered up with more fashionable wall treatments. The house was in such poor condition when it was donated to the National Trust that it has been gradually taken to pieces and rebuilt over a number of years. All the original materials have been reused wherever possible. New materials replicate the methods of construction and decoration of the originals, even if they are to be covered up. All the layers have been reassembled so that it now replicates its appearance when it came into Trust hands. Both the National Trust and English Heritage believe that the important element of this method is that all historical evidence is preserved for the future.

A number of problems exist in the preserved as found method. One is that the interiors will continue to decay. Keeping the original objects on display will eventually damage them. The conditions that prevail when the house is 'found' can only be preserved up to a point.[74]

Some aesthetic judgement also seems to be commonly practised when the rooms are presented for visitors. Phillips comments on the interpretation process at Brodsworth saying that English Heritage had made some changes and compromises. For example, during the purchase of the property, some objects were returned to the family. There were originally many small items around the house, some of which are now missing or have been redistributed. And some items of furniture had to be moved to a different location to ease visitor flow. In one bedroom there appears a casual arrangement of draped curtains across the bed. Phillips suggests that this arrangement was contrived since the room had undergone many disturbances during the work on the house. 'It seems a quintessential image of atmospheric decay, but true decay is messier.'[75]

A further example of aesthetic judgement being made is in the treatment of Calke Abbey, owned by the National Trust. The house presents neglected interiors, but what we see is selected neglect. In the dining room, for example, the last member of the family to live there had cleaned it up by using modern emulsion paint. Rather than exhibit this as part of the authentic history of the house, the Trust made the decision to restore the room, using thorough methods of research to recreate the original decorative scheme.[76]

Generally, however, compared to other methods, there is a lack of aesthetic judgements being made and less editing out of cheap, ugly or 'inappropriate' objects. But it must be acknowledged that these interiors show only a tiny part of the history of the house: the last sad days. This method seems to celebrate romantic decay, but on an overcast day these interiors can look especially depressing. There seems to be a fashion at the moment for 'shabby chic', so once again this will almost certainly be a temporary solution of what to do with historic interiors.

Interpretation Methods in Practice

Historic house museums then, can be restored, have their layers of occupation preserved, or they are preserved as found. It is not so much the method chosen but how it is carried out that provides the key to accessing the material culture of the past. Houses need to be interpreted in such a way that visitors are brought into contact with the narratives of domestic lived experience; through the presentation of the material culture the lives of the inhabitants can be explored. It is possible to accomplish this through each of the methods described. The next section examines some examples of houses that have adopted a variety of methods of representing the lived experience of homes in the past.

For the purposes of the present discussion, the overriding issues to be addressed in relation to the interpretation methods and their realization at particular sites are whether any methods are able to 'capture' the particular circumstances of individual homes in the past. Chapters 1–5 highlighted in particular the prevalence of homes that were ordinary rather than wealthy and fashionable, the transient nature of many home furnishings, and the clutter that accumulated in rooms and cupboards. The tendency to recycle furnishings and to purchase second-hand goods was stressed. The need for homes to accommodate additional people, especially servants, and the public role of homes to entertain visitors contrasted with the homes of single men and women that were somewhat disadvantaged in this respect, although it was noted how these homes could achieve an individual quality that reflected the gender of their occupant. It would not be advantageous to separate out these aspects when houses open to the public are considered. Such issues operated alongside each other in people's homes and indeed other issues were relevant too, such as the space occupied by children in the home, the cultural influence of religion and ethnic background. The examples of historic house museums that will be highlighted in the remainder of this chapter have all engaged with a variety of issues and have sought ways to represent them effectively in their interpretation strategies.

Emphasizing ordinary and provincial homes, rather than elite homes that led the way in new fashions, has been achieved in a number of houses recently made into historic house museums. The use of social history to inject a sense of lived experience has been an important influence in this respect.[77] Many of the National Trust's recently acquired buildings reflect its move to widen the scope of the properties that it manages and also to broaden its appeal to the visiting public. Recent acquisitions have included a Victorian workhouse, a Chartist cottage, the Liverpool homes of John Lennon and Paul McCartney, and the back-to-back houses in Birmingham.[78]

A suburban house in Worksop, Nottinghamshire, called simply Mr Straw's house, is another example of the Trust breaking away from its grand country house image. But ownership and interpretation of the house has been criticized. William Straw gave 1.5 million pounds to the Trust along with his house in 1990, expecting the Trust to sell it. But the Trust decided to preserve the house as found and to use the legacy to maintain it. William Straw had already begun this process by keeping the house just as it was when his widowed mother died in 1939. He had thrown nothing away. Paula Weideger is critical of opening this house to the public since it is so small it can only accommodate four visitors at a time. But she is also critical of preserving a house of this type and in this condition. 'It is not of historic or architectural importance or even an illustration of how people lived in a particular period. It is merely the not especially attractive suburban home of a cranky bachelor who hated to throw things out.'[79]

Mr Straw's house does present problems due to its size but the critics cannot have it both ways. If the Trust is to be more representative of society as a whole then modest sized homes with little architectural merit will be preserved;

and why not a suburban house in Worksop? Weideger is entirely correct in stating that this house is not representative of society in general. It does not show how most middle-class people lived in the twentieth century. Mr Straw's House preserves exactly how this one individual lived and is entirely authentic in that respect. The Trust has recognized that this is a rare thing to have survived and therefore worth preserving.

The documentary evidence, used in Chapters 1–5, provides a snapshot of the process of homemaking: a continuously changing and transient process. The past is about change, whereas museums are static, they preserve a moment. Therefore the qualitative methods used for analysing documentary sources also need to be incorporated in museum interpretation. This process is often referred to as trying to achieve a 'lived-in' look. Perhaps the most difficult aspect of recreating the lived experience of daily life in a home is making believable the clutter and temporary arrangements that might suggest the inhabitants had just left the room.[80] The Harriet Beecher Stowe house, built in 1871, has been restored to show the home of the writer of *Uncle Tom's Cabin* and numerous books on domestic management. In the 1980s these interiors were reinterpreted to show how Beecher Stowe is thought to have lived – in a less than tidy way. But visitors were shocked by this interpretation since Beecher Stowe was so well known for her advice on good household management. The interiors have now been tidied up.[81]

Aesthetic judgements about clutter still hark back to the Colonial Revival and the country house style ideas. Clutter is often arranged aesthetically rather than in a realistic manner. In houses designed according to Modern Movement principles clutter is also banished. The National Trust now owns several Modern houses that are presented in an immaculate state. Erno Goldfinger's home at 2 Willow Road, Hampstead, has been tidied up so that what was once a family home is presented as the perfect example of Modernist aesthetics.[82]

Interpretation around activities invites clutter to be taken seriously. Various stories about the inhabitants and their daily lives have been recreated at the Read House, in Newcastle, Delaware, due to its interpretation method and how the site is presented to the public. Begun in 1801 by a lawyer, George Read II, the Read House is owned by the Historical Society of Delaware. The house was restored in the 1980s using paint analysis, bills and inventories and even X-rays of parts of the decoration.[83] The house was well documented and the Society produced a careful reconstruction of the interiors of the 1830s, although approximations of the furniture had to be acquired using the inventory of 1836 and tradesmen's bills for guidance. The restoration does, however, break with that of most house museums in the US: rooms are restored to reflect two different time periods and owners. As well as a number of rooms reflecting the early-nineteenth century life of George Read and his family, three rooms retain the decorative schemes created by Mr and Mrs Philip Laird, the owners in the 1930s. This allowed important interiors, including the dining room with its individually commissioned hand-painted wallpaper, to remain intact. Also, furnishings were retained that had been bequeathed to the Society along with the house by Mrs Laird in 1975.[84] This departure from interpreting to a strict and single date allows the Read House to preserve well-documented interiors with their original furnishings and to relate the whole history of the house.[85] But the course taken at the house has caused some mystification. A reader of *Historic Preservation*, the magazine published by the National Trust for Historic Preservation, commented on an article detailing the restoration of the Read House. The writer could not understand the 'philosophy' involved and was worried by the selective exhibition of several eras. Charles Lyle, director of the Historical Society of Delaware, was forced to respond to the letter to explain their intentions.[86]

Each year the Read House adopts a theme to present aspects of the daily life of the inhabitants.[87] In 2005 it was women's work. The theme is interpreted in different ways throughout the house; in the drawing room small work tables were dotted about the room with sewing and embroidery in progress, rather than displayed as artwork, as they would have been in the Colonial Revival style. The dining room had silver and ceramics in the process of being chosen for a dinner party with piles of plates rather than the more usual formal table setting. In Mrs Laird's bedroom this woman's work was consistent with her leisured lifestyle and a painting had arrived for her approval still in its box on the floor with tissue paper spilling out. Making the house superficially untidy allows the curators at the Read House to go a long way in the difficult task of recreating believable tableaux of daily life. At the same time this interpretation allows for a variety of narratives to be conveyed to visitors concerning the whole history of the house.

Accentuating frugal lifestyles and makeshift methods of homemaking are just some of the themes of the Lower East Side Tenement Museum in New York. The museum uses four restored apartments to tell the stories of different immigrant families, of different religions and nationalities. They do not avoid sensitive subjects but rather make a point of exploring the lives of illegal immigrants, broken families and prejudice. As the founder Ruth J. Abrams has declared, too often historic sites shy away from sensitive issues and edit the history of the site. This is an important point since many visitors think that a historic site, by offering tangible evidence, is the reality of the past.[88] The humble belongings and the appearance of arrested use are full of pathos but they are also used as props to recount stories of ingenuity, family and community life. The stories told at this museum are further explored through an extensive outreach programme.

While poor homes are often used to emphasize social history the interpretation used at large country houses have also been affected by these methods.[89] At Erddig, the Trust's house in Wales, near the English border, a particularly full version is provided of both below stairs life for servants and that of the upstairs life of eccentric aristocrats. Their interpretation of the house takes a different form to that which is usual for a large country house. The normal practice has been to cater to the interests of the connoisseur, the furniture and architectural historian. At Erddig the estate carpenter had fashioned a table with legs made from discarded window poles. This incongruous item of furniture remains in situ on an upper landing whereas it may well have been removed if furniture history and aesthetics dominated the presentation. But now that social history is allowed to play a part in the interpretation so such individual objects are included. A comparison of the Trust's *Guidebooks* demonstrates the changing emphasis very clearly; older guides almost exclusively concentrated on furniture and art history style narratives, newer guides are more inclusive of the context of houses and their inhabitants.

In the old style of interpretation the areas used by servants tended to be ignored and often made into offices. In many houses they have not survived intact since by the twentieth century the resident family wanted more modern facilities. However, at Erddig the remarkably full survival of the servants' quarters has prompted a special treatment. In addition the history of this house and the relationship between the servants and family over several centuries has survived in documents, paintings, and more recently recorded in oral history research, the last family member as well as some surviving servants making contributions. In his study of the servants at Erddig, Merlin Waterson concludes that while the family were eccentric still the completeness of the service areas give a good idea of the complexity of running country houses of this size.[90] The effect is heightened by the tour of the house beginning in the servants' quarters, the outbuildings and the carpentry shop followed by the laundry and then kitchens, gradually emerging into the service corridor and proceeding through the green baize door into the main house.

The complete opposite of Erddig is offered at Kedleston Hall in Derbyshire. This house had undergone no significant changes to its structure since it was built in the 1760s. The internal furnishings were also mostly intact. The Trust, therefore, decided to restore the interiors to their eighteenth-century appearance. The tour at Kedleston is principally of the staterooms in the central section; the family wing is still occupied by the Curzon family, and the service wing is now the tea room and gift shop. To enhance the visitor's experience, the tour begins by entering the house at the main entrance, up an imposing flight of steps. Here in the entrance hall the visitor is sometimes met by the 'housekeeper' who then conducts the tour, thereby recreating the eighteenth-century experience of many visitors to country houses and described by Jane Austen in *Pride and Prejudice* when Elizabeth Bennett visited the home of Darcy.

But social history is not the only way to capture the reality of domestic interiors that were created by individual homemakers. The cultural history of accumulating the contents of a home can also be emphasized. Many houses open to the public have unique collections that can be incorporated in a positive way into the interpretation. Just as the structure is a historical document of the past so too is the collection that it contains. Furniture, paintings and other decorative objects amassed over the years by a family or families constitute a 'collection' that is unique, as is its arrangement.[91] Problems arise if a collection has been broken up previous to the house coming into public hands. It is impossible to recreate the sense of the 'whole' of the objects that previously existed and their unique relationship to each other. When replacements are used the interior inevitably becomes a collection of antiques. While they give a suggestion of how rooms might have been furnished they lose the individuality of the particular family who occupied the house and how they lived with their possessions. This is not generic room settings but it is inevitably a tidied up version where the interior decorator has more input in creating an aesthetically pleasing 'melange'.

Evergreen, an Italianate house on the outskirts of Baltimore, Maryland, was begun in the 1850s but grew over several generations of the Garret family, who were wealthy collectors and patrons of the arts. While the interiors have been restored to their appearance in the mid-twentieth century, this interpretation still allows the changing tastes and varied collecting interests of the family to remain in evidence. This is aided by previous generations variously retaining the decoration and furnishings in some rooms, completely renovating others, and adding new rooms over time. So, one reception room has had its restoration based on a 1880s photograph, whereas the gold bathroom was renovated but had always been preserved by the family, and the reading room and drawing room both reflect the last generation's creations with specially commissioned murals and collection of twentieth-century paintings. The tour of the house allows the history of the building and its occupants to be told layer after layer.[92]

Preserving various periods and layers gathered together by successive generations also shows to some extent how many people lived with their objects since it was the exception rather than the rule to furnish as a complete scheme with everything new, although there have been periods when this was done in the staterooms of grand houses. But the tendency to retain ancient artefacts is perhaps a demonstration of aristocratic taste that does not hold true for other sections of society. The retention of eighteenth-century silk chair covers or a hand-painted Chinese wallpaper was not an option for less wealthy sections of society; nor would it have been seen as desirable. Middle- and working-class households throughout the later-nineteenth and most of the twentieth century thought changing wallpaper on an almost yearly basis desirable. Retaining furnishings and artefacts became a sign of old money in the twentieth century for aristocratic and gentry families in England. Just as leading fashion was their role in earlier centuries, so by the twentieth they sidestepped fashion and adopted 'timeless' good taste.

While the notion of a collection is inappropriate for less wealthy homes, still historic houses of non-aristocratic families that retain layers of occupation can reflect the idiosyncratic choices made by individuals or families over several generations. As at Brodsworth with the ordinary bathroom fittings added to this once grand house, so at the Codman House a mixture of qualities exists in its furnishings. The Codman House in Lincoln, Massachusetts has been owned since the 1960s by the SPNEA.[93] The house was originally built in 1740 but enlarged in the 1790s. Five generations of the Codman family lived there, each making changes to the structure and interiors. The SPNEA originally planned in the late 1960s to preserve the interior, as it was when the house came into their hands. They called this the 'bell jar' approach. Several rooms were piled with lumber and the interiors generally looked neglected and forlorn. The SPNEA decided in the 1980s to conserve objects and to adopt a less drastic approach. The context of the layered history of the house was retained but some cleaning up and tidying up was carried out. As the site's curator Richard Nylander explains:

> The significance of this house is that it contains an overwhelming accumulation of objects amassed by successive generations of a single family. The visitor to Codman House sees the actual furnishings the

family lived with, not those determined by a curator who would be likely to furnish a room with objects of a consistent quality. At Codman House there are masterpieces in the same room with factory-made goods next to cheap souvenirs brought back from world travels. Each object is made more meaningful by its relation to the others around it.[94]

At Greyfriars in Worcester, the National Trust shows the house much as the last inhabitants, the brother and sister Mately and Elsie Moore, lived in it. Although they made over the property in 1966, they remained in the house and inhabited the space until their deaths in the 1980s. This ancient merchant's house had a chequered history, and this is told to visitors through the evidence of the architecture and biographical information on its various inhabitants along with some surviving artefacts that have been brought back to the house.[95] But the overriding narrative at Greyfriars is the work of the Moores to preserve the building and to display there their collection of objects that consists of a mixture of antiques, family pieces, art objects and curiosities that they collected, and objects fashioned by them. The latter include the tapestry covers for a chair embroidered by Mately, watercolours and embroidery by Elsie along with her work-bag and scissors hanging in their habitual place beside the fire. This house displays a particular attitude to collecting, displaying and preserving artefacts that was prevalent in the earlier-twentieth century. The Arts and Crafts Movement influenced the Moores' tastes and accomplishments. This is clear in the collection of books in the library: while not of great interest to bibliophiles, it is nonetheless highly demonstrative of the Moores' particular tastes. The Moores succeeded in preserving Greyfriars when it was threatened with demolition due to its precarious state. Restoration was carried out in the post-war period when both labour and materials were scarce. In addition their attitudes to preservation were different to present-day fastidious preservation and conservation views. For example, the extensive restoration work on the house was poorly documented. Mately used pieces of embossed leather that was saved from another house in Worcester that was being demolished in the 1960s to cover small wooden boxes of his own construction. Similarly, Elsie acquired some fine late-seventeenth century embroideries and cut off the damaged sections to make wall hangings and a valance to go over a window. In all respects then Greyfriars and its contents present a unique creation that demonstrates tastes and attitudes held by the preservationists of the first half of the twentieth century.

A house that had been carefully preserved during the nineteenth and twentieth centuries was Uppark in Sussex. The National Trust intended to continue to preserve its romantic untouched atmosphere. But this intention was severely challenged when the house was badly damaged by fire in 1989. The decision to restore was controversial. Many people thought that the house should be left as a ruin or pulled down, although the insurance terms did not allow for this – only total reinstatement. Some critics thought any restoration would produce a 'fake' and some still think this is the result. But the decision to restore Uppark and how this restoration was carried out is closely related to the National Trust's preservation philosophy. The crucial point about the restoration was that the Trust decided to restore to the day before the fire and to incorporate as much original material as possible. Indeed the latter would not have been possible without the former. Thus the 'patina of history' is preserved and in some instances 'recreated'. The wallpaper in the Red Room provides a good example. A replica flock paper was made to cover the walls and the surviving fragments were put back in their original position. Since the paper had faded to a variety of reds and browns in different parts of the room these circumstances were replicated in the replacement paper.[96]

The approach adopted at Uppark also preserves the context for the contents of the collection, 95 per cent of which in the staterooms were saved. 'The National Trust, a champion of the historically authentic, non-museum display of works of art' preserves interiors for which they had been purchased and collected by the inhabitants.[97] In this instance the individual objects had the patina of age and therefore required a patinated interior to display them effectively.

In their description of the restoration of Uppark Rowell and Robinson link the approach taken there with British attitudes to restoration espoused by Ruskin and Morris, and the SPAB. They are, therefore, also making a link between such ideas and the efforts of the Trust to preserve the 'patina of history' at Uppark.[98] However, they also suggest that the SPAB's approach to preserving historic buildings was developed with reference to medieval and vernacular buildings. That is using an archaeological approach to preserving everything of historical interest. Whereas, they claim it is difficult to apply the same principles to Victorian and Georgian buildings, since they depend less on texture, natural materials, hand-craftsmanship and patina.[99] This comment was felt necessary since the SPAB had been critical of the project to save Uppark, especially the reinstatement of an exact copy of the staircase since none of the original had survived. A final and telling point was made by Rowell and Robinson saying that the 'later decoration and restoration work is surely as much part of the history of the building as anything that went before.'[100] In other words, the restoration work is now part of Uppark's history. And displaying and explaining the process is now part of the interpretation of Uppark for visitors.

But just as the decision to restore Uppark to its appearance the day before the fire may eventually result in uneven ageing in the future so it will also inevitably be seen to reflect the period of its restoration. This is true of the interpretation methods used at all historic houses open to the public. The dual challenge is for them to continue to be relevant in the future and for no work to be done that irrevocably destroys their unique tangible evidence of the past.

The final example of a historic house museum to be highlighted in this section is Locust Lawn, in New Paltz, New York. This house was built in 1814 for the Hasbrouck family.[101] Here the interpretation has yet to be fixed since the house is not permanently open to visitors. Usually by the time the public are admitted to a house there is no hint of what it had looked like or its condition before the conservation work was completed. The decisions have already been made about what objects are to remain, how they are to be arranged and what furnishings need to be changed or added.[102] At Locust Lawn this process is still ongoing. The extensive collections that came with the house are being inventoried.[103] Cupboards and chests of drawers are packed full of objects, especially textiles, that all need to be assessed for conservation. Here too is the material evidence that together with biographical information can be incorporated into interpretation narratives. The lives of the past inhabitants, their skills, aspirations, individual tastes are stored here amongst layers of acid-free tissue paper. Three objects give a taste of the richness of the collection and the possibilities it possesses for relating narratives. These are a rose blanket, a piece of unfinished patchwork and some blue and white printed bed hangings.

The term rose blanket was given to later-eighteenth to early-nineteenth century English-made bed covers produced in Bolton, Lancashire. The name derived from the geometric design that resembled the compass rose on old maps. The design was woven into each of the four corners. The example at Locust Lawn displays the usual characteristics for this type of counterpane. It proclaims its English and professional manufacture in the expert weaving, the even and fine quality of the thread, and the absence of a centre seam. These were all attributes that could not be easily imitated by local or home production at this period. This rose blanket was a demonstration of refined taste in the early nineteenth century. It shows that rural New Paltz, in the Hudson valley area, had access to imported goods.[104] The Hasbroucks had created a stylish house that contrasted with the vernacular buildings nearby and they furnished it with professionally made goods to add comfort and gentility.

The piece of unfinished patchwork is by contrast a decidedly home-made item and not one that demonstrates the great needlework and design skills that are often apparent in patchwork quilts. The patchwork was abandoned when it was large enough to cover a single bed but no backing fabric or quilting had been done. Just two designs of cotton fabric were used with small flower prints. One has a white background and the other is lilac with mauve flowers. The latter fabric has faded in uneven patches to a dark brown, showing the fugitive nature of fabric dyes at the period it was made. The patchwork design is composed of simple rectangles of cloth, three inches wide, and some at the edges are several feet in length. In a good light the rectangles of the lilac and mauve fabric display tiny puckers along some of the short edges. These creases were produced by the fabric having been tightly gathered for some considerable period, probably around the waistband of a dress. It was not unusual to reuse fabric from clothing when making a patchwork quilt but in this instance the use of fabric that so clearly betrayed its former use seems to suggest either poor workmanship or extreme frugality. Many items of home-produced needlework were of this level of skill and equally lacking in aesthetic charm, but these items survive in far fewer numbers than the examples of exquisite workmanship that are passed on as heirlooms. In this instance a piece of unfinished patchwork was put away and forgotten until it was found by a later generation that revered their heritage to such an extent that all the possessions of past generations were kept and cherished.[105]

The textile bed hangings at Locust Lawn were the grandest item of the three described. They were also the oldest, dating from about 1770 so they were a cherished item from an earlier generation when Josiah Hasbrouck built his fine house. The fabric of the hangings is heavy cotton printed in blue by use of a copper plate. The fabric would have been imported from England and then made up into the hangings at home. The curtains and valance are all bound with a blue tape to match the printed design. In the 1770s cotton fabric for bed hangings was prestigious. It was expensive to produce before the industrialization of the cotton industry brought prices down. The earlier use of wood blocks was giving way to copper plates finely engraved with designs. Large repeats required more skill to engrave and print and were therefore more expensive than compact designs. The repeat of the pattern on the Locust Lawn bed hangings is approximately two feet. By the early-nineteenth century copper plates were made into cylinders that greatly speeded up the printing process, but these were generally designs with small repeats.[106] All of these aspects of the manufacture of the fabric would have given these hangings status and made them worth passing on to future generations. However, there is a further dimension to these particular hangings that would have marked them out as special to their owners and visitors to the home of the Hasbroucks. The design is made up of florid medallions of roses, fruit and rococo ornaments. In amongst these medallions are individual and grouped depictions of birds. Some perch on branches with their tail feathers luxuriantly displayed, a group of ducks nestle amongst bull rushes and a hen flirts coquettishly with a cockerel.[107] This unusual print and the size of the repeat pattern would have created a dramatic statement in the bed room where they were hung.

The bed hangings at Locust Lawn will present the curator at this house museum with a dilemma. If the US policy of retiring original textiles is followed then only reproduction fabrics could be used in the house when it opens to the public. It is unlikely that this particular design is available commercially and to have it specially made would be too costly. So a similar design would need to be selected. But a similar design would not recreate the highly individual choice that these hangings represent.

At Locust Lawn, as at Brodsworth Hall and the Codman House, described above, fine and common place items existed side by side. Original objects demonstrate the true homemaking choices practised by individual homemakers. Only through their retention in situ can these choices be made apparent to visitors of historic house museums.

Conclusion

This chapter set out to examine the methods employed at historic houses open to the public to see if they were able to capture something of the experiences of people's domestic lives that had been the subject of the preceding chapters. Homes in the past may have generally followed the trends of their period but all homes reflected the personalities of their occupants. These homes were unique and demonstrated the particular circumstances of the lived experience of individuals.

The homes looked at in Chapters 1–5 explored homemaking as consumption practice. Homemakers had to reconcile the tensions inherent in creating a home. So, work continued to intrude in some homes long after separation was thought to be desirable. Old-fashioned objects sat alongside fashionable ones. Furnishings were repaired, and objects that displayed patina existed alongside new. Different levels of society responded in a variety of ways to housing servants, and to providing a public role for the home. Bachelors and independent women produced gendered furnishing solutions.[108] Each home generated its own narratives produced by objects with personal associations. And all of these homemaking solutions were temporary ones since the circumstances of homemakers changed during their lives. To capture this context of homemaking historic house museums need to include an interpretation programme that narrates the stories of the past, and articulates the interpretation process to its visitors.

The premise of this chapter has been that historic houses are interpreted for visitors. Curators and historians who interpret the past inevitably make subjective decisions. In addition, different methods have been used over time and although ideas have moved forward some houses continue to display methods that were current perhaps 50 or more years ago. The differences and proclivities of the methods used in England and the United States have also been highlighted; clearly this is a subject warranting far more analysis. However some conclusions can be drawn from the methods examined.

Restored houses have perhaps the strongest tendency to produce generic period rooms particularly when they rely on insufficient evidence. Even when there is good documentation for what rooms contained some guesswork is still needed. There is a tendency to fill gaps with obvious and fashionable choices of furnishings whereas, as we have seen in the previous chapters in real homes, this was not always the case. Interpretation based on what is aesthetically pleasing is slightly less in evidence now that documentation of authentic interiors is adhered to. But there is still the possibility of editing out items or choosing what we think *should* be in a room. The use of replicas too encourages an over-pristine and too-perfect creation to be achieved. Over-tidy rooms are often the result. However, restored houses do allow narratives about domestic interiors of the past to be told. And they are the only way for pre-twentieth century working-class interiors to be represented since such homes do not survive intact.

Preserving layers should be 'authentic' and individual but inevitably includes much tidying up of stray and what appear extraneous elements; ornaments of lesser value and family mementoes. This method is most inclined towards the use of aesthetic judgements. While it might avoid generic period room settings it can result in rooms that merely present a collection of antiques. This occurs when much of the furniture has been sold or retained by the donor. Since this method is most often employed for wealthy homes such houses often do not offer much scope for an inclusive presentation beyond attempts to show 'downstairs' life for servants. However, it could be argued that for many people this is not the reason for visiting a large and grand house. As Clive Aslet, editor of *Country Life* has observed, 'The country house is the product of an elitist culture and you can't escape that.'[109]

Preserved as found is then the method that most accurately reflects lived experience, providing that not too much tidying up is allowed beyond safety issues. Use of this method avoids generic room settings since the contents and their disposition are retained. However, this method can only present rooms as they appeared when the house became a museum. This is a serious limitation. If all houses were treated like this there could be no tangible recreations of rooms in the past. And in most cases it would not be suitable for working-class housing since invariably this status of building has seen the most changes. Wealthier families, especially those that have fallen on hard times, are the most likely to keep interiors intact. Apart from the lack of social inclusion then this method is also in danger of almost exclusively celebrating eccentric and rather sad lives.

As the final section demonstrated, houses that have been interpreted using any of the above methods can employ demanding and enlightening display techniques to enable visitors to gain understanding about objects, interiors and the people who inhabited them. Gaynor Kavangh suggests that 'to make any sense of the past, the cultural context has to be reconstructed.'[110] She is referring to traditional museums where the context needs to be provided in the display and interpretation provided. At historic houses the context is readily available. But that context is fragile and can easily be upset by insensitive treatment. Protecting and preserving the tangible evidence should be paramount in all decisions that affect the interiors. Historic houses provide a unique educational tool that objects in a museum cannot match. Finding new ways to access that material and protect it for the future is an ongoing challenge.

Notes

[1]   Jane Austen (1954 originally published 1813), *Pride and Prejudice*, London: Zodiac Press, p. 188.

[2]   Of the homes examined in the previous chapters only two are open to the public with 'historic interiors', although a number of others still exist as buildings. Soho House in Birmingham, the home of Matthew Boulton, has restored interiors. It is owned by Birmingham Museums. Benthall Hall is now owned by the National Trust and is shown with layers of occupation that relate to several families but not the Harries family whose occupation was examined in Chapter 2.

[3]   Diane Barthel (1996), *Historic Preservation: Collective Memory and Historical Identity*, New Brunswick NJ: Rutgers University Press, p. 10.

[4]   See George W. McDonald (1982), *Hearth and Home: Preserving a People's Culture*, Philadelphia: Temple University Press.

[5]   England has been chosen for the comparison rather than the UK as certain trends in preservation differ between the countries of the UK.

[6]   Stuart Hall (ed.) (1997), Introduction, *Representation: Cultural Representations and Signifying Practices*, London: Sage in association with the Open University, p. 8.

[7]   Select bibliography for the history of the preservation movement in England: James Lees-Milne (ed.) (1945), *The National Trust: A Record of Fifty Years' Achievement*, London: Batsford; Robin Feddon (1968), *The National Trust: Past and Present*, London: Jonathan Cape; Gervase Jackson-Stops (ed.) (1985), *The Treasure Houses of Britain*, Washington DC: National Gallery of Art; David Lowenthal (1985), *The Past is a Foreign Country*, Cambridge: Cambridge University Press; Patrick Wright (1985), *On Living in an Old Country*, London: Verso; Robert Hewison (1987), *The Heritage Industry: Britain in a Climate of Decline*, London: Methuen; *Treasures for the Nation* (1988), exhibition catalogue, London: British Museum for the National Heritage

Memorial Fund; Jennifer Jenkins and Patrick James (1994), *From Acorn to Oak Tree: The Growth of the National Trust 1895–1994*, London: National Trust; Paula Weideger (1994), *Gilding the Acorn: Behind the Façade of the National Trust*, London: Simon and Schuster; Merlin Waterson (1994), *The National Trust: The First Hundred Years*, London: National Trust and BBC Books; Emma Barker (1999), 'Heritage and the Country House', in Emma Barker (ed.), *Contemporary Cultures of Display*, New York and London: Yale University Press; Peter Mandler (1997), *The Fall and Rise of the Stately Home*, New York and London: Yale University Press; Gill Chitty and David Baker (1999), *Managing Sites and Buildings: Reconciling Presentation and Preservation*, London: Routledge; John Cornforth (1998), *The Country Houses of England, 1948–98*, London: Constable; Adrian Tinniswood (1998), *The Polite Tourist: a History of Country House Visiting*, London: National Trust; David Lowenthal (1998*)*, *The Heritage Crusade and the Spoils of History*, Cambridge: Cambridge University Press.

8   Mandler (1997), *The Fall and Rise*, gives an economic explanation for some owners opening their homes.

9   Although the legislation was in place by 1937 World War II intervened to prevent progress for some years.

10   John Ruskin quoted in Nikolaus Pevsner (1976), 'Scrape or Anti-Scrape', in Jane Fawcett (ed.), *The Future of the Past: Attitudes to Conservation 1174–1974*, London: Thames and Hudson, p. 49.

11   Mark Girouard 'Living with the Past: Victorian Alterations to Country Houses', in Fawcett (1976), *The Future of the Past*, p. 133.

12   Girouard in Fawcett (1976), *The Future of the Past*, p. 134.

13   Girouard in Fawcett (1976), *The Future of the Past*, p. 136.

14   The overlap of people involved in both organizations and the continued close connections is acknowledged by Simon Jervis (1997), 'Far from Uniform', *SPAB Newsletter*, volume 18, number 4, pp. 12–15.

15   For an account of the Country House Scheme see Waterson (1994), *The National Trust*.

16   Christopher Rowell and John Martin Robinson (1996), *Uppark Restored*, London: National Trust, p. 172.

17   *Guide to Hanbury Hall, Worcestershire* (1981), London: The National Trust.

18   Michael Saunders Watson foreword to Anna Sproule and Michael Pollard (1988), *The Country House Guide: Family Homes in the Historic Houses Association*, London: Century, p. 10.

19   Sproule and Pollard (1988), *The Country House*, p. 14.

20   Carla Carlisle (2004), editorial, *Country Life*, 20 May 2004, p. 220.

21   Hewison (1987), *The Heritage Industry*, p. 71.

22   Visit made in 2001.

23   Watson foreword to Sproule and Pollard (1988), *The Country House*, p. 7.

24   Anthony Mitchell (1999), 'Conservation in Context: the Conservation of Historic Interiors by the National Trust', in Velson Horie (ed.), *The Conservation of Decorative Arts*, London: Archetype Publications, p. 29.

25   Mandler (1997), *The Rise and Fall*, p. 413.

26   Louise Ward (1996), 'Chintz, swags and bows: The myth of the English Country-House Style', *Things*, number 5, pp. 7–37. For an account of John Fowler's involvement with the Trust see John Cornforth (1978), 'John Fowler and the National Trust', in Gervase Jackson-Stops (ed.), *National Trust Studies 1979*, London: Sotheby Parke Bernet.

27 Mitchell (1999), 'Conservation in Context', p. 29.

28 Mitchell (1999), 'Conservation in Context', p. 30.

29 Mitchell (1999), 'Conservation in Context', p. 33. Rowell and Robinson attribute the idea of restoring decorative schemes to match faded colours to John Fowler, although due to the then inadequate conservation technique of using paint scrapes, it was not possible to be accurate. Rowell and Robinson (1996), *Uppark Restored*, p.173.

30 *Guidebook to Eastnor Castle, Ledbury, Herefordshire* (c. 2003), pp. 13 and 20. Privately owned houses continue with this method but the National Trust and English Heritage have adopted more rigorous methods informed by current conservation techniques that will be dealt with later in this chapter.

31 Barthel (1996), *Historic Preservation*. The restoration of historic houses in the US has allowed for explicit stories of the past to be told. However, these stories have been dominated by political and nationalistic tendencies as explained in Patricia West (1999), *Domesticating History: the Political Origins of America's House Museums*, Washington and London: Smithsonian Institution Press. When social history became more influential in museum interpretation so the difficult stories of the past, such as slavery, have been included at sites but again this has not escaped criticism. See for example Richard Handler and Eric Gable (1997), *The New History in an Old Museum: Creating the Past at Colonial Williamsburg*, Durham and London: Duke University Press.

32 Weideger (1994), *Gilding the Acorn*, p. 68.

33 Fiona Reynolds, who became director general of the National Trust in 2001, quoted in Sandy Mitchell (2001), 'Upstairs, downstairs', *Daily Telegraph Magazine*, 20 October 2001, pp. 23–25.

34 Charles B. Hosmer (1965), *Presence of the Past: a History of the Preservation Movement in the United States Before Williamsburg*, New York: G.P. Putnam, p. 36.

35 Hosmer (1965), *Presence of the Past*, pp. 41–49.

36 In the US a guide to historic house museums lists the sites together with a description of the site and a definition of the interpretation method used. For example, one entry has as its primary interpretive period and themes described as '1820, The social, both public and private, uses of the spaces; relationships between householders and slaves; Richmond's place in transatlantic trade.' Patricia Chambers Walker and Thomas Graham (2000), *Directory of Historic House Museums in the US*, AltaMira Press, p. xii. No guide explicitly describes the interpretation of UK historic houses this way. In the US it is also quite usual to have guides take visitors through the house to explain the interiors, the objects and their use in the past. In the UK this is rarely the case.

37 Select bibliography of US heritage movement: Hosmer (1965), *Presence of the Past*; William T. Alderson and Shirley Payne Low (1976), *Interpretation of Historic Sites*, Nashville TN: American Association for State and Local History; William Seale (1979), *Recreating the Historic House Interior*, Nashville TN: American Association for State and Local History; Charles B. Hosmer (1981), *Preservation Comes of Age: From Williamsburg to National Trust, 1926–1949*, Charlottesville: University of Virginia; William J. Murtagh (1988), *Keeping Time: the History and Theory of Preservation in America*, Pittstown NJ: Main Street Press; Sherry Butcher-Younghans (1993), *Historic House Museums: A Practical Handbook for their Care, Preservation and Management*, New York: Oxford University Press; James M. Lindgren (1995), *Preserving New England*, New York and Oxford: Oxford University Press; Barthell (1996), *Historic Preservation*; Jessica Foy Donnelly (ed.) (2002), *Interpreting Historic House Museums*, Walnut Creek CA: AltaMira Press.

38 Jan Cohn (1979), *The Palace or the Poorhouse: the American House as a Cultural Symbol*, East Lansing: The Michigan State University Press, p. x.

39 Unlike Historic Deerfield, Greenfield and Colonial Williamsburg both moved buildings to the site and recreated others.

40 Hosmer (1965), *Presence of the Past*, p. 239. The British Arts and Crafts architect and designer C.R. Ashbee had attempted to found an American National Trust in 1901 but had not succeeded. The aims of the SPNEA were the closest to the English National Trust. Hosmer (1965), *Presence of the Past*, p. 255. The SPNEA is now called Historic New England.

41 Quoted in Lindgren (1995), *Preserving New England*, p. 141.

42 See Lindgren (1995), *Preserving New England*; Richard Nylander (1995), 'The Codman House: A Case Study in Preserving and Interpreting Context', in Wendy Claire Jessup (ed.), *Conservation in Context: Finding a Balance for the Historic House Museum*, Proceedings from the Symposium 7–8 March 1994, Andrew Mellon Foundation and National Trust for Historic Preservation.

43 To distinguish between the two, the full title National Trust for Historic Preservation will always be used to refer to the US organization.

44 For more on Colonial Revival taste in furniture see T.A. Denenberg and T.E. Bowman (January 2003), 'Wallace Nutting and the Invention of Old America', *The Magazine Antiques*, pp. 130–137.

45 Jane C. Nylander (1993), *Our Own Snug Fireside: Images of the New England Home 1760–1860*, New Haven and London: Yale University Press, p. 16.

46 Helen Hughes (ed.) (2000), *Layers of Understanding: Setting Standards for Architectural Paint Research*, Papers taken from the proceedings of English Heritage national seminar in London, 28 April 2000, Shaftsbury: Donhead.

47 Roger W. Moss (1998), *Historic Houses of Philadelphia: a Tour of the Region's Museum Homes*, Philadelphia: University of Pennsylvania Press.

48 Hosmer (1965), *Presence of the Past*, pp. 282–283.

49 Edward O. Welles (1982), 'George Washington Slept Here…And Here's How It Really Looked: Scientific Paint Analysis and Washington's Own Writings Help Conservators Give Mount Vernon a Surprising New Look', *Historic Preservation*, volume 34, number 3, pp. 22–27.

50 See Elaine Green (ed.) (1986), 'The Period Room Reconsidered: A House and Garden Symposium', *House and Garden* (US), October 1986, pp. 219–225, 256–265; Michael Olmert (1985), 'The New, No-frills Williamsburg', *Historic Preservation*, volume 37, number 5, October 1985, pp. 27–33.

51 Rowell and Robinson (1996), *Uppark Restored*, p. 172.

52 Peter Thornton was also influenced by Scandinavian museum practice. He was Keeper of the Furniture and Woodwork Department from 1966 to 1984.

53 Ham and Osterley were owned by the National Trust but administered until 1990 by the Victoria and Albert Museum. Apsley House has now passed to English Heritage.

54 Barthel (1996), *Historic Preservation*, pp. 147–148.

55 The public outcry against the reinterpretation at Colonial Williamsburg is commented on in Greene (1986), 'The Period Room'.

56 If all the originals are kept on display then the most fragile elements, especially the textiles, are liable to deteriorate. To counter this, lighting levels are kept low and conditions are carefully monitored. Even the visiting public walking through the rooms creates additional threats to the textiles by causing dust to move around and harm them.

A seminar entitled 'Dust to Dust: Science, Perception and Management in Historic Interiors' was held at the British Library, London, 12 April 2005. The seminar was the culmination of a three-year research project by the University of East Anglia, Historic Royal Palaces, and English Heritage.

57 David Phillips (1997), *Exhibiting Authenticity*, Manchester: Manchester University Press, p. 129.

58 Murtagh, (1988), *Keeping Time*, p. 84. For the debates within the conservation community surrounding this problem see Deborah Lee Trupin (1997), 'Exhibiting Textiles in Historic House Furnished Rooms: Balancing Conservation and Interpretation', *Fabric of an Exhibition: An Interdisciplinary Approach*, Preprints of a Conference, Ottawa: Canadian Conservation Institute, pp. 45–49; Bonnie Halvorson (2000), 'Modern Replacement Fabrics in Historic Interiors: Ethical and Practical Concerns', *The Conservation of Heritage Interiors*, Preprints of a Conference, Ottawa: Canadian Conservation Institute, pp. 107–112.

59 George L. Wrenn (1971), 'What is a Historic House Museum?', *Historic Preservation*, volume 23, number 1, pp. 55–58, p. 56.

60 See the Prentis house at the Shelburne Museum, Vermont. This house preserves the arrangements created by the collector and interior decorator Katherine Prentis Murphy in the 1950s. Although the interiors were later somewhat restored to authentic eighteenth-century decoration and arrangements, those of Katherine Prentis Murphy have been reinstated, and in some instances elements, commonly used by her elsewhere, have been introduced to 'honour Mrs Murphy'. *A Souvenir of Shelburne Museum* (2005), Shelburne VT. See also H. Joyce and J.E. Edwards (April 2002), 'Three Historic Houses at the Shelburne Museum Reinterpreted', *The Magazine Antiques*, pp. 104–113.

61 Jervis (1997), 'Far from Uniform', p. 13.

62 English Heritage hosted a symposium 'Inspired by the Past: John Fowler's Approach to Decoration and Restoration in a Changing World', London, 4 July 2001. A publication is forthcoming.

63 Simon Jervis (1997), 'Far from Uniform', p. 14. Jervis states that the Trust still wishes to preserve the 'spirit of place' in its properties. He suggests that between restoring and preserving as found there are 'many steps in between' where a 'complex balance' is desirable, p. 13.

64 Amelia Peck (1998), *Lyndhurst: A Guide to the House and Landscape*, Tarrytown, NY: The National Trust for Historic Preservation.

65 Barthel (1996), *Historic Preservation*, p. 2.

66 Murtagh (1988), *Keeping Time*, pp. 80–81.

67 Ward (1996), 'Chintz, Swags and Bows', pp. 7–8.

68 The United Kingdom Institute of Conservators (UKIC), an organization that united conservators as a single profession despite differences between specialisms. Even more recent has been the UKIC interiors subdivision that holds seminars and conferences to bring together discussion about objects in context and the interior decoration of houses; aspects that had previously been neglected. The US equivalent of UKIC is the AIC (American Institute for Conservation). Select bibliography for conservation principals and codes of practice: Sharon Timmons (ed.) (1976), *Preservation and Conservation: Principles and Practices*, The proceedings of the North American International Regional Conference, Williamsburg, Virginia and Philadelphia, Pennsylvania, 10–16 September, 1972, Washington, DC: Smithsonian Institution Press; Robert F. McGriffin (1983), *Furniture Care and Conservation*, Nashville, Tennessee: American Association for

State and Local History; Sheila Landi (1992), *The Textile Conservator's Manual*, 2nd edition, London: Butterworth-Heinemann; Jessica S. Johnson (1993), 'Conservation and Archaeology in Great Britain and the United States: A Comparison', *Journal of the American Institute for Conservation*, volume 32, number 3, pp. 249–269; Wendy Claire Jessup, (1995), *Conservation in Context: Finding a Balance for the Historic House Museum*, Symposium 7–8 March 1994, Andrew W. Mellon Foundation and National Trust for Historic Preservation, Washington DC; Kysnia Marko (ed.) (1997), *Textiles in Trust*, Proceedings of the Symposium at Blickling Hall, Norfolk, September 1995, London: Archetype Publications in association with the National Trust; Jane Henderson and Diane Dollery (2000), 'Growing Pains: The Development of a Conservation Profession in the UK', in Ashrok Roy and Perry Smith (eds) (2000), *Tradition and Innovation: Advances in Conservation*, Contributions to the Melbourne Congress, 10–14 October 2000; Dinah Eastop and K. Gill (eds.) (2001), *Upholstery Conservation: Principles and Practice*, Oxford: Butterworth-Heinemann; Kate Clark (2001), *Informed Conservation*, London: English Heritage; Hughes (2000), *Layers of Understanding*.

[69] Phillips (1997), *Exhibiting Authenticity*, p. 126.

[70] Phillips (1997), *Exhibiting Authenticity*, p. 128.

[71] Drayton Hall visitor leaflet 2005.

[72] Guidebooks were not available for this property or Drayton Hall. Information was taken from publicity material and personal visits in 2005.

[73] For a full discussion of Brodsworth see Phillips (1997), *Exhibiting Authenticity*, pp. 129–132.

[74] Phillips (1997), *Exhibiting Authenticity*, p. 130.

[75] Phillips (1997), *Exhibiting Authenticity*, p. 131. A photograph of this room is shown with less romantic drapery in Emma Barker (1999), 'Heritage and the Country House', in Emma Barker (ed.), *Contemporary Cultures of Display*, New York and London: Yale University Press, p. 225.

[76] Phillips (1997), *Exhibiting Authenticity*, p. 132.

[77] David Flemming (1993), *Social History in Museums: a Handbook for Professionals*, London: HMSO.

[78] For a discussion of the Trust's desire to widen its appeal see Sandy Mitchell (2001), 'Upstairs, downstairs'.

[79] Weideger (1994), *Gilding the Acorn*, p. 383.

[80] See for example Handler and Gable (1997), *The New History*, on the debate at Colonial Williamsburg over whether to leave horse manure in the streets.

[81] For images of the interiors in the 1970s see Catherine Beecher Stowe and Harriet Beecher Stowe (1994 with an introduction by Joseph Van Why), *The American Woman's Home*, Hartford CT: The Stowe-Day Foundation. I am grateful to Elif Armbruster for the information on the reinterpretation of the Beecher Stowe house.

[82] Jervis (1997), 'Far from Uniform', p. 14. For a description of the clutter at 2 Willow Road see Gillian Naylor (1999), 'Modernism and Memory: Leaving Traces', in Marius Kwint, Christopher Breward and Jeremy Aynsley (eds), *Material Memories: Design and Evocation*, Oxford: Berg.

[83] The restoration project is fully detailed in editions of the *Newsletter* of the Historical Society of Delaware, 1984–86.

[84] Charles T. Lyle (1986), *The George Read II House*, Offprint from the Delaware Antiques Show Catalog, Reprinted by the Historical Society of Delaware, no page numbers.

85 The house had only three owners. The late-nineteenth century owners are not fully represented in the interpretation; however, a sparsely furnished room on the second floor gives the guide the opportunity to talk about their occupation of the house.

86 Letters page, *Historic Preservation*, volume 37, number 4, August 1985, pp. 4–5.

87 It is not unusual for American houses to display signs of habitation but it is difficult to do well. For a discussion on this subject see Nancy E. Villa Bryk (2002), '"I wish you could take a peek at us at the present moment": Infusing the Historic House with Characters and Activity', in Jessica Foy Donnelly (ed.), *Interpreting Historic House Museums*, Walnut Creek CA: AltaMira Press. In houses displayed in the Colonial Revival style it is usual to have artefacts supposedly in use but displayed as art objects. This is especially the case in kitchens and pantries.

88 Ruth J. Abrams (2000), 'Planting Cut Flowers', *History News: the Magazine of the American Association for State and Local History*, volume 55, number 3, pp.4–10.

89 English Heritage along with private and state-owned country houses in Yorkshire staged special exhibitions during 2004 called 'Maids and Mistresses: Celebrating 300 Years of Women and the Yorkshire Country House'.

90 Merlin Waterson (1990), *The Servants' Hall: a Domestic History of Erddig*, London: The National Trust, p. 9.

91 There is now an extensive literature on the subject of collecting and collections. For example see Susan M. Pearce (ed.) (1994), *Interpreting Objects and Collections*, London: Routledge; John Elsner and Roger Cardinal (eds) (1994), *The Cultures of Collecting*, London: Reaktion Books.

92 *Evergreen House*, guidebook (n.d.); Susan Stiles Dowell (1994), 'Ever Beautiful', *Southern Accents*, November/December 1994 (no page numbers).

93 Their publicity material declares that the organization 'offers a unique opportunity to experience the lives and stories of New Englanders through their homes and possessions'. www.HistoricNewEngland.org

94 Nylander (1995), 'The Codman House', pp. 71–72.

95 *The Greyfriars Guidebook* (2002), London: The National Trust.

96 This process is described and illustrated in Rowell and Robinson (1996), *Uppark Restored*, pp. 107–126.

97 Rowell and Robinson (1996), *Uppark Restored*, p. 45.

98 Rowell and Robinson (1996), *Uppark Restored*, pp. 35–36.

99 Rowell and Robinson (1996), *Uppark Restored*, p. 36.

100 Rowell and Robinson (1996), *Uppark Restored*, p. 42.

101 Locust Lawn is now owned by the Huguenot Historical Society. The house passed down through the Hasbrouck family and most of the contents were retained. However, the last occupants did add some objects and unfortunately this information was not always recorded.

102 It may be the case that increasingly houses will open during the process of interpretation. Tyntesfield, a house owned by the National Trust near Bristol, is being treated in this way.

103 I volunteered for several weeks at this site in 2004 and revisited in 2005. I am grateful to the Huguenot Historical Society for allowing me access to their collections. In particular I am indebted to the curator Leslie LeFevre-Stratton and her interns, Ashley Hurlbert and Korri Krajacek, for sharing ideas and information with me for this publication.

104 Ulrich suggests that there were patriotic reasons for the home production and consumption of imitations of rose blankets at this period. Laurel Thatcher Ulrich (2001),

The Age of Homespun: Objects and Stories in the Creation of an American Myth, New York: Alfred A. Knopf.

[105] The Huguenot Historical Society was primarily founded as a genealogical society. See Nylander (1994), *Our Own Snug Fireside*, for comments on the home production of clothing and bedding and the retention of textile objects by historical societies in New England.

[106] Adrian Forty (1986), *Objects of Desire: Design and Society 1750–1980*, London: Thames and Hudson.

[107] This design is reproduced in Florence M. Montgomery (1970), *Printed Textiles: English and American Cottons and Linens 1700–1850*, New York: Viking Press, p. 235.

[108] Homes inhabited by independent women are the least represented in historic house museums.

[109] Quoted in Sandy Mitchell (2001), 'Upstairs, downstairs', p. 25.

[110] Gaynor Kavangh (1990), *History Curatorship*, Washington DC: Smithsonian Institute, p. 65.

Appendix

Homemakers and Tradespeople

Listed here are the homemakers and tradespeople who appear in the text. Since a number of them are featured several times the lists should be used in conjunction with the index.

Homemakers

Name	Place	Occupation	Date
Charles Bowyer ADDERLEY	Hams Hall, near Birmingham	Gentleman	1837
John ALCOTT	Coventry	Stonemason	1827
Jonah BISSELL	Birmingham	Merchant in fancy and hardware metal goods	1842
Anne BOULTON	Birmingham	Spinster	1819–1829
Matthew BOULTON	Birmingham	Metal wares manufacturer	1790s
Matthew Robinson BOULTON	Birmingham	Metal wares manufacturer	1826–1838
Mary BUCKNILL	Coventry	Widow	1838
Mr BRADBURY	Stone, Staffordshire	–	1823
Ann BURGE	Chichester	Laundress?	1841
Anne CAVE	Clifton upon Dunsmore, Warwickshire	Gentlewoman	1755
Ann CHANDLER	Shrewsbury	Widow	1814
Harriet and Margaret CROFT	Chichester	Spinsters	1840s
Ann DEVEY	Bridgnorth, Shropshire	Widow	1767
William DIXON	Stone	Gentleman	1825–1826
Fanny DOWNES	Coventry	Spinster	1858
Marie Ann DRINKWATER	Chichester	Spinster	1806–1841
Col. EGERTON	Severn Hills, near Shrewsbury	Gentleman	1814
Richard EVASON	Cardington, Shropshire	Farmer	1777

James EYKYN	Wolverhampton	Upholsterer	1780
Thomas FARNEL	Sutton Coldfield	Brickmaker and farmer	1830
William FIELD	Rumboldswhyke, West Sussex	Farmer	1841
Mary FISHER	Chichester	Spinster	1841
Ann FOX	Cleobury Mortimer	Spinster	1813
Thomas FRANCIS	Birmingham	Gentleman	1849
Elizabeth GOODALL	Coventry	Plumber and glazier	1837
Richard GREVIS	King's Norton, Worcestershire	Gentleman	1759
John HAINES	Coventry	Silk dyer	1821
Francis Blythe HARRIES	Broseley	Gentleman	1840s
Ann and Thomas HEELEY	Birmingham	Grocer and toy maker	1764
Margaret HIGGINSON	Bridgnorth	Widow	1762
Avery HOMER	Birmingham	Tanner	1834
Joseph HUNT	Birmingham	Gunsmith	1770
Rev. Mr HUNTLEY	Shifnal, Shropshire	Vicar	1794
Catherine HUTTON	Birmingham	Spinster	1791–1825
Samuel HUTTON	Ward End Hall, near Birmingham	Stationer	1837
William HUTTON	Birmingham	Stationer and historian	1791
Elizabeth JEFFRIES	Bridgnorth	Widow	1768
Mary Ann LIVINGSTON	Chichester	Spinster	1840–1843
Thomas LOVATT	Claverley, Shropshire	Farmer	1786
John and Susannah MARRIAN	Bobbington, Staffordshire	Farmer	1761 & 1770
Miss MARSHALL	Stone	Milliner	1825–1828
Mary Ann MASON	Chichester	–	1836
Miss MAYOR	Meole Brace, Shrewsbury	Spinster	1831
Fairfax MORESBY Esq.	Lichfield	Gentleman	1816
MORRIS	Lewes, Sussex	–	Mid-19th c.
James MULLOCK	Whitchurch, Shropshire	Farmer	1804

Robert MYNOR	Birmingham	Surgeon and midwife	1790
Mrs G. NEWLAND (Alithia)	Chichester	Widow	1840s–1851
William Charles NEWLAND	Chichester	Gentleman	1806–1851
James Wakeman NEWPORT	Hanley William, Worcestershire	Gentleman	1785
Celia PARKER	Chichester	Spinster	1848
David PARKES	Shrewsbury	Schoolmaster, artist and antiquarian	1833
Elizabeth PARSONS	Wolston, Warwickshire	Widow	1849
William PICKARD	Walgrave, Warwickshire	–	1856
Hannah and Catherine POYNER	Bridgnorth	Gentlewomen	1765
Joseph PRIESTLEY	Birmingham	Presbyterian minister & scientist	1791
Charles RIDGE	Chichester	Proprietor, Chichester Old Bank	1839–1842
Thomas ROBINSON	Coventry	Confectioner	1853
Caroline SMELT	Chichester	Spinster	1847
Elizabeth STAMPER	Chichester	Spinster	1844
John STAUNTON	Kenilworth	Gentleman	1800–1811
Thomas STEVENS	Stone	Gentleman	1831
Thomas THOMAS	Bobbington, Shropshire	Farmer	1796
Henry WACE	Shrewsbury	Solicitor	1861
Joseph WILSON	Chichester	Surgeon	1841
Catherine WRIGHT	Withybrooke, Warwickshire	Widow	1843
Mary YOUNG	Coventry	Milliner	1841

Tradespeople

Name	Place	Occupation	Date
APLETREE	Birmingham	Cabinetmaker & upholsterer	1838
Thomas BARKE	Shifnal, Shropshire	Cabinetmaker, upholsterer, appraiser & auctioneer	1835
Richard BRIDGENS	Birmingham (and London)	Architect and designer	1820s
Mr CAMPIONE	Itinerant	Seller of Italian and French paintings and ornaments	1770
Elizabeth COOKE	Birmingham	Upholsterer	1819–1823
Cornelius DIXON	Birmingham	Interior decorator	1790s
Thomas DONALDSON	Shrewsbury	Carver and gilder	1811
ELD and CHAMBERLAIN	Birmingham	Furnishing draper	1861
James EYKYN	Wolverhampton	Upholsterer	1780
John FALLOW	Birmingham	Auctioneer	1849
John FODEN	Stone, Staffordshire	Furniture maker (wheelwright)	1827–1866
Richard FRANCE	Shrewsbury	Cabinetmaker, chair maker and furniture broker	1794
Thomas HARRIS	Birmingham	Cabinetmaker and upholsterer	1851
HENSMAN	Birmingham	Cabinetmaker & upholsterer	1812
James HOPKINSON	Nottingham	Cabinetmaker	1840s
KENDALL and Son	Birmingham	Toilet case makers	1858
John LUSH	Chichester	Portrait painter	1830–1840s
James MILLAR	Birmingham	Portrait painter	1790
J. MILLS	Birmingham	Cabinetmaker	1840s
James NEWTON	London	Cabinetmaker	1797–1805
ONIONS	Birmingham	Furniture broker	1840s
Samuel PEARSON	Birmingham	Cabinetmaker and furniture broker	1824
Henry PEAT	Chichester	Cabinetmaker and appraiser	1806–1840s

Samuel PEAT	Chichester	Cabinetmaker	1840s–1850s
Jonathan PERRY	Shrewsbury	Auctioneer	1814
J. PHILLIPS	London	Broker and appraiser	1791
John RODDERICK	Birmingham	Auctioneer	1840s
Thomas SHAKSHAFT	Middleton, Warwickshire	Joiner	1751–1763
Thomas SMALLWOOD	Birmingham	Cabinetmaker & upholsterer	1795
Mr SMITH	Shropshire	Auctioneer	1845
TANNER	Birmingham	Cabinetmaker & upholsterer	1815
Robert URWICK	Shrewsbury	Joiner	1744
Elizabeth VOWLES	Birmingham	Furniture broker	1826
Thomas WARREN	Birmingham	Auctioneer	1787

Bibliography

Primary Sources

Birmingham City Archives, Birmingham Central Library
Inventory and papers relating to Jonah Bissell, MS319/1–31
Matthew Boulton papers [MBP]
Eld and Chamberlain catalogue and bills, MS1081/1–8
Hutton Beale family papers 106/12
Inventory of home of James Wakeman Newport, MS394886
Norton papers, inventory of Ham Hall (2182) 820–824
Inventory for the home of Joseph Priestley, 399801 (IIR30)
Notebook of Thomas Shakshaft, MSS 556647 (IIR41)
Pershouse Collection of Ephemera, volumes I and II, MS897
Account book and inventory relating to the Staunton family, 397968–71,
MS585/53, MS723, 73128 (IIR63)
Trade Directories for West Midlands
Trading ephemera
*A Supplement to the London Cabinet Makers' Price Book of 1797 As Agreed in
Birmingham January 1 1803*, (1803), Birmingham: Printed by M. Swinney, MS
108061
Aris's *Birmingham Gazette*

Coventry Archives, Coventry
Warwickshire wills

East Sussex Record Office, Lewes
Morris family notebook, AMS 5569/66

Lichfield Joint Record Office, Lichfield
Probate Records

Public Record Office, Kew
James Eykyn inventory, PROB 31/678/155
Richard Grevis inventory, PROB 31/436/91

Shropshire Record Office, Shrewsbury
Inventory for Richard Evason, 6000/17750
Inventory and family papers for Ann Fox, 6000/15298–15347
Inventory and family papers for Thomas Blythe Harries, 6000/12839/2–3, 15277
Inventory and family papers for Thomas Mullock, 6000/12167
Papers relating to David Parkes, 6001/153, D87.7, MSS3060, MSS4073, MSS6856

Salopian Journal

Staffordshire Record Office, Stafford
Account book of John Foden, 3161

West Sussex Record Office, Chichester
Chronology of Chichester, Add Mss 29,710
Family papers for Miss Drinkwater, Add Mss 8454, and 'Chichester Papers',
volume 5, Add Mss 11,128
Family papers for Mary Ann Fisher, Add Mss 16,607
Diary of John Lush, Add Mss 19026
Diary of Mary Ann Mason, Add Mss 29,830
Notebooks of Peat cabinetmakers, Add Mss 2235–45
Trade Directories for Sussex
Sussex Chronicle and Chichester Advertiser
Sussex Agricultural Express

Winterthur Library, Winterthur, Delaware, USA
Society of London Cabinetmakers Job Settling Committee Book, MSS 742

Secondary Sources

Abrams, Ruth J. (2000), 'Planting Cut Flowers', *History News: the Magazine of the American Association for State and Local History*, volume 55, number 3, pp.4–10.
Acton, Eliza (1860 first published in 1845), *Modern Cookery for Private Families*, London: Longman, Green, Longman and Roberts.
Alderson, William T. and Shirley Payne Low (1976), *Interpretation of Historic Sites*, Nashville TN: American Association for State and Local History.
Arscott, Caroline (1988), 'Employer, husband, spectator: Thomas Fairburn's commission of The Awakening Conscience', in J. Wolff and J. Seed (eds), *The Culture of Capital: Art, Power and the Nineteenth-Century Middle Class*, Manchester: Manchester University Press.
Attfield, Judy (1996), '"Give 'em something dark and heavy": The Role of Design in the Material Culture of Popular British Furniture 1939–1965', *Journal of Design History*, volume 9, number 3, pp. 185–201.
Attfield, Judy (2000), *Wild Things: the Material Culture of Everyday Life*, London: Berg.
Attfield, Judy and Pat Kirkham (eds) (1995), *A View from the Interior*, London: The Women's Press.
Austen, Jane (1954 originally published 1813), *Pride and Prejudice*, London: Zodiac Press.
Austen, Jane (1994 originally published in 1811), *Sense and Sensibility*, Harmondsworth: Penguin.

Ayres, James (1993), 'Domestic Interiors in Britain: a Review of the Existing Literature', in David Flemming (ed.), *Social History in Museums: a Handbook for Professionals*, London: HMSO.

Ayres, James (2003), *Domestic Interiors: The British Tradition 1500–1850*, New Haven and London: Yale University Press.

Barker, Emma (1999), 'Heritage and the Country House', in Barker, Emma (ed.), *Contemporary Cultures of Display*, New York and London: Yale University Press.

Barker, Hannah (1996), 'Catering for Provincial Tastes: Newspapers, Readership and Profit in Late-Eighteenth Century England', *Historical Research*, volume 69, number 168, pp. 42–61.

Barthel, Diane (1996), *Historic Preservation: Collective Memory and Historical Identity*, New Brunswick, NJ: Rutgers University Press.

Beale, Catherine Hutton (ed.) (1891), *Reminiscences of a Gentlewoman of the Last Century: Letters of Catherine Hutton*, Birmingham: Cornish Brothers.

Beard, Geoffrey and Christopher Gilbert (eds) (1986), *Dictionary of English Furniture Makers 1660–1840*, Leeds: Furniture History Society and W.S. Maney and Sons Ltd.

Beckett, John and Catherine Smith (2000), 'Urban Renaissance and Consumer Revolution in Nottingham, 1688–1750', *Urban History*, 27, pp. 31–50.

Beeton, Mrs Isabella (1861), *The Book of Household Management*, London: Ward, Lock & Co.

Benson, John (1996), 'Working-Class Consumption, Saving, and Investment in England and Wales, 1851–1911', *Journal of Design History*, volume 9, number 2, pp. 87–99.

Berg, Maxine (1996), 'Women's Consumption and the Industrial Classes of Eighteenth-Century England', *Journal of Social History*, volume 30, number 2, pp. 415–434.

The Book of the Household (c. 1870), London: The London Printing and Publishing Company.

Borsay, Peter (1989), *The English Urban Renaissance: Culture and Society in the Provincial Town, 1660–1770*, Oxford: Clarendon Press.

Borsay, Peter (1994), 'The London Connection: Cultural Diffusion and the Eighteenth-Century Provincial Town', *London Journal*, 19, pp. 21–35.

Borsay, Peter (ed.) (1990), *The Eighteenth-Century Town 1688–1820*, London: Longman.

Bourdieu, Pierre (1984), *Distinction: A Social Critique of the Judgement of Taste*, London: Routledge and Kegan Paul.

Bowett, Adam (1994), 'The Commercial Introduction of Mahogany and the Naval Stores Act of 1721', *Furniture History*, volume 30, pp. 43–56.

Branca, Patricia (1974), 'Image and Reality: The Myth of the Idle Victorian Woman' in Mary S. Hartman and Lois Banner (eds), *Clio's Consciousness Raised*, New York: Harper.

Brassington, W.S. (1894), *Historic Worcestershire*, Birmingham: The Midland Education Co. and Simpkin, Marshall, Hamilton and Kent.

Braudel, Ferdinand (1973), *Capitalism and Material Life 1400–1800*, London: Weidenfeld and Nicolson.

Brewer, John (1997), *The Pleasures of the Imagination: English Culture in the Eighteenth Century*, Chicago: University of Chicago Press.

Brewer, John and Roy Porter (eds), *Consumption and the World of Goods*, London: Routledge.

Bristow, Ian C. (1996), *Architectural Colour in British Interiors 1615–1840*, New Haven and London: Yale University Press.

Bryden, I. and J. Floyd (eds) (1999), *Domestic Space: Reading the Nineteenth-Century Interior*, Manchester: Manchester University Press.

Bryk, Nancy E. Villa (2002), '"I wish you could take a peek at us at the present moment": Infusing the Historic House with Characters and Activity', in Jessica Foy Donnelly (ed.), *Interpreting Historic House Museums*, Walnut Creek, CA: AltaMira Press.

Burman, Sandra (ed.) (1979), *Fit Work for Women*, London: Croom Helm.

Burnett, John (1978), *A Social History of Housing 1815–1970*, Newton Abbot: David and Charles.

Butcher-Younghans, Sherry (1993), *Historic House Museums: A Practical Handbook for their Care, Preservation and Management*, New York: Oxford University Press.

Campbell, Colin (1987), *The Romantic Ethic and the Spirit of Modern Consumerism*, Oxford: Blackwell.

Caraccioli, Charles (1775), *The Life of Robert, Lord Clive, Baron Plassey*, London: T. Bell.

Carlisle, Carla (2004), editorial, *Country Life*, 20 May 2004.

Cassell's Household Guide (1870–74), London: Cassell, Petter, and Galpin, volumes 1–4.

Chalklin, C.W. (1974), *The Provincial Towns of Georgian England: a Study of the Building Process, 1740–1820*, London: Edward Arnold.

Chapple, J.A.V. (1980), *Elizabeth Gaskell: A Portrait in Letters*, Manchester: Manchester University Press.

Cherry, Gordon E. (1994), *Birmingham: A Study in Geography, History and Planning*, Chichester: Wiley.

Chinn, Carl (1998), Introduction to *The Life of William Hutton*, Studley, Warwickshire: Brewin Books.

Chippendale, Thomas (1754), *The Gentleman and Cabinet Maker's Director*, London: published by the author.

Chitty, Gill and David Baker (1999*)*, *Managing Sites and Buildings: Reconciling Presentation and Preservation*, London: Routledge.

Cieraad, Irene (1999), At *Home: An Anthropology of Domestic Space*, Syracuse NY: Syracuse University Press.

Clark, Kate (2001), *Informed Conservation*, London: English Heritage.

Clarke, P. (ed.) (1984), *The Transformation of English Towns 1600–1800*, London: Hutchinson.

Cohn, Jan (1979), *The Palace or the Poorhouse: the American House as a Cultural Symbol*, East Lansing: The Michigan State University Press.

Collins, Diane (1993), 'Primitive or Not? Fixed-shop Retailing before the Industrial Revolution', *Journal of Regional and Local Studies*, volume 3, number 1, pp. 23–35.

Corfield, Penelope (1982), *The Impact of English Towns 1700–1800*, Oxford: Oxford University Press.

Cornforth, John (1978), 'John Fowler and the National Trust', in Gervase Jackson-Stops (ed.), *National Trust Studies 1979*, London: Sotheby Parke Bernet.

Cornforth, John (1998), *The Country Houses of England, 1948–98*, London: Constable.

Cosnett, Thomas (1825), *The Footman's Directory and Butler's Remembrance*, London: Simpkin, Marshall and Henry Colburn.

Cotton, Bernard D. (1990), *The English Regional Chair*, Woodbridge: Antique Collectors' Club.

Cox, Jeff and Nancy Cox (1984), 'Probate Inventories: the Legal Background', Part 1, *The Local Historian*, volume 16, number 1, pp. 133–145; Part 2, volume 16, number 2, pp. 217–228.

Cox, Jeff and Nancy Cox (2000), 'Probate 1500–1800: a System in Transition', in Tom Arkell, Nesta Evans and Nigel Goose, *When Death Do Us Part: Understanding the Probate Records of Early Modern England*, Oxford: Leopards Press.

Cox, Nancy (2000), The *Complete Tradesman: a Study of Retailing 1550–1820*, Aldershot: Ashgate.

Cruikshank, Dan and Neil Burton (1990), *Life in the Georgian City*, London: Viking.

Cwerne, Saulo B. and Alan Metcalf (2003), 'Storage and Clutter: Discourses and Practices of Order in the Domestic World', *Journal of Design History*, volume 16, number 3, pp. 229–239.

Davidoff, Leonore and Catherine Hall (1987), *Family Fortunes: Men and Women of the English Middle Class 1780–1850*, London: Routledge.

Davidson, Caroline (1985), *The World of Mary Ellen Best*, London: Chatto and Windus.

Davies, Kathleen M. (1981), 'Continuity and change in literary advice on marriage', in R.B. Outhwaite (ed.), *Marriage and Society: the Social History of Marriage*, London: Europa

Decker, Paul (1759), *Chinese Architecture*, London: printed for the author and sold by Henry Parker.

Denenberg, T.A. and T.E. Bowman (January 2003), 'Wallace Nutting and the Invention of Old America', *The Magazine Antiques*, pp. 130–137.

Denholm, A. F. (1988), 'The Impact of the Canal System on Three Staffordshire Market Towns 1760–1850', *Midland History*, volume 13, pp. 59–76.

Dent, Robert K. (1973 first published 1878–80), *Old and New Birmingham: A History of the Town and its People*, London: EP Publishing.

Dickens, Charles (1960 first published 1865), *Our Mutual Friend*, Oxford: Oxford University Press.

Donnelly, Jessica Foy (2002) (ed.), *Interpreting Historic House Museums*, Walnut Creek, CA: AltaMira Press.

Duggan, Audrey (2000*)*, *A Lady of Letters: Catherine Hutton 1757–1846*, Studley, Warwickshire: Brewin Books.

Durant, David N. (1988), *Living in the Past*, London: Aurum Press.

Earle, Peter (1989), *The Making of the English Middle Class*, London: Methuen.

Eastop, Dinah and K. Gill (eds) (2001), *Upholstery Conservation: Principles and Practice*, Oxford: Butterworth-Heinemann.

Edwards, Clive D. (1993), *Victorian Furniture: Technology and Design*, Manchester: Manchester University Press.

Edwards, Clive D. (1996), *Eighteenth-Century Furniture*, Manchester: Manchester University Press.

Elias, Norbert (1978), *The Civilising Process*, Oxford: Basil Blackwell.

Ellis, Mrs (1844), *Family Monitor and Domestic Guide: The Women of England, their Social Duties and Domestic Habits*, New York: Henry G. Lanley.

Ellis, Mrs (1845), *Daughters of England*, London and Paris: Fisher, Son and Co.

Ellwood, Giles (1995), 'James Newton', *Furniture History*, volume 31, pp. 129–205.

Elsner, John and Roger Cardinal (eds) (1994), *The Cultures of Collecting*, London: Reaktion Books.

Everitt, A. (1966), 'Social Mobility in Early Modern England', *Past and Present*, number 33, pp. 56–73.

The Family Economist: a Penny Monthly Magazine for the Industrious Classes, (1851), volume 5, London: Groombridge and Sons.

Fawcett, Jane (ed.) (1976), *The Future of the Past: Attitudes to Conservation 1174–1974*, London: Thames and Hudson.

Feddon, Robin (1968), *The National Trust: Past and Present*, London: Jonathan Cape.

Finn, Margot (1996), 'Women, Consumption and Coverture in England, c. 1760–1860', *Historical Journal*, 39, pp. 703–722.

Finn, Margot (2000), 'Men's Things: Masculine Possessions in the Consumer Revolution', *Social History*, volume 25, number 2, pp. 133–155.

Forty, Adrian (1987), *Objects of Desire: Design and Society 1750–1980*, London: Thames and Hudson.

Flemming, David (1993*)*, *Social History in Museums: a Handbook for Professionals*, London: HMSO.

Franklin, Jill (1981*)*, *The Gentleman's Country House and its Plan, 1835–1914*, London: Routlegde and Kegan Paul.

Gilbert, Christopher (1977), *Backstairs Furniture from Country Houses*, Leeds: Temple Newsam.

Gilbert, Christopher (1991), *English Vernacular Furniture*, New Haven and London: Yale University Press.

Gilbert, C. and P. Kirkham (eds) (1982), 'London and Provincial Books of Prices: Comment and Bibliography', *Furniture History*, volume 18, pp. 1–266.

Girouard, Mark (1976), 'Living with the Past: Victorian Alterations to Country Houses', in Fawcett, Jane (ed.), *The Future of the Past: Attitudes to Conservation 1174–1974*, London: Thames and Hudson.

Girouard, Mark (1978), *Life in the English Country House*, New York and London: Yale University Press.

Girouard, Mark (1990), *The English Town*, New Haven and London: Yale University Press.

Grier, Katherine C. (1988), *Culture and Comfort: People, Parlors, and Upholstery, 1850–1930*, Rochester, NY: The Strong Museum and Massachusetts University Press.

Glenn, Virginia (1979), 'George Bullock, Richard Bridgens and James Watt's Regency Furnishing Schemes', *Furniture History*, volume 15, pp. 54–67.

Goodman, Jocelyne Baty (ed.) (1968), *Victorian Cabinet Maker: The Memoirs of James Hopkinson 1819–1894*, Routledge and Kegan Paul.

Graves, Jane (1998), 'Clutter', *Art, Architecture and Design*, volume 5, number 2, pp. 63–68.

Green, Elaine (ed.) (1986), 'The Period Room Reconsidered: A house and Garden Symposium', *House and Garden* (US), October, pp. 219–225, 256–265.

Gregson, Nicky and Louise Crew (2003), *Second-hand Cultures*, London: Berg.

Guide to Aston Hall (1973), Birmingham: City of Birmingham Museum and Art Gallery.

Guide to Attingham Park, Shropshire (1998), London: National Trust.

Guide to Benthall Hall, Shropshire (1997), London: The National Trust.

Guide to Greyfriars (2002), London: The National Trust.

Guide to Hanbury Hall, Worcestershire (1981), London: The National Trust.

Guillery, Peter (2004), *The Small House in Nineteenth-Century London*, New York and London: Yale University Press.

Hall, Catherine (1979), 'The Early Formation of Victorian Domestic Ideology', in Sandra Burman (ed.), *Fit Work for Women*, London: Croom Helm.

Hall, Stuart (ed.) (1997), *Representation: Cultural Representations and Signifying Practices*, London: Sage in Association with Open University.

Halvorson, Bonnie (2000), 'Modern Replacement Fabrics in Historic Interiors: Ethical and Practical Concerns', *The Conservation of Heritage Interiors*, Preprints of a Conference, Ottawa: Canadian Conservation Institute, pp. 107–112.

Handler, Richard and Eric Gable (1997), *The New History in an Old Museum: Creating the Past at Colonial Williamsburg*, Durham NC and London: Duke University Press.

Hardyment, Christina (Introduction) (1987*)*, *The Housekeeping Book of Susanna Whatman 1776–1800*, London: Century in association with The National Trust.

Henderson, Jane and Diane Dollery (2000), 'Growing Pains: The Development of a Conservation Profession in the UK', in Roy, Ashrok and Perry Smith (eds), *Tradition and Innovation: Advances in Conservation*, Contributions to the Melbourne Congress, 10–14 October 2000, London: International Institute for Conservation of Historic Art Works.

Hetherington, Kevin (2004), 'Secondhandness: Consumption, Disposal and Absent Presence', *Environment and Planning, D: Society and Space*, volume 22, pp. 157–173.

Hewison, Robert (1987), *The Heritage Industry: Britain in a Climate of Decline*, London: Methuen.

Hopkins, Eric (1989), *Birmingham: the First Manufacturing Town in the World 1760–1840*, London: Weidenfeld and Nicolson.

Horie, Velson (ed.) (1999), *The Conservation of Decorative Arts*, London: Archetype Publications.

Hosmer, Charles B. (1965), *Presence of the Past: a History of the Preservation Movement in the United States Before Williamsburg*, New York: G.P. Putnam.

Hosmer, Charles B. (1981), *Preservation Comes of Age: From Williamsburg to National Trust, 1926–1949*, Charlottesville VA: University of Virginia.

House, Madeline and Graham Storey (eds) (1965), *The Letters of Charles Dickens*, Oxford: Clarendon Press.

Hudson, Pat (2000), *History by Numbers: An Introduction to Quantitative Approaches*, London: Arnold.

Hughes, Helen (ed.) (2000), *Layers of Understanding: Setting Standards for Architectural Paint Research*, Papers taken from the proceedings of English Heritage national seminar in London 28 April 2000, Shaftsbury: Donhead.

Hutchinson, Maxwell (2003), *Number 57: The History of a House*, London: Headline.

Hunt, Margaret (1996), *The Middling Sort: Commerce, Gender and the family in England, 1680–1780*, Berkeley: University of California Press.

Ionides, Julia (1999), *Thomas Farnolls Pritchard of Shrewsbury: an Architect and 'Inventor of Cast Iron Bridges'*, Ludlow: Dog Rose Press.

Jackson-Stops, Gervase (ed.) (1978), *National Trust Studies 1979*, London: Sotheby Parke Bernet.

Jackson-Stops, Gervase (ed.) (1985), *The Treasure Houses of Britain*, Washington DC: National Gallery of Art.

Jackson-Stops, Gervase (ed.) (1989), *The Fashioning and Functioning of the British Country House*, Washington: National Gallery and University of New England.

Jenkins, Jennifer and Patrick James (1994), *From Acorn to Oak Tree: The Growth of the National Trust 1895–1994*, London: National Trust.

Jenkins, Simon (2003), *England's Thousand Best Houses*, Harmondsworth: Allen Lane.

Jervis, Simon (1997), 'Far from Uniform', *SPAB Newsletter*, volume 18, number 4, pp. 12–15.

Jessup, Wendy Claire (1995*)*, *Conservation in Context: Finding a Balance for the Historic House Museum*, Symposium 7–8 March 1994, Andrew W. Mellon Foundation and National Trust for Historic Preservation, Washington DC.

Johnson, Jessica S. (1993), 'Conservation and Archaeology in Great Britain and the United States: A Comparison', *Journal of the American Institute for Conservation*, volume 32, number 3, pp. 249–269.

Joyce, H. and J.E. Edwards (April 2002), 'Three Historic Houses at the Shelburne Museum Reinterpreted', *The Magazine Antiques*, pp. 104–113.

Kavangh, Gaynor (1990), *History Curatorship*, Washington DC: Smithsonian Institute.

Keating, P. (1976) Introduction to Elizabeth Gaskell, *Cranford*, Harmondsworth: Penguin.

Kerr, Robert (1864), *The Gentleman's House or How to Plan English Residences from the Parsonage to the Palace*, London: Murray.

Kidd, Alan and David Nicholls (eds) (1999), *Gender, Civic Culture and Consumerism: Middle-Class Identity in Britain, 1800–1940*, Manchester: Manchester University Press.

Kinchin, Juliet (1996), 'Interiors: Nineteenth-Century Essays on the "Masculine" and the "Feminine" Room', in Pat Kirkham (ed.), *The Gendered Object*, Manchester: Manchester University Press.

King, Thomas (1839), *The Modern Style of Cabinet Work Exemplified*, London: Architectural Library.

Kirkham, Pat (1988), 'The London Furniture Trade 1700–1870', *Journal of the Furniture History Society*, volume 24, pp. 1–219.

Kirkham, Pat (1995), '"If you have no sons": Furniture-making in Britain', in Judith Attfield and Pat Kirkham (eds), *A View from the Interior: Women and Design*, London: The Women's Press.

Kirkham, Pat, Rodney Mace and Julia Porter (1987), *Furnishing the World: the East London Furniture Trade 1830–1980*, London: Journeyman.

Kowaleski-Wallace, Elizabeth (1997), *Consuming Subjects: Women, Shopping and Business in the Eighteenth Century*, New York: Columbia University Press.

Kwint, Marius, Christopher Breward and Jeremy Aynsley (eds) (1999), *Material Memories*, London: Berg.

A Lady (1829), *The Home Book: or Young Housekeeper's Assistant*, London: Smith, Elder and Co.

A Lady (1838), *The Workwoman's Guide*, London: Simpkin, Marshall and Co.

Lambert, Miles (2004), '"Cast-off Wearing Apparell?": The Consumption and Distribution of Second-hand Clothing in Northern England during the long Eighteenth Century', *Textile History*, volume 38, number 1, pp. 1–26.

Landi, Sheila (1992), *The Textile Conservator's Manual*, 2nd edition, London: Butterworth-Heinemann.

Lawton, Richard (ed.) (1978), *The Census and Social Structure*, London: Frank Cass.

Lees-Milne, James (ed.) (1945*)*, *The National Trust: A Record of Fifty Years' Achievement*, London: Batsford.

Lemire, Beverly (1991), *Fashion's Favourite: The Cotton Trade and the Consumer in Britain, 1660–1800*, Oxford: Oxford University Press.

Lemire, Beverly (1997), *Dress, Culture and Commerce: the English Clothing Trade Before the Factory, 1660–1800*, London: Macmillan.

Lindgren, James M. (1995), *Preserving New England*, New York and Oxford: Oxford University Press.

Lloyd, Nathaniel (1975), *History of the English House*, London: Architectural Press.

Loudon, J.C. (1833), *Encyclopaedia of Cottage, Farm and Villa Architecture*, London: Longman, Orme, Brown, Green and Longman.

Loudon, J.C. (1838), *The Suburban Gardener and Villa Companion*, published by the author.

Lowenthal, David (1985), *The Past is a Foreign Country*, Cambridge: Cambridge University Press.

Lowenthal, David (1998), *The Heritage Crusade and the Spoils of History*, Cambridge: Cambridge University Press.

Lyle, Charles T. (1986), *The George Read II House*, Offprint from the Delaware Antiques Show Catalog, Reprinted by the Historical Society of Delaware.

McCracken, Grant (1990), *Culture and Consumption*, Bloomington and Indianapolis: Indiana University Press.

McDonald, George W. (1982), *Hearth and Home: Preserving a People's Culture*, Philadelphia: Temple University Press.

McGriffin, Robert F. (1983), *Furniture Care and Conservation*, Nashville, Tennessee: American Association for State and Local History.

McInnes, Angus (1988), 'The Emergence of a Leisure Town: Shrewsbury 1660–1760', *Past and Present*, number 120, pp. 53–87.

McKendrick, Neil (1974), 'Home Demand and Economic Growth: a New View of the Role of Women and Children in the Industrial Revolution', in Neil McKendrick (ed.) *Historical Perspectives: Studies in English Thought and Society in Honour of J. H. Plumb*, Cambridge: Cambridge University Press.

McKendrick, Neil, John Brewer and J.H.Plumb (1982), *The Birth of a Consumer Society*, London: Europa.

MacLeod, Dianne Sachko (1996), *Art and the Victorian Middle Class: Money and the Making of Cultural Identity*, Cambridge: Cambridge University Press.

Mandler, Peter (1997), *The Fall and Rise of the Stately Home*, New York and London: Yale University Press.

Marko, Kysnia (ed.) (1997), *Textiles in Trust*, Proceedings of the Symposium at Blickling Hall, Norfolk, September 1995, London: Archetype Publications in association with the National Trust.

Medlam, Sarah (1993), 'The Decorative Arts Approach: Furniture', in David Flemming, *Social History in Museums: a Handbook for Professionals*, London: HMSO.

Meldrum, Tim (1999), 'Domestic Service, Privacy and the Eighteenth-Century Metropolitan Household', *Urban History*, volume 26, number 1, pp. 27–39.

Miller, Daniel (1998), *Material Culture: Why Some Things Matter*, London: UCL.

Miller, Daniel (ed.) (1995), *Acknowledging Consumption*, London: Routledge.

Mitchell, Anthony (1999), 'Conservation in Context: the Conservation of Historic Interiors by the National Trust', in Velson Horie (ed.), *The Conservation of Decorative Arts*, London: Archetype Publications.

Mitchell, Sandy (2001), 'Upstairs, downstairs', *Daily Telegraph Magazine*, 20 October 2001, pp. 23–25.

Montgomery, Florence M. (1970), *Printed Textiles: English and American Cottons and Linens 1700–1850*, New York: Viking Press.

Moss, Roger W. (1998), *Historic Houses of Philadelphia: a Tour of the Region's Museum Homes*, Philadelphia: University of Pennsylvania Press.

Murtagh, William J. (1988), *Keeping Time: the History and Theory of Preservation in America*, Pittstown NJ: Main Street Press.

Naylor, Gillian (1999), 'Modernism and Memory: Leaving Traces', in Marius Kwint, Christopher Breward and Jeremy Aynsley (eds), *Material Memories: Design and Evocation*, Oxford: Berg.

Nenadic, Stana (1994), 'Middle-rank Consumers and Domestic Culture in Edinburgh and Glasgow 1720–1840', *Past and Present*, number 145, pp. 122–156.

Nylander, Jane C. (1994), *Our Own Snug Fireside: Images of the New England Home, 1760–1860*, New Haven and London: Yale University Press.

Nylander, Richard (1995), 'The Codman House: A Case study in Preserving and Interpreting Context', in Wendy Claire Jessup (ed.), *Conservation in Context: Finding a Balance for the Historic House Museum*, Proceedings from the Symposium 7–8 March 1994, Andrew Mellon Foundation and national Trust for Historic Preservation.

Olmert, Michael (1985), 'The New No-frills Williamsburg', *Historic Preservation*, volume 37, number 5, October 1985, pp. 27–33.

Parker, Rozsika (1984), The Subversive Stitch: Embroidery and the Making of the Feminine, London: The Women's Press.

Parkin, David (1999), 'Mementoes as Transitional Objects in Human Displacement', *Journal of Material Culture*, volume 4, number 3, pp. 303–320.

Pearce, Susan M. (ed.) (1994), *Interpreting Objects and Collections*, London: Routledge.

Pearson, W. (1807), *Antiquities of Shropshire*, London.

Peck, Amelia (1998), *Lyndhurst: A Guide to the House and Landscape*, Tarrytown, NY: The National Trust for Historic Preservation.

Perkin, Harold (1968), *The Origins of Modern English Society*, London: Routledge and Kegan Paul.

Perkin, J. (1989), *Women and Marriage in Nineteenth Century England*, London: Routledge.

Pevsner, Nikolaus (1976), 'Scrape or Anti-Scrape', in Jane Fawcett (ed.), *The Future of the Past: Attitudes to Conservation 1174–1974*, London: Thames and Hudson.

Phillips, David (1997), *Exhibiting Authenticity*, Manchester: Manchester University Press.

Pointon, Marcia (1993), *Hanging the Head: Portraiture and Social Formation in Eighteenth-Century England*, Paul Mellon Centre for Studies in British Art and Yale University Press.

Pointon, Marcia (1997), *Strategies for Showing: Women, Possession, and Representation in English Visual Culture 1665–1800*, Oxford: Oxford University Press.

Pointon, Marcia (1999), 'Materializing Mourning: Hair, Jewellery and the Body', in Kwint, Marius, Christopher Breward and Jeremy Aynsley (eds), *Material Memories*, London: Berg.

Ponsonby, Margaret (1994), 'Samuel Peat: Chichester Cabinet Maker', *Regional Furniture*, volume 3, pp. 64–72.

Ponsonby, Margaret (2003), 'Ideals, Reality and Meaning: Homemaking in England in the first Half of the Nineteenth Century', *Journal of Design History*, volume 16, number 3, pp. 201–214.

Read, Donald (1964), *The English Provinces c. 1760–1960: a Study in Influence*, London: Edward Arnold.

Richards, Sarah (1999), *Eighteenth-Century Ceramics: Products for a Civilised Society*, Manchester: Manchester University Press.

Rowell, Christopher and John Martin Robinson (1996), *Uppark Restored*, London: National Trust.

Saumarez Smith, Charles (1993), *Eighteenth-Century Decoration*, London: Weidenfeld and Nicolson.

Schoelwer, Susan Prendergast (1979), 'Form, Function and Meaning in the Use of Fabric Furnishings: a Philadelphia Case Study, 1700–1775', *Winterthur Portfolio*, volume 4, number 1, pp. 25–40.

Schoeser, Mary and Celia Rufey (1989), *English and American Textiles: 1790 to the Present*, New York: Thames and Hudson.

Schor, H. M. (1992), *Scheherezade in the Marketplace: Elizabeth Gaskell and the Victorian Novel*, New York and Oxford: Oxford University Press.

Seale, William (1979), *Recreating the Historic House Interior*, Nashville TN: American Association for State and Local History.

Shammas, Carole (1990), *The Pre-Industrial Consumer in England and America*, Oxford: Oxford University Press.

Shoemaker, Robert B. (1998), *Gender in English Society, 1650–1850: the Emergence of Separate Spheres?*, London and New York: Longman.

Sparke, Penny (1995), *As Long As It's Pink*, London: Harper Collins.

Sparkes, Ivan (1973), *The English Country Chair*, Buckinghamshire: Spur.

Sproule, Anna and Michael Pollard (1988), *The Country House Guide: Family Homes in the Historic Houses Association*, London: Century.

Stillinger, Elizabeth (1980), *The Antiquers*, New York: Alfred Knopf.

Stobart, Jon (1998), 'Shopping Streets as Social Space: Leisure, Consumerism and Improvement in an Eighteenth-Century Town', *Urban History*, volume 25, number 1, pp. 3–21.

Stone, Lawrence (1979), *The Family, Sex and Marriage in England 1500–1800*, Harmondsworth: Penguin.

Stowe, Catherine Beecher and Harriet Beecher Stowe (1994 with an introduction by Joseph Van Why), *The American Woman's Home*, Hartford CT: The Stowe-Day Foundation.

Styles, John (2000), 'Product Innovation in Early Modern London', *Past and Present*, Number 168, pp. 124–169.

Sweet, Rosemary (1999), *The English Town, 1680–1840: Government, Society and Culture*, London: Longman.

Taylor, Alec Clifton (1978), *Six English Towns*, London: BBC.

Timmons, Sharon (ed.) (1976), *Preservation and Conservation: Principles and Practices*, The proceedings of the North American International Regional Conference, Williamsburg VA and Philadelphia, 10–16 September, 1972, Washington DC: Smithsonian Institution Press.

Tinniswood, Adrian (1998), *The Polite Tourist: a History of Country House Visiting*, London: National Trust.

Todd, Barbara J. (1996), 'The Remarrying Widow: a Stereotype Reconsidered', in Mary Prior (ed.), *Women in English Society 1500–1800*, London: Routledge.

Tosh, John (1999), *A Man's Place: Masculinity and the Middle-Class Home in Victorian Britain*, New Haven and London: Yale University Press.

Treasures for the Nation (1988), exhibition catalogue, London: British Museum for the National Heritage Memorial Fund.

Trupin, Deborah Lee (1997), 'Exhibiting Textiles in Historic House Furnished Rooms: Balancing Conservation and Interpretation', *Fabric of an Exhibition: An Interdisciplinary Approach*, Preprints of a Conference, Ottawa: Canadian Conservation Institute, pp. 45–49.

Uglow, Jenny (2002), *The Lunar Men: The Friends Who Made the Future*, London: Faber and Faber.

Ulrich, Laurel Thatcher (2001*)*, *The Age of Homespun: Objects and Stories in the Creation of an American Myth*, New York: Alfred A. Knopf.

Veblen, Thorstein (1994 first published 1899), *The Theory of the Leisure Class*, with an introduction by R. Lekachman, Harmondsworth: Penguin.

Vicinus, Martha (ed.) (1972), *Suffer and Be Still: Women in the Victorian Age*, London: Methuen.

Vickery, Amanda (1993), 'Golden Age to Separate Spheres? A review of the categories and chronology of English women's history', *The Historical Review*, volume 36, number 2, pp. 383–414.

Vickery, Amanda (1993), 'Women and the World of Goods: a Lancashire Consumer and her Possessions, 1751–81', in Brewer, John and Roy Porter (eds), *Consumption and the World of Goods*, London: Routledge.

Vickery, Amanda (1998), *The Gentleman's Daughter: Women's Lives in Georgian England*, New Haven and London: Yale University Press.

Wahrman, Dror (1995), *Imagining the Middle Class*, London: Cambridge University Press.

Wainwright, Clive (1988), *George Bullock Cabinet Maker*, London: John Murray.

Wainwright, Clive (1989), *The Romantic Interior*, New Haven and London: Yale University Press.

Wall, Cynthia (1997), 'The English Auction: Narratives of Dismantlings', *Eighteenth-Century Studies*, volume 31, number 1, pp. 1–25.

Walsh, Claire (1995), 'Shop Design and the Display of Goods in Eighteenth-Century London', *Journal of Design History*, volume 8, number 3, pp. 157–176.

Wanklyn, Malcolm (1993), 'Urban Revival in Early Modern England: Bridgnorth and the River Trade, 1660–1800', *Midland History*, volume 28, pp. 37–64.

Wanklyn, Malcolm (ed.) (1998), *Inventories of Worcestershire Landed Gentry 1537–1786*, Worcestershire Historical Society New Series, volume 16, Worcester: Worcestershire Historical Society.

Ward, Louise (1996), 'Chintz, Swags and Bows; the Myth of the English Country-House Style', *Things*, number 5, pp. 7–37.

Waterhouse, Ellis (1981), *The Dictionary of British 18th Century Painters*, Woodbridge: Antique Collectors' Club.

Waterson, Merlin (1990), *The Servants' Hall: a Domestic History of Erddig*, London: The National Trust.

Waterson, Merlin (1994), *The National Trust: The First Hundred Years*, London: National Trust and BBC Books.

Watson, Michael Saunders (1988), foreword to Anna Sproule and Michael Pollard, *The Country House Guide: Family Homes in the Historic Houses Association*, London: Century.

Weatherill, Lorna (1986), 'A Possession of One's Own: Women and Consumer Behaviour in England, 1660–1740', *Journal of British Studies*, volume 25, pp. 131–156.

Weatherill, Lorna (1988), *Consumer Behaviour and Material Culture in Britain 1660–1760*, London: Routledge.

Weatherill, Lorna (1993), 'The Meaning of Consumer Behaviour in Late-Seventeenth and Early-Eighteenth Century England', in Brewer, John and Roy Porter (eds), *Consumption and the World of Goods*, London: Routledge.

Weideger, Paula (1994), *Gilding the Acorn: Behind the Façade of the National Trust*, London: Simon and Schuster.

Welles, Edward O. (1982), 'George Washington Slept Here…And Here's How it Really Looked: Scientific Paint Analysis and Washington's Own Writings Help Conservators Give Mount Vernon a Surprising New Look', *Historic Preservation*, volume 34, number 3, pp. 22–27.

West, Patricia (1999), *Domesticating History: the Political Origins of America's House Museums*, Washington: Smithsonian Institute Press.

West, Veronica (1982) 'Broseley Hall and Thomas Farnolls Pritchard', *Journal of the Wilkinson Society*, number 10, pp. 10–11.

Whorwood, R.W. (2001), The Notebook of Thomas Shakeshaft, 1751–1764, Ashbourne, Derbyshire: Published by the author.

Whorwood, R.W. (2004), 'The Notebook (1751–1764) of Thomas Shakeshaft Carpenter and Cabinetmaker of Middleton, Warwickshire, *Furniture History Society Newsletter*, number 155, pp. 4–5.

Williams, James (1847 4th edition), *The Footman's Guide*, London: Thomas Deane and Son (Winterthur Library).

Wilson, H.R. (1978), *David Parkes*, published by the author (Shropshire Record Office, BP24)

Wrenn, George L. (1971), 'What is a Historic House Museum?', *Historic Preservation*, volume 23, number 1, pp. 55–58.

Wright, Patrick (1985), *On Living in an Old Country*, London: Verso.

Wright, Susan (1989), '"Holding Up Half the sky": Women and their Occupations in Eighteenth-Century Ludlow', *Midland History*, volume 14, pp. 53–74.

Wright, Susan (1990), 'Sojourners and Lodgers in a Provincial Town: The evidence from Eighteenth-Century Ludlow', *Urban History*, volume 17, pp. 14–35.

Wrigley, E.A. (1967), 'A Simple Model of London's Importance in Changing English Society and Economy 1650–1750', *Past and Present*, Number 37, pp. 44–70.

Index

Homemakers that feature in the text are listed by name. See also the Appendix.